N. Bell

To Jill, who also
cares for the loss of Cranmer's Liturgy

For Services Rendered

In Memoriam
Archbishop Thomas Cranmer,
who, among his many talents,
included the spicileging art.

For Services Rendered

An anthology in thanksgiving for the Book of Common Prayer

compiled by

Norman Taylor

The Lutterworth Press
Cambridge

Published by
The Lutterworth Press
P.O. Box 60
Cambridge
CB1 2NT
England

British Library Cataloguing in Publication Data:
A catalogue record is available from the British Library.

ISBN: 0 7188 2877 1

copyright © 1993, Norman Taylor

First published in 1993 by The Lutterworth Press.

Printed by
St Edmundsbury Press
Bury St Edmunds, Suffolk

CONTENTS

LIST OF ILLUSTRATIONS

The illustrations from The Book of Common Prayer are here reproduced by kind permission of the Syndics of Cambridge University Library. Illustrations I, II, VI will be found under classification Rel.b.75.3; numbers III and IV under Adams.7.67.14; and number V under Rit.d.775.1.

ACKNOWLEDGEMENTS

I wish to express my deep gratitude to all those correspondents who so kindly supplied me with relevant references from their own reading; and especially to the Revd Professor Raymond Chapman, who also read the first two chapters in draft form and encouraged me to continue, and to Lady Elton F.S.A., whose never-failing enthusiasm strengthened my resolve. Members of the staff of the Cambridge University Library, especially the Revd Nigel Hancock, Senior Under Librarian, Jerry Bye and Dr Frederick Ratcliffe, the University Librarian, were most patient in helping me to find books, and I thank them. I am most grateful also to those authors and publishers, literary executors and agents, who have permitted me to use quotations from their books: the anthology would have been sadly lacking in completeness without them. Nor would it ever have been completed but for the skill of Mrs Eileen Gayfer at the word processor - to her I am particularly indebted.

N.T.
Shire End West
Lyme Regis

PROLOGUE

'Young men and women beginning to write are generally given the plausible but utterly impracticable advice to write as shortly as possible, as clearly as possible, and without other thought in their minds except to say exactly what is in them. Nobody ever adds on these occasions the one thing needful: "And be sure you choose your patron wisely", though that is the gist of the whole matter. For a book is always written for somebody to read, and since the patron is not merely the paymaster, but also in a very subtle and insidious way the instigator and inspirer of what is written, it is of the utmost importance that he should be a desirable man.'[1]

The anthologist need not heed the generally given advice because, though he feels kindly disposed to most of the authors from whose work he borrows, he does not feel answerable on their account. All the more reason, perhaps, to heed Mrs Woolf's advice, and consider his patrons. There are four to whom he addresses himself:

First, to the lover of the Book of Common Prayer, in the hope that he will enjoy discovering what its services have meant to others and how much mention is made of them in our literature.

Secondly, to the lover of anthologies, who delights both in finding that another shares his favourite authors, and in the discovery of books unknown to him before.

Thirdly and fourthly, to the lover of great literature and to the lover of God (sometimes, though not always, one and the same) who have not been brought up on the Prayer Book, and who may begin to discover and enjoy the literary and spiritual genius of Cranmer, Coverdale and others in this tangential approach.

'And having thus endeavoured to discharge our duties in this weighty affair, . . . although we know it is impossible (in such variety of apprehensions, humours and interests, as are in the world) to please all; nor can expect that men of fractious, peevish and perverse spirits should be satisfied with anything that can be done in this kind by any other than themselves, yet we have good hope that what is here presented. . . will be well accepted and approved by all sober, peaceable and truly conscientious sons of the Church of England.'[2]

And indeed by all other men and women of good will.

1. Virginia Woolf, 'The Patron and the Crocus', *The Common Reader*, 1925.
2. The Preface to the 1662 Book of Common Prayer.

Despise Profane
not the *his holy*
Word Things
of
GOD *or his*
Ordin
neather ances

S. Wale inv et del.   C. Grignion sculp.

The Principal Figure (   ) decently habited and
regally crown'd, represents the Church of England, of whom ŷ King is the Head;
she tramples on Swords, Chains &c, to show her Abhorence of Persecution and
Love of Peace, signified by the Olive Branch, with her Right Hand she points to ŷ
open Bible, (held by Boy Angels with the Cap of Liberty) to denote her Love of
Truth & Liberty of searching ŷ Scriptures, allow'd to all her Members. The Mitre &
Crozier denote her Episcopal Government, as ŷ Bread & Wine do the Sacrament Administer'd in both kinds to ŷ Laity

CHAPTER 1
Morning Prayer or Mattins

THE OPENING SENTENCES AND INVITATION TO CONFESSION

At Pankot in India after Independence a new Indian priest comes to the church for Easter Day.

1. They went to morning service on Sunday, April 2nd. The church was fuller than she had seen it for years. Lucy stared in dismay and fascination at Father Sebastian. She was glad Tusker hadn't insisted on eight o'clock communion. But when the new priest began to intone the sentences of the scriptures prescribed for opening the order of morning prayer in a loud ringing voice she was struck first by their beauty and then by the recollection of her Father mumbling them and then by the resonance of Father Sebastian's voice and the curious appropriateness of the Indian lilt to the lilt and rhythm of the words. She opened her eyes and saw that his were shut and that he was speaking words known by heart.

"I will arise and go to my Father, and will say unto him, Father, I have sinned against heaven and before thee, and am no more worthy to be called thy son."

"Dearly beloved brethren, the Scripture moveth us in sundry places to acknowledge and confess our manifold sins and wickedness," Father Sebastian continued, without a break, and the service was away, flowing through the church and through Lucy's mind and heart and soul.

Country controversy: squire versus parson

2. The service was in truth a pitched battle between the two. First one and then the other would be worsted. Occasionally my mother joined in to separate them. For the Vicar and my father had very different temperaments. Each exasperated the other. Each feared and yet respected the other. My father feared the Vicar's sanctity. This unworldly, learned and lonely clergyman was tolerant, except of one thing, betting. He profoundly disapproved of racing and his cup of misery overflowed when my father presented the church with a new roof, new panelling or lighting, out of his winnings. If the bush telegraph announced to the vicarage that my father had during the previous week won a race - if he lost the Vicar would be all smiles - Morning Prayer opened with the following sentence from Scripture: "When the wicked man turneth away from his wickedness that he hath committed, and doeth that which is lawful and right, he shall save his soul alive." The Vicar would read these words from his desk while looking my father sternly in the eye. The victim would visibly squirm in the manor pew. Not satisfied with this awful

warning the Vicar would after a pause give the answer in a voice so like my father's as to be an unmistakeable imitation, "I acknowledge my transgressions, and my sin is ever before me." All my father could do was to shake his head. In this way the Vicar won the first round.

Farm labourers chat in Warren's Malthouse
3. "And he's the fearfullest man, bain't ye, Joseph? Ay, another time ye were lost by Lambing-Down Gate, weren't ye, Joseph?"

"I was," replied Poorgrass, as if there were some conditions too serious even for modesty to remember itself under, this being one.

"Yes; that were the middle of the night, too. The gate would not open, try how he would, and knowing there was the Devil's hand in it, he kneeled down."

"Ay," said Joseph, acquiring confidence from the warmth of the fire, the cider, and a perception of the narrative capabilities of the experience alluded to. "My heart died within me, that time; but I kneeled down and said the Lord's Prayer, and then the Belief right through, and then the Ten Commandments, in earnest prayer. But no, the gate wouldn't open; and then I went on with Dearly Beloved Brethren, and, thinks I, this makes four, and 'tis all I know out of book, and if this don't do it nothing will, and I'm a lost man. Well, when I got to Saying After Me, I rose from my knees and found the gate would open - yes, neighbours, the gate opened the same as ever."

A meditation on the obvious inference was indulged in by all, and during its continuance each directed his vision into the ashpit, which glowed like a desert in the tropics under a vertical sun, shaping their eyes long and liny, partly because of the light, partly from the depth of the subject discussed.

THE GENERAL CONFESSION

Reflections on attendance at Silocene Baptist chapel from the age of 8 to 16
4. The long so-called extempore prayers I recall with embarrassment and distaste. They seldom expressed what I felt and, to use a Quaker phrase, they failed 'to speak to my condition' or of my condition. For one thing, we Nonconformists were disinclined to acknowledge, once we had been 'saved', that we were sinners and preferred to confess only to 'shortcomings'. I knew myself to be rather more than a short-comer and there were many, including the village policemen, P.C. Powell, who would gladly have testified to the fact! When later I got to know the General Confession in the Book of Common Prayer of the Anglicans I said to myself 'That's more like it'. 'Erred and strayed from thy ways like lost sheep.' Having looked for lost sheep on the mountains with my farmer grandfather I realized how perfectly apt that phrase was. And 'followed too much the devices and desires of our own hearts.' Exactly! And 'left undone those things which we ought to have done: and . . . done those things which we ought not to have done.' All neatly summarized in a few marvellously inspired lines! For the long-winded and high-flown extempore prayers, therefore, a debit.

All creatures great and small!
5. Inside, the church, though crammed with people, was cool and quiet, and the roof seemed very high. From outside the roar of Cairo came faintly, the muted ting and rumble of the trams along Boulac, the cries of men with carts. A few flies

zizzed in the aisles. The parson, the Reverend C. T. Horan, a retired merchant navy captain, gave off an uncomplicated seafaring holiness, conducting the service in an authoritative but gentle manner. Praying, one could feel the pattern of the hassocks imprinting itself interestingly on one's bare knees. How strange that a few pews in front the proud knees of Kitchener should also be bent to implore the forgiveness of God, which surely could not, in the face of so much glory, be necessary? I implored it with some vigour myself; there had been that business of lying to Nanny over having finished my scrambled eggs at breakfast, when they were, in fact, reposing in the bignonia creeper just below the sewing-room window. Down where I knelt there was a special dusty prayer-bookish smell. For hymns and psalms one stood on the pew, but even then my father seemed very remote and far up.

'Sing the gloria, darling, you know that.' My mother had a veil tied over her large hat; what would happen if she wanted to blow her nose? Behind the lectern, Kitchener, in implacable tones, was reading the Gospel according to St Mark. Over his shoulder one could just see the figure of Christ in a red cloak in the stained glass east window; they looked unlike, but were they relations? How did people stick in hat-pins without sticking them into their heads?

Sitting on the pew, one could swing one's legs as hard as one liked without their actually hitting the pew behind and causing remonstrance. Wonderful sonorous words emerged from the lined simplicity of Mr Horan's face; his reassuring saintliness came out and embraced one for a fleeting moment of time. The matchless prose of the Book of Common Prayer swam in my ears like some majestic and unearthly sea. There was no question of coming out before the sermon. William and I, aged five and three and unaware of hardship, underwent the full superb stretch.

THE ABSOLUTION OR REMISSION OF SINS

On board ship, when there is no chaplain or the chaplain is sick, a problem arises.
6. From long practice Masters-at-Arms have an astonishing facility for summing up a Captain's decision at the Request table. A religious and litigious Engine Room Artificer once put in a request to see the Captain regarding church the previous Sunday.
Captain: Well, what about church?
E.R.A.: It's about your reading it, Sir.
Captain: The Chaplain was sick. You know perfectly well it was my duty to take church in his absence.
E.R.A.: Yes, Sir, but not to read the Absolution, Sir.
Captain: Why not?
E.R.A.: Only an ordained priest is entitled to give Absolution, Sir.
Captain: Never heard of it. Fetch me a Prayer Book.
A messenger scurried away and returned with a Prayer Book which the Captain inspected.
Captain: Bless my soul, he's right.
For one brief, very brief moment the Captain and the Engine Room Artificer faced each other in silence. Then the smug expression on the E.R.A.'s face was shattered by a bark from the Master-at-Arms:

"Sins not absolved. Right turn. Double march."

THE EASTER ANTHEM

The first psalm at Mattins is always Psalm 95, the Venite, except on the nineteenth day of the month when it takes its place with the psalms of the day; and on Easter Day, when it is replaced by some sentences from St Paul's Epistles, known as the Easter anthems, which are found before the Collect, Epistle and Gospel for Easter Day.

7. During Father Sebastian's sermon, the text for which he took from one of the anthems prescribed to be said or sung on Easter Day instead of a psalm ('Christ our Passover is sacrificed for us: therefore let us keep the feast; not with the old leaven, nor with the leaven of malice and wickedness: but with the unleavened bread of sincerity and truth'), Lucy thought his attention was drawn to her rather frequently as if she were someone he felt he had seen before, which of course he had done, if he'd yet studied the photographs Mr Bhoolabhay must have sent him days ago.

8. Easter, with its new broad sunshine, the warm smell of grass, the great full moon, became for me a page of golden romance. For several weeks beforehand I anticipated and sensed that thrilling and abounding antiphon:

Christ our passover is sacrificed for us: therefore let us keep the feast . . . .
Christ is risen from the dead: and become the first-fruits of them that slept.
For since by man came death: by man came also the resurrection of the dead.

The golden bowl was here unbroken. The ancient and adapted Easter hymn ranged and rang alongside the *Te Deum*:

Jesus Christ is risen to-day, Alleluia!
Our triumphant holy day, Alleluia!
Who did once, upon the Cross, Alleluia!
Suffer to redeem our loss. Alleluia!

THE PSALMS, CANTICLES, AND LESSONS

9. In the course of a few weeks Tess revived sufficiently to show herself so far as was necessary to get to church one Sunday morning. She liked to hear the chanting - such as it was - and the old Psalms, and to join in the Morning Hymn. That innate love of melody, which she had inherited from her ballad-singing mother, gave the simplest music a power over her which could well-nigh drag her heart out of her bosom at times.

To be as much out of observation as possible for reasons of her own, and to escape the gallantries of the young men, she set out before the chiming began, and took a back seat under the gallery, close to the lumber, where only old men and women came, and where the bier stood on end among the churchyard tools.

Parishioners dropped in by twos and threes, deposited themselves in rows before her, rested three-quarters of a minute on their foreheads as if they were praying, though they were not; then sat up, and looked around. When the chants came on one of her favourites happened to be chosen among the rest - the old double chant 'Langdon' - but she did not know what it was called, though she would much have liked to know. She thought, without exactly wording the thought, how strange and godlike was a composer's power, who from the grave could lead through sequences of emotion, which he alone had felt at first, a girl like her who had never heard of his name, and never would have a clue to his personality.

The Prayer Book has a "Table of Proper Lessons to be read at Morning and Evening Prayer on the Sundays and Holy Days throughout the year." To ignore this Table is to invite disaster, especially when Squire battles with parson.
10. But the choice of lessons was my father's absolutely, whenever he did attend church. I am quite sure his extraordinary choice of Old Testament Lessons was a means of getting his own back on the Vicar. This was when he actually took the stage, and could give as good as he got. In the first place an old bone of contention was that the Vicar would not allow him to read from the desk. Over this matter the Vicar displayed an uncharacteristic lack of charity, not to say dog-in-the-manger attitude. He was extremely jealous of the three-decker and would even hound Mrs Hartwell out of the clerk's stall to which, strictly speaking, she was entitled. He liked to use all three decks himself, although even he could not do so at the same time, and would bob about from one to the other, expecting Mrs Hartwell to open and shut the three doors before and after him. Therefore my father was obliged to stand rather ignominiously under the chancel arch, to which he would advance with impeccable dignity. He pointedly refused to make use of a modern lectern which the Vicar had offered as a compromise. He thought the offer insulting and the lectern a shoddy affair, which indeed it was. So he would hold the large bible in both hands, ostentatiously conveying to all of us how extremely awkward and heavy it was. On one occasion in a particularly vindictive mood he announced: 'Here beginneth the 36th chapter of the Book of Genesis, verses 1 to 43.'

After transfixing the Vicar in his turn with a steely eye, he started off: 'Now these are the generations of Esau, who is Edom. Esau took his wives of the daughters of Canaan; Adah the daughter of Elon the Hittite, and Aholibamah the daughter of Annah the daughter of Zibeon the Hivite; and Bashemath Ismael's daughter, sister of Nebajoth. And Adah bare to Esau, Eliphaz: and Bashemath bare Reuel.' On and on he droned. This was what he called enjoying his pound of flesh. First the farmers' wives, then Miss Empey, although so devout, then the school-mistress dropped off, and last of all the servants from the manor at the risk of a severe reprimand after the service. Not so the Vicar. He shifted, took off his pince-nez, cleared his throat, and puffed out his cheeks to no avail. My father relentlessly continued: 'And the sons of Eliphaz were Teman, Omah, Zepho, and Gatam, and Kenaz. And Timna was concubine to Eliphaz, Esau's son. And these are the sons of Reuel; Nahath, and Zerah, Shammah and Mizzah . . .' The Vicar becoming desperate made a sign for help to my mother who up to now had been remarkably patient. She nodded assent, and in her turn made signs to my father to stop. He took no notice and went on: 'And the children of Ezer are these; Bilhan, and Zaavan, and Achan; and of Dishan, Uz and Fuz. These are the dukes that come of the Horites; Duke Lotan, Duke Shobal, Duke Zibeon, Duke Anah.'

My mother could bear it no longer. She half rose in her seat, and making a face of painful embarrassment, mouthed the words, 'Your buttons!' while nodding a downward glance at my father's trousers. Instantly he turned scarlet, slid a hand across his stomach, and abruptly halted at the words, 'And the name of the city was Pau.' Mumbling, 'Here endeth the first lesson,' he sidled back into the pew. My mother was triumphant. She nudged him in the ribs and said, 'April fool!' My father looked perplexed. 'But it isn't April,' he retorted, 'It's August.'

The Old Testament lesson is followed by the Te Deum. Priscilla Napier tells of her intoxication with this hymn when she was a child at Brulos Beach in Egypt during the First World War.

11. We wore no shoes all summer, even the pleasures of worship were unmarred by the tightness of clean white socks, by the scratchiness of starched muslin dresses round the neck and under the arms. "We praise Thee, O God," I shouted delightedly in the rush-matting church, "we acknowledge Thee to be the Lord." The Te Deum was splendid, vision building, whether sung in the coolness of All Saints at Cairo, in the plunging saloon of the P & O ship in the Atlantic, on grey summer mornings in the mossy parish church at Sidmouth, or as here in the rush-matting hut with the sun splintering through the roof and the breeze blowing the candle flames on the altar at right angles to the candles. "To Thee Cherubim and Seraphim continually do cry." The cherubim sat on the cumulus clouds; their fat legs swung in the blue. Some had trumpets and some had drums, but all were having fun. They were naked and the sun shone on them and the breeze blew through their toes. "To Thee Cherubim and Seraphim continually do cry, Holy, Holy, Holy, Lord God of Sabaoth. Heaven and earth are full of the majesty of Thy Glory." If one pressed one's feet into the sand, it could be felt fountaining up between one's toes. Kneeling down, one's knees sank gratefully into the softness of it. "Oh Almighty God, who alone canst order the unruly wills and affections of sinful men . . . ." Sitting during the lesson, one could lift the sand up on to one's foot as if it were a spade and feel the sand pour off like water. "To Thee Cherubim and Seraphim continually do cry." Let others sing of prophets and martyrs; they were old, bearded, boring. In a passion of enjoyment at both ends, I corkscrewed my feet down into the sand and lifted up my voice still more enjoyably and less tunefully. "To Thee Cherubim and Seraphim continually do cry." My mother leant over me and kindly pointed out that we had got to "Vouchsafe, Oh Lord, to keep us this day without sin," but like a stuck gramophone needle, I took no notice. "To Thee Cherubim and Seraphim continually do cry, Holy, Holy, Holy."

12. The second summer at Brulos was less dreamy, more eventful than the first. The English passion for activity, that accompanies them through no matter what climate, was given full rein. Perhaps a general parental feeling had crept in that Satan would find some mischief still for idle hands to do; anyway there was more organisation. Sports every Saturday, sand-castle competitions, handicraft exhibitions, a general encouragement to Do and not to Dream. Morning lessons set in, in a small room behind the billiard-room, though not, alas, with Miss Quibell. Perhaps Miss Quibell felt happier to preserve her mystique by remaining in the large cool museum among the Pharaohs in Cairo and not risking the relaxed bathing-dress atmosphere of Brulos.

Church this summer was unexpectedly around the billiard table; perhaps the rush-matting chapel with its guttering candles had burnt down. Here at morning Sunday School we were organised by charming Mrs Lasbery into marching round the billiard table singing hymns, which was splendidly active, and enjoyed by all, as long as the hymn was "Bright the vision that delighted", or "The Son of God goes forth to war, A kingly crown to gain", or "Onward Christian Soldiers, marching as to war". "Soldiers of Christ, Arise", we shouted; our bare feet thumped pleasurably on the boards in a manner that might have surprised John Milton. Feeling perhaps that the whole thing was becoming a bit off-key and martial, the authorities confronted us next Sunday with a new hymn on a different note.

"Praise Him, Praise Him," we sang doubtfully, "all ye little children, He is Love, He is Love,"

Mrs Lasbery, kind and sweet as ever, urged us on, but this hymn is a lurid example of the sort of thing that the adult world erroneously supposes that children will be able to stomach, being too sweet and innocent to know better. I noticed with horrified delight that my partner in the march, Peter Dudgeon, was loudly singing, "Praise Him, Praise Him, all ye little donkeys." Thus introduced to the pleasures of blasphemy, I longed, but did not quite dare, to join in. "Love Him, Love Him, all ye little brickbats," Peter continued in the next verse, "He is Love, He is Love." Eleanor Gairdner from behind tapped him on the shoulder, but he continued unmoved. "Serve Him, Serve Him, all ye little soapsuds," Peter carolled. I listened entranced, to see where the flight of his fancy would carry him next. His face was radiant with enjoyment, his feet beat out the rhythm, no fire from Heaven descended to consume him. "Crown Him, Crown Him, all ye little wigwams," Peter sang on. This was too much for me, and I was told sternly to go outside until I could stop laughing.

The Te Deum still held its undisputed grip upon my soul; not even Peter Dudgeon could or would take the mickey out of that. "To Thee Cherubim and Seraphim continually do cry," I shouted, slightly more in tune than last summer, on Sunday mornings across the green stretches of the billiard table. "Heaven and earth are full of the majesty of Thy glory. To thee Cherubim and Seraphim continually, continually, CONTINUALLY do cry". It was the same idea, only how much less soppily expressed.

Readers who were young girls at any time during the first half of this century may well have read "Rebecca of Sunnybrook Farm" by the authoress of the following extract from "A Cathedral Courtship" - a short novel written in the form of a diary by a young American visiting England with her high-church Aunt. She here writes from York.

13. We go to two services a day in the Minster, and sometimes I sit quite alone in the nave drinking in the music as it floats out from behind the choir screen. The Litany and the Commandments are so beautiful heard in this way, and I never listen to the fresh, young voices chanting "Write all these thy laws in our hearts, we beseech thee," without wanting passionately to be good. I love, too, the joyful burst of music in the Te Deum: "Thou didst open the Kingdom of heaven to all believers". I like that word "all"; it takes in foolish me, as well as wise Aunt Celia.

The Benedicite is the alternative canticle to the Te Deum, and is sung especially during Advent and Lent.

14. I found in this service at All Saints a complete contrast each Sunday to the world as I knew it. My own world held beauty and happiness, but it was continually in shadow from my inability to keep pace with that normal progress which youth at that age should be making, and my disability, instead of lessening, was increasing. A keener realisation only broadened the viciousness of the circle. But here was not only a spectacle, but one in which I could share. I could take part in a living action, entirely unhampered by any inhibition, for I could always read, sing (though never in tune), or intone, in company with others. I have always, I think, had a sensitive ear for the spoken language, and I was never tired of listening to this tender yet virile and touching rendering of the sixteenth-century liturgy. Although not understanding, or having much ear for music, I was suddenly caught up in the cloud of prayers not always accompanied, yet with music ever on their heel. A great event for me was when Sunday evening fell on the last day of the month, and the hundred-and-fiftieth Psalm (*O Praise God in his holiness: praise him in the firmament of his power*) was played and sung in sustained *fortissimo*. I could conceive nothing grander. I grew to know my way about the Prayer Book, and to look forward in Advent and Lent to the canticle substituted for the *Te Deum*, in which I loved the Winter and Summer, the Green Things and the Wells, the Spirits and Souls of the Righteous, and the Holy and Humble Men of Heart, who were all to bless the Lord.

15. The irresistible, universal, automatic tendency to find sweet pleasure some- where, which pervades all life, from the meanest to the highest, had at length mastered Tess. Being even now only a young woman of twenty, one who mentally and sentimentally had not finished growing, it was impossible that any event should have left upon her an impression that was not in time capable of transmu- tation.

And thus her spirits, and her thankfulness, and her hopes, rose higher and higher. She tried several ballads, but found them inadequate; till, recollecting the psalter that her eyes had so often wandered over of a Sunday morning before she had eaten of the tree of knowledge, she chanted: "O ye Sun and Moon . . . O ye Stars . . . ye Green Things upon the Earth . . . ye Fowls of the Air . . . Beasts and Cattle . . . Children of Men . . . bless ye the Lord, praise Him and magnify Him for ever!"

She suddenly stopped and murmured: "But perhaps I don't quite know the Lord as yet."

And probably the half-unconscious rhapsody was a Fetichistic utterance in a Monotheistic setting; women whose chief companions are the forms and forces of outdoor Nature retain in their souls far more of the Pagan fantasy of their remote forefathers than of the systematized religion taught their race at later date. However, Tess found at least approximate expression for her feelings in the old Benedicite that she had lisped from infancy; and it was enough.

Church Parade

16. The accents of Allways are many and various, and nowhere are they heard to better advantage than in church. Especially during the singing of the *Benedicite*. For each verse of this great canticle, as you may remember, begins with the interjection O. And as the chant progresses, it is difficult not to be struck by the

extraordinary number of different sounds which different people make, on being confronted by the same vowel.

The vicar, for example, says "*Oooh!*" He says it with a bright smile, like a child who has climbed a fence and suddenly sees an orchard whose trees are fiery with fruit.

"*Oooh, ye Ice and Snow, bless ye the Lord!*" cries the vicar, with such boyish exultation that one feels he would like to run out and make a snowball, here and now, and throw it up with a shout of glee, to the grey sky . . . up and up till a white hand fluttered out, far above, and caught it, and turned it into a star. . . .

"*Oh, ye Wells, bless ye the Lord!*" cries Mrs M. She goes down deep on the word "wells", thereby showing her sense of the dramatic.

And as I stand there, with the sunlight splintering through the stained glass, and making little pools of blue and orange on the flimsy paper of my Prayer Book, I think that Mrs M may indeed call upon the wells to bless the Lord, for hers is the only well in the village which did not run bone-dry last summer. And it is difficult to forget the very ungodly look of exultation which always appeared on her face as she looked over the hedge to watch the water-cart passing down the dusty road, to fetch a few buckets of muddy fluid for the rest of us. . . .

"*Ow! Ye Whiles, and all that move in the Waters, bless ye the Lord.*"

And when you hear that Ow! you blink, and start, and look nervously across to the choir to see if anybody has been hurt. But all you see is a mild little man with glasses and a moustache, and that fascinating form of *coiffure* which consists in three or four long strands of hair carefully plastered across a bald head, horizontally, from the left ear to the right.

"*Ow! ye Whiles . . .*"

It is Mr Joy who gives us the *Ow!* Mr Joy is the keeper of the village shop. And though he has lived in Allways for fifteen years he is still an unrepentant Cockney. He still smiles in a kindly but pitying way at the simple manners of the villagers. He loves Allways, and he is a fierce defender of its rights and customs, but he will have his little joke. "This way to the bargain basement, sir," he always says, when he opens the trap door that leads to his cellar. "Early doors, seven-thirty," he chuckles, when there is a village concert. I am devoted to Mr Joy, but I do wish he would modify that "ow!" when he is singing the *Benedicite*.

Oooh!

Oh!

Ow!

The voices boom out, the little organ manfully accompanies them, and thus the chant continues. It is a sunny morning in spring, and through the windows one sees a blowing tapestry of sky and branches and cloud, threaded with many a fleeting pattern as the birds fly to and fro.

"*Oh! ye Servants of the Lord, bless ye the Lord, praise Him and magnify Him for ever* . . . .

Oh . . . ye Servants of the Lord . . . .

You look up, quickly. Why did you hear that "Oh" so clearly? It was very soft, very gentle, but somehow, it rang out above all the other warring interjections, it had a shining clarity that compelled attention. There it is again!

"*Oh! Ye holy and humble men of heart, bless ye the Lord* . . . .

You peer across the church, striving to find the singer of this bird-like note. And there, in the shadows, you see the plain, bespectacled face of a woman of about fifty. Her mouth is wide open, ridiculously wide open, and the hands that clutch her shabby Prayer Book are worn and gnarled. Her throat is swelling with the effort of her song, and there is a strand of mouse-like hair drifting into her eyes.

But you say to yourself "That woman is beautiful. Terribly, austerely beautiful. Her cheeks are painted with a colour that is not of this world, and a wild bird is singing in her throat . . . a bird that has strayed from some divine thicket."

And you will be right. For you are looking at Miss Hazlitt, plain, grey Miss Hazlitt, singing her heart out, in the shadows.

As the Benedicite provides an alternative to the Te Deum, so to the Benedictus does the Jubilate, mentioned here by a great modern poet.
17. As a boy, both before and after it broke, I had the luck to possess a voice which, though certainly not of solo quality, was good enough for a choir.

As a choirboy, I had to learn, not only to sight-read music, but also to enunciate words clearly - there is a famous tongue twister in the *Jubilate* - "For why, it is He that hath made us and not we ourselves" - and to notice the difference between their metrical values when spoken and when sung, so that, long before I took a conscious interest in poetry I had acquired a certain sensitivity to language which I could not have acquired in any other way.

THE BANNS
The Marriage Service (The Solemnization of Matrimony) begins with a rubric that orders the Banns of Marriage to be read at Morning Service immediately after the 2nd lesson.

Lord Peter Wimsey has been asked by Mr Venables, the Rector of Fenchurch St Paul, to stay at the Rectory and investigate a murder in the parish.
18. It was Sunday morning. As he lifted his head from his calculations, he heard the bells begin to ring for matins. He hastened out in the hall, where he found his host winding the grandfather clock.

"I always wind it when the bells begin on a Sunday morning," explains Mr Venables, "otherwise I might forget. I fear I am none too methodical. I hope you will not feel obliged to come to church, merely because you are our guest. . ."

Wimsey turned to find Bunter at his elbow, offering him with one hand his hat and with the other two leather-bound volumes on a small salver.

"You see, padre, we have every intention of going to church; we have, in fact, come prepared. Hymns A & M - I suppose that is the right work? . . . Why, padre, what's the trouble? Have you lost anything?"

"I - er - it's very odd - I could have declared that I laid them down just here. Agnes! Agnes, my dear! Have you seen those banns anywhere?"

"What is it Theodore?"

"The banns, my dear. Young Flavel's banns. I know I had them with me. I always write them out on a slip of paper, you see, Lord Peter; it is so very inconvenient to carry the register to the lectern. Now what in the world — ?"

"Are they on top of the clock, Theodore?"

"My dear, what a——! Bless me, though, you are quite right. How did that come about, I wonder? I must have put them up there unconsciously when I was picking up the key. Very strange indeed, but the little mishap is now remedied, thanks to my wife. She always knows where I have put things. I believe she knows the workings of my mind better than I do myself. Well, I must go across to the Church now. I go early, because of the choirboys. My wife will show you the Rectory pew." . . . .

The service was devoid of incident, except that Mr Venables again mislaid the banns, which had to be fetched from the vestry by the tenor on the cantoris side.

According to the first Prayer Books, Banns were simply to be published 'in the service time'. Later the rubric was made more specific: 'immediately before the sentences for the offertory'. However, many went out of church after the sermon and before these, so that statute 26 of George II 'To prevent clandestine marriages', stipulated an earlier position in the service, 'immediately after the second lesson', when everyone would be present.

Parson Adams goes his own way, and reads the Banns as unaware of the likely consequences as he is of the cause of them.

19. The morning after her arrival, being Sunday, Lady Booby went to church, to the great surprise of everybody, who wondered to see her ladyship, being no very constant churchwoman, there so suddenly upon her journey. Joseph was likewise there; and I have heard it was remarked that she fixed her eyes on him more than on the parson; but this I believe to be only a malicious rumour. When the prayers were ended, Mr Adams stood up, and with a loud voice pronounced, "I publish the banns of marriage between Joseph Andrews and Frances Goodwill, both of this parish," &c. Whether this had any effect on Lady Booby or not, who was then in her pew, which the congregation could not see into, I could never discover: but certain it is that in about quarter of an hour she stood up, and directed her eyes to that part of the church where the women sat, and persisted in looking that way during the remainder of the sermon in so scrutinizing a manner, and with so angry a countenance, that most of the women were afraid she was offended at them. The moment she returned home she sent for Slipslop in her chamber, and told her she wondered what that impudent fellow Joseph did in that parish? Upon which Slipslop gave her an account of her meeting Adams with him on the road, and likewise the adventure with Fanny. At the relation of which the lady often changed her countenance; and when she had heard all, she ordered Mr Adams into her presence, to whom she behaved as the reader will see in the next chapter.

Chapter ii . *A dialogue between Mr Abraham Adams and the Lady Booby*
Mr Adams was not far off, for he was drinking her ladyship's health below in a cup of her ale. He no sooner came before her than she began in the following manner: "I wonder, sir, after the many great obligations you have had to this family" (with all which the reader hath in the course of this history been minutely acquainted), "that you will ungratefully show any respect to a fellow who hath been turned out of it for his misdeeds. Nor doth it, I can tell you, sir, become a man of your character, to run about the country with an idle fellow and wench. Indeed, as for the girl, I know no harm of her. Slipslop tells me she was formerly bred up in my house, and behaved as she ought, till she hankered after this fellow, and he spoiled

her. Nay, she may still, perhaps do very well, if he will let her alone. You are, therefore, doing a monstrous thing in endeavouring to procure a match between these two people, which will be to the ruin of them both." - "Madam," said Adams, "if your ladyship will but hear me speak, I protest I never heard any harm of Mr Joseph Andrews; if I had, I should have corrected him for it; for I never have, nor will, encourage the faults of those under my cure. As for the young woman, I assure your ladyship I have as good an opinion of her as your ladyship yourself or any other can have. She is the sweetest-tempered, honestest, worthiest young creature; indeed, as to her beauty, I do not commend her on that account, though all men allow she is the handsomest woman, gentle or simple, that ever appeared in the parish." - "You are very impertinent," says she, "to talk such fulsome stuff to me. It is mighty becoming truly in a clergyman to trouble himself about handsome women, and you are a delicate judge of beauty, no doubt. A man who hath lived all his life in such a parish as this is a rare judge of beauty! Ridiculous! Beauty indeed! A country wench a beauty! I shall be sick whenever I hear beauty mentioned again. And so this wench is to stock the parish with beauties, I hope. But, sir, our poor is numerous enough already; I will have no more vagabonds settled here" - "Madam," says Adams, "your ladyship is offended with me, I protest, without any reason. This couple were desirous to consummate long ago, and I dissuaded them from it; nay, I may venture to say, I believe I was the sole cause of their delaying it" - "Well," says she, "and you did very wisely and honestly too, notwithstanding she is the greatest beauty in the parish." - "And now, madam," continued he, "I only perform my office to Mr Joseph." - "Pray, don't mister such fellows to me," cries the lady. "He," says the parson, "with the consent of Fanny, before my face, put in the banns." "Yes," answered the lady, "I suppose the slut is forward enough; Slipslop tells me how her head runs upon fellows; that is one of her beauties, I suppose. But if they have put in the banns, I desire you will publish them no more without my orders." - "Madam," cries Adams, "if any one puts in a sufficient caution, and assigns a proper reason against them, I am willing to surcease." - "I tell you a reason," says she: "he is a vagabond, and he shall not settle here, and bring a nest of beggars into the parish; it will make us but little amends that they will be beauties." - "Madam," answered Adams, "with the utmost submission to your ladyship, I have been informed by lawyer Scout that any person who serves a year gains a settlement in the parish where he serves." - "Lawyer Scout," replied the lady, "is an impudent coxcomb; I will have no lawyer Scout interfere with me. I repeat to you again, I will have no more incumbrances brought on us: so I desire you will proceed no farther." - "Madam," returned Adams, "I would obey your ladyship in everything that is lawful; but surely the parties being poor is no reason against their marrying. God forbid there should be any such law! The poor have little share enough of this world already; it would be barbarous indeed to deny them the common privileges and innocent enjoyments which nature indulges to the animal creation." - "Since you understand yourself no better," cries the lady, "nor the respect due from such as you to a woman of my distinction, than to affront my ears by such loose discourse, I shall mention but one short word; it is my orders to you that you publish these banns no more; and if you dare, I will recommend it to your master, the doctor, to discard you from his service. I will, sir, notwithstanding your poor family; and then you and the greatest beauty in the parish may go and beg together." - "Madam," answered Adams, "I know not what your ladyship means by the terms master and service. I am in the service of a Master who will never discard me for doing my duty; and if the doctor (for indeed I have never been able to pay for a licence) thinks proper to turn me from my cure, God will provide me, I hope another. At least, my family, as well as myself, have hands; and he will prosper, I doubt not, our endeavours to get our bread honestly with them. Whilst my conscience is pure, I shall never fear what man can do unto me." - "I condemn my humility." said the lady, "for demeaning myself to converse with you so long. I shall take other measures; for I see you are a confederate with them. But the sooner you leave me the better; and I shall give orders that my doors may no longer be open to you. I will suffer no parsons who run about the country with beauties to be entertained here." - "Madam," said Adams, "I shall enter into no persons' doors against their will; but I am assured, when you have enquired farther into this matter, you will applaud, not blame, my proceeding; and so I humbly take my leave:" which he did with many bows, or at least many attempts at a bow.

THE CREED

It is an ancient custom to turn eastwards to say the Creed; but the congregation normally face eastward in any case, and only the clergy and choir need to turn. In churches of an evangelical tradition this symbolic action is often left unperformed.

20. I fell into a low state of health at St James's School, and finally after a serious illness my parents took me away. Our family doctor, the celebrated Robson Roose, then practised at Brighton; and as I was now supposed to be very delicate, it was thought desirable that I should be under his constant care. I was accordingly, in 1883, transferred to a school at Brighton kept by two ladies. This was a smaller school than the one I had left. It was also cheaper and less pretentious. But there was an element of kindness and of sympathy which I had found conspicuously lacking in my first experiences.

My partiality for Low Church principles which I had acquired from Mrs Everest *[his nurse]* led me into one embarrassment. We often attended the service in the Chapel Royal at Brighton. Here the school was accommodated in pews which ran North and South. In consequence, when the Apostles' Creed was recited, everybody turned to the East. I was sure Mrs Everest would have considered this practice Popish, and I conceived it my duty to testify against it. I therefore stood stolidly to my front. I was conscious of having created a "sensation". I prepared myself for martyrdom. However, when we got home no comment of any kind was made upon my behaviour. I was almost disappointed, and looked forward to the next occasion for a further demonstration of my faith. But when it came, the school was shown into different pews in the Chapel Royal facing East, and no action was called for from any one of us when the Creed was said. I was puzzled to find my true course and duty. It seemed excessive to turn away from the East. Indeed I could not feel that such a step would be justified. I therefore became willy-nilly a passive conformist.

It was thoughtful and ingenious of these old ladies to have treated my scruples so tenderly. The results repaid their care. Never again have I caused or felt trouble on such a point. Not being resisted or ill-treated, I yielded myself complacently to a broad-minded tolerance and orthodoxy.

Contrariwise, Edward, also sitting in the transept, was only too ready to turn eastwards.

21. Nobody would have suspected Edward of being in love, had it not been that after breakfast, with an overacted carelessness, "Anybody who likes," he said, "can feed my rabbits," and he disappeared with a jauntiness that deceived nobody, in the direction of the orchard. . . .

Harold found Edward, pacing the orchard, with the sort of set smile that mountebanks wear in their precarious antics, fixed painfully on his face, as with pins. Harold opened well on the rabbit subject, but, with a fatal confusion between the abstract and the concrete, had then gone on to remark that Edward's lop-eared doe, with her long hindlegs and contemptuous twitch of the nose, always reminded him of Sabina Larkin (a nine year old damsel, child of a neighbouring farmer): at which point Edward, it would seem, had turned upon and savagely mistreated him, twisting his arm and punching him in the short-ribs. . . .

Edward's general demeanour during morning service was safe to convict him; but there was also a special test for the particular case. It happened that we sat in a transept, and, the Larkins being behind us, Edward's only chance of feasting on Sabina's charms was in the all-too-fleeting interval when we swung round eastwards. I was not mistaken. During the singing of the Benedictus the impatient one made several false starts, and at last he slewed fairly round before "As it was in the beginning, is now, and ever shall be" was half finished. The evidence was conclusive: a court of law could have desired no better.

THE LORD'S PRAYER

The Lord's Prayer is said at the beginning of the service after the Confession and Absolution in accordance with ancient tradition, whereby the priest always began a service with the pater noster. In 1662 the doxology (for thine is the kingdom .. .) was added, as it is found in ancient Eastern Liturgies, and as it found its way into St Matthew's gospel; but the second time that the Lord's Prayer is said, the prayer ends in accordance with the earliest gospel texts at "deliver us from evil". Here indeed is a trap for the unwary.

For various reasons, Richard Cadogan - a poet - and his friend Gervase Fen - professor of English - are following a girl in Oxford, and are themselves being followed by two hired thugs, referred to in this passage as Scylla and Charybdis. They enter the chapel of St Christopher's college as Mattins is beginning. The "Witches Kitchen" is the nick-name for a separate enclosure for women.

22. The President frowned when a young woman with golden hair and blue eyes entered the Witches Kitchen during the first hymn; he frowned still more when, a few moments later, Fen and Cadogan arrived, noisily whispering; and he openly scowled when after a brief interval they were followed by two men in dark blue suits whose knowledge of the Anglican liturgy was plainly sketchy to a degree.

In order to get as near to the girl as possible, Fen and Cadogan made their way up to a public pew by the choir. Scylla and Charybdis settled themselves nearby. The ritual went its way with an effortless grace, and until it was over no one moved. Fen, who disapproved of congregational singing, occupied himself with glaring at anyone who opened his mouth. Cadogan, abandoning reflection on the tortured series of events in which he was involved, joined the President in a muted craving for lunch (by an unfortunate chance the First Lesson was largely concerned with the comestibles in favour with ancient Jewry). The girl worshipped unobtrusively. Scylla and Charybdis rose and fell with evident unease. Only the Lord's Prayer seemed to strike a chord, and then they were unhappily unaware that at one point in the proceedings it is curtailed, and so said "For Thine is the Kingdom" when everyone else was pronouncing the Amen.

VERSICLES AND RESPONSES

23. "What is the matter with Candlestickmaker?" Sandy said. "I don't dig him."
    "I just figured him out, Sandra, honey. He's what used to be called an immitigable blatherskite. That was when people knew how to talk."
    "The days when they said 'damnable,'" I threw in.
    "The way you and he talk together. This kind of antiphonal conversation. It's like an Episcopal ritual."

24. After breakfast we dawdled about till it was time to dress for church, and as most of the ladies took about five minutes more than they had allowed for, it seemed likely that we should be late. At the last moment, Miss Lucy lost her Prayer Book, and it was not till another five minutes had gone in the search that she remembered having left it in the church the Sunday before. This being settled we all stowed away in the carriages and drove off. It was only a short drive; but when we came in sight of the quaint little church there was no sound of bells, and it became evident that we were late. In the porch we shook out our dresses, the Irishman divided the burden of Prayer Books he had been gallantly bearing, and we swept up the little church into a huge square pew.
    "My dear Ida, I must tell you that we had been brought up to have a just horror of being late for service, this being a point on which my father was what is called "very particular". Fatima and I therefore felt greatly discomposed by our late and disturbing entrance, though we were in no way to blame. We had also been taught to kneel during the prayers, and it was with a most uncomfortable sensation of doubt and shame-facedness that we saw one lady after another sit down and bend her bonnet over her lap, and hesitated ourselves to follow our own customs in the face of such a majority. But the red-haired young lady seemed fated to help us out of our difficulties. She sank at once on her knees in a corner of the pew, her green silk falling round her; we knelt by her side, and the question was settled. The little Irishman cast a doubtful glance at her for a moment, and then sat down, bending his head deeply into his hat. We went through a similar process about responding, which did not seem to be the fashion with our hostess and her friends. The red-haired young lady held to her own customs, however, and we held with her. Our responses were the less conspicuous as they were a good deal drowned by the voice of an old gentleman in the next pew. Diversity seemed to prevail in the manners of the congregation. This gentleman stood during prayers, balancing a huge Prayer Book on the corner of the pew, and responding in a loud voice, more devout than tuneful, keeping exact time with the parson also, as if he had a grudge against the clerk and felt it due to himself to keep in advance of him.

THE COLLECTS AND ANTHEM

Of the three collects appointed to be read, only the first changes with the seasons and is found with the Epistle and Gospel to be used at Holy Communion. The second for peace and the third for grace are said at every morning prayer.

25. I knew the seasons of the church's year including that funny trio of Sundays which come before Lent known as Septuagesima, Sexagesima and Quinquagesima which I always visualized as three rather old, quaintly-dressed women. And I could name the colours associated with each season. All these were a hangover from the days of universal illiteracy but in Warcop School they still had to be learnt.

The Collects, many of which I had to memorize were pleasanter, self-contained and therefore easier to learn than the rather arid theology of the catechism. Some of them became so much a part of me that when Tony Benn was trying to persuade the Cabinet to continue to support Concord (it had no 'e' then) the words: "Lover of concord", from the second collect for peace at matins came into my mind and ever afterwards I have thought of Tony as the lover of concord.

Though I loathed learning it at the time, I am glad now that I had to learn by heart so much memorable prose from the Book of Common Prayer which surely represents the high water mark of the English language. I can think of no more beautiful or economical language than that, for example, in the collect to which I have just referred nor any which expresses better that central theme of the Christian ethic, the reconciling of service and freedom ". . . . whose service is perfect freedom."

26. As usual at Mattins, St Lawrence's was about half-full. It was pleasanter inside than out, the light softened by the clear pale green glass with which Maurice had replaced some lurid windows shattered by blast, and warmed by the new red matting in chancel and nave. It had two treasures: a fine brass lectern of Flemish design in the shape of a spread eagle, and a reredos donated by an Episcopalian soldier from Long Island who, having wandered by sheer chance into the church ten minutes before the small bomb struck the east wall, and having escaped with nothing more than a cut on the cheek, had expressed his gratitude in this way. Otherwise, it was a typical church of the early nineteen-hundreds, bleak, draughty and without style. . . .

Plymmer stopped playing, then plunged in a rather perfunctory manner into the processional hymn. The congregation rose. The choir streamed in, headed by Derek, who was the son of the Pelhams' grocer, and looked a different boy on Sundays, remote, almost lunar, infinitely good. He was the youngest singer in the choir, which had men and women, but no children. The cross bobbed along towards the chancel, throwing off lemony gleams of light, for the rain had stopped and the sun had come out. As Maurice passed the pew where Libby sat she turned her face full upon him, uplifted, unashamed, and smiling: just perceptibly, with one corner of his mouth, he smiled in return. The Pelhams, moved, remembering the facts if not the emotions of old pleasures, smiled at each other and touched forefingers under cover of their respective prayer books.

An English Sunday, Humphrey thought, may not be flashy, but there is nothing like it. He made a mental note to say this to Georgina.

She was thinking that the vicar looked tired: but then, poor man, he would. They did too much, all of them did. She thought he rushed the service a little.

"Funny old girl," Humphrey murmured, under cover of the lesson, jerking his head in the direction of Miss Falls, whose only eccentricity - but it was enough - was to wear the skirt of a perfectly ordinary suit down to her ankles. In the eyes of some parishioners, but not of the Pelhams, she had another eccentricity: she turned up unfailingly to the service at 8 a.m. Georgina nodded to show that she had heard. Miss Falls was funny every Sunday.

"'Grant that this day,'" Maurice was saying in his clear, rather dull voice, "'we fall into no sin neither run into any kind of danger—'" He twitched his head towards the gallery, where there had been some faint sound of giggle and scuffle - "'but that all our doings may be ordered by Thy governance to do always that is righteous in Thy sight . . .'"

"'In Quires and Places where they sing,'" said Humphrey, quoting in a whisper, "'here followeth the Anthem." Heaven help us.'

This was Plymmer's moment, this was where he came into his own. Where he got his anthems from, the Pelhams did not know; nor why the vicar did not restrain him. Humphrey, though uninterested in music, had a good ear; he had recognised that Plymmer's anthems were not infrequently too much for the choir.

The performance that morning was ambitious and ragged; also it was long. Only Peter Betts and Louis Waterer, in their front pew, maintained an attitude of enthusiasm, even of excitement. Peter sat rigid, with parted lips, his first and second fingers to the knot of his tie. Louis, much smaller, much younger, much darker, glanced at him now and then, beaming and sharing.

THE PRAYERS FOR THE KING'S MAJESTY
AND FOR THE ROYAL FAMILY

27. The sudden death of King Charles the Second threw all things into confusion, and all minds into a panic.

We heard of it first in church, on Sunday, the eighth day of February, 1684-5, from a cousin of John Fry, who had ridden over on purpose from Porlock. He came in just before the anthem, splashed and heated from his ride, so that every one turned and looked at him. He wanted to create a stir (knowing how much would be made of him), and he took the best way to do it. For he let the anthem go by very quietly - or rather I should say very pleasingly, for our choir was exceedingly proud of itself, and I sang bass twice as loud as a bull, to beat the clerk with the clarionet - and then just as Parson Bowden, with a look of pride at his minstrels, was kneeling down to begin the prayer for the King's Most Excellent Majesty (for he never read the Litany, except upon Easter Sunday), up jumps young Sam Fry, and shouts, -

"I forbid that there prai-er."

"What!" cried the parson, rising slowly, and looking for some one to shut the door: "have we a rebel in the congregation?" For the parson was growing short-sighted now, and knew not Sam Fry at that distance.

"No," replied Sam, not a whit abashed by the staring of all the parish; "no rebel, parson; but a man who mislaiketh popery and murder. That there prai-er be a prai-er for the dead."

"Nay," cried the parson, now recognising and knowing him to be our John's first cousin, "you do not mean to say, Sam, that His Gracious Majesty is dead."

"Dead as a sto-un: poisoned by they Papishers." And Sam rubbed his hands with enjoyment, at the effect he had produced.

"Remember where you are, Sam," said Parson Bowden, solemnly; "when did this most sad thing happen? The King is the head of the Church, Sam Fry; when did His Majesty leave her?"

"Day afore yesterday. Twelve o'clock. Warn't us quick to hear of 'un?"

"Can't be," said the minister: "the tidings can never have come so soon. Anyhow, he will want it all the more. Let us pray for His Gracious Majesty."

And with that he proceeded as usual; but nobody cried "Amen," for fear of being entangled with popery. But after giving forth his text, our parson said a few words out of book, about the many virtues of His Majesty, and self-denial, and devotion, comparing his pious mirth to the dancing of the patriarch David before the ark of the covenant; and he added, with some severity, that if his flock would not join their pastor (who was much more likely to judge aright) in praying for the King, the least they could do, on returning home, was to pray that the King might not be dead, as his enemies had asserted.

Morning Prayer ends with the quotation from St Paul's 2nd Epistle to the Corinthians, commonly called The Grace. Cranmer hoped that Mattins and Evensong would be said daily, and Psalms and Lessons were arranged to this purpose.

28. Mr Copley's study was at the back of the Old Rectory, looking out over the unkempt lawn and the three rows of wind crippled bushes which the Copleys called the shrubbery. It was the only room in the rectory which Meg would not dream of entering without first knocking and it was accepted as his private place as if he were still in charge of a parish and needing a quiet sanctum to prepare his weekly sermon or counsel those parishioners who sought his advice. It was here each day he read Morning Prayer and Evensong, his only congregation his wife and Meg, whose low feminine voices would make the responses and read alternate verses of the psalms. On her first day with them he had said gently but without embarrassment: "I say the two main offices every day in my study, but please don't feel that you need to attend unless you wish to."

She had chosen to attend, at first from politeness, but later because this daily ritual, the beautiful, half-forgotten cadences, seducing her into belief, gave a welcome shape to the day.

For most generations the service on Sundays and Holy Days has consisted of Mattins, Litany and Ante-Communion, and monthly, or more frequently, Communion. Thus the sermon was preached after the Creed in the Ante-Communion as the Rubric demands.

Today, Mattins, or alternatively Holy Communion, are generally considered sufficient for our spiritual needs, and sadly the Litany is rarely used. Where Mattins still prevails over a sung Communion, the Sermon and Blessing, divided by hymns, follow the prayers.

"Here endeth the Order of Morning Prayer throughout the Year."

REFERENCES

1. Paul Scott, *Staying On,* Heinemann 1977, Ch. 11.
2. James Lee-Milne, *Another Self,* Hamish Hamiton 1970.
3. Thomas Hardy, *Far From the Madding Crowd,* Macmillan 1902, Ch. 8.
4. A.H. Jones , *His Lordship's Obedient Servant,* Gomer Press 1987, Recollections of a South Wales Borderer.
5. Priscilla Napier, *A Late Beginner,* Michael Joseph 1966, Ch. 1 p. 16.
6. Geoffrey Lowis, *Fabulous Admirals,* Putnam 1957, Ch. Requestmen and Defaulters.
7. Paul Scott, *Staying On,* op. cit., Ch. 11.
8. Eric Bligh, *Tooting Corner,* Secker & Warburg 1946, p. 260.
9. Thomas Hardy, *Tess of the D'Urbervilles,* Macmillan 1891, Ch. Maiden no More.
10. James Lee-Milne, *Another Self,* op. cit., Ch. Tobias and the Angel.
11. Priscilla Napier, *A Late Beginner,* op. cit., Ch. 13.
12. Ibid, Ch. 15.
13. Kate Douglas Wiggin, *A Cathedral Courtship,* Gay & Hancock Ltd. 1901.
14. Eric Bligh, *Tooting Corner,* op. cit., p. 259.
15. Thomas Hardy, *Tess of the D'Urbervilles,* op. cit., Ch. The Rally.
16. Beverley Nichols, *A Village in a Valley,* Jonathan Cape 1934, Ch. 1.
17. W.H. Auden, *A Certain World,* Faber & Faber 1971, Choirboys p. 73.
18. Dorothy L. Sayers, *The Nine Tailors,* Victor Gollancz 1935, Lord Peter is called into the hunt.
19. Henry Fielding, *The Adventures of Joseph Andrews,* Millar 1742, Book IV Ch. 2.
20. Winston Churchill, *My Early Life,* Collins 1930, Ch. 2 Childhood.
21. Kenneth Grahame, *The Golden Age,* Methuen 1932, Young Adam Cupid.
22. Edmund Crispin, *The Moving Toyshop,* Victor Gollancz 1946, pp. 77-8.
23. Peter de Vries, *Consenting Adults,* Victor Gollancz 1981, Ch. 13.
24. J.H. Ewing, *Mrs Overtheway's Remembrances,* Henry Frowde & Hodder & Stoughton 1911, Ch. The Snoring Ghost.
25. Edward Short, *I Knew My Place,* MacDonald & Co. 1983, p. 182.
26. Pamela Hansford Johnson, *The Humbler Creation,* Macmillan 1959.
27. R.D. Blackmore, *Lorna Doone,* (1869) Everyman Library, J.M. Dent & Sons 1906, Ch. The King must not be prayed for.
28. P.D. James, *Devices & Desire,* Faber & Faber 1988, Ch. 51.

CHAPTER 2
Evening Prayer or Evensong

A famous German scholar, Rudolf Otto, during a visit to England in 1928, reflected on his experience of Evensong in a conversation with a former Dean of St Paul's who writes:

1. We corresponded at intervals particularly on one subject which was near his heart - to compose a Book of Common Prayer for the German people.

My connection with this began in a conversation which took place in London the evening before Otto returned to Marburg, after giving his lectures on "Mysticism, Eastern or Western". He had not been in England for thirty five years, though he lectured in English with no manuscript except one sheet of notepaper. While staying with us, he had moved about the country and formed a judgement on its condition. I asked him what he thought of England now. I have often thought about his answer: "England is still the most religious country in Europe." I was surprised and implored him to say what he meant. His answer could be summarily stated as "that England is the one country in Europe in which large sections of the population are guided in public and private affairs by Christian principles." So far as I remember, he did not include Scotland in his verdict - and this has some bearing on the next stage of the conversation. I said, "Supposing you to be right in your estimate of the religion of the nation, to what causes would you attribute its relative soundness?" He replied, "Very largely to the Book of Common Prayer." I can remember verbatim his elaboration of this idea. "Last Sunday evening I was in Canterbury Cathedral at Evensong. The congregation of over a thousand people was a mixture of all kinds of citizens: tradesmen with their wives, soldiers with their girls and so on through a long range of occupations - a cross section of the population. And these people had thoughts given them which they could never have conceived by themselves, in language which they could not have chosen themselves, but which stays in their mind like a song.

A weekday Evensong at "Silbury"

2. Alethea *[the new Dean's wife]* loved a weekday Evensong. The congregation was rarely more than 20 or 30, but the emptiness of the building, the very absence of worshippers, seemed rather paradoxically to create in a supreme degree the sense of worship. She felt no longer Alethea Mallinson held down by a weight of petty worries, by bodily aches and pains, but someone or something which had a place in a great act of praise, an act which was not in time but in eternity. Before she came to Silbury she had had this feeling when she was alone in the country, and most of all if she were walking in mountains; but it was stronger in the Cathedral than she

31

had ever known it. She wondered sometimes if it could be good, it was not allied with thought, hardly even with mental pictures. She returned from it always with a feeling of exaltation, a conviction that the centre of her life was somewhere beyond, but she was never sure that her faults were fewer, or her prayers more earnest.

This afternoon she forgot her anxiety, forgot she was tired, and for a little while became one with the beauty of the Service, with the pillars fading into the dark roof, the lights on the altar, the dim windows, young Collins's voice answered by the harmony of the choir. She left the Cathedral hardly conscious of who had been there, and entered her house with a mind at rest.

THE GENERAL CONFESSION AND ABSOLUTION

3. I think, as Mr Irwine looked round to-day, his eyes rested an instant longer than usual on the square pew occupied by Martin Poyser and his family. And there was another pair of dark eyes that found it impossible not to wander thither, and rest on that round, pink-and-white figure. But Hetty was at that moment quite careless of any glances - she was absorbed in the thought that Arthur Donnithorne would soon be coming into church, for the carriage must surely be at the church gate by this time. She had never seen him since she parted with him in the wood on Thursday evening, and oh! how long the time had seemed! Things had gone on just the same as ever since that evening; the wonders that had happened then had brought no changes after them; they were already like a dream. When she heard the church door swinging, her heart beat so, she dared not look up. She felt that her aunt was curtsying; she curtsied herself. That must be old Mr Donnithorne - he always came first, the wrinkled small old man, peering round with short-sighted glances at the bowing and curtsying congregation; then she knew Miss Lydia was passing, and though Hetty liked so much to look at her fashionable little coal-scuttle bonnet, with the wreath of small roses round it, she didn't mind it to-day. But there were no more curtsies - no, he was not come; she felt sure there was nothing else passing the pew door but the housekeeper's black bonnet, and the lady's maid beautiful straw that had once been Miss Lydia's, and then the powdered heads of the butler and the footman. No, he was not there; yet she would look now - she might be mistaken - for, after all, she had not looked. So she lifted up her eyelids and glanced timidly at the cushioned pew in the chancel: - there was no one but old Mr Donnithorne rubbing his spectacles with his white handkerchief, and Miss Lydia opening the large gilt-edged prayer-book. The chill disappointment was too hard to bear: she felt herself turning pale, her lips trembling; she was ready to cry. Oh, what *should* she do? Everybody would know the reason; they would know she was crying because Arthur was not there. And Mr Craig, with the wonderful hot-house plant in his buttonhole, was staring at her, she knew. It was dreadfully long before the General Confession began, so that she could kneel down. Two great drops *would* fall then, but no one saw them except good-natured Molly, for her aunt and uncle knelt with their backs towards her. Molly, unable to imagine any cause for tears in church except faintness, of which she had a vague traditional knowledge, drew out of her pocket a queer little flat blue smelling-bottle, and after much labour in pulling the cork out, thrust the narrow neck against Hetty's nostrils. "It donna smell," she whispered, thinking this was a great advantage which old salts had over fresh ones: they did you good without biting your nose. Hetty pushed it away peevishly; but this little flash of

temper did what the salts could not have done - it roused her to wipe away the traces of her tears, and try with all her might not to shed any more. Hetty had a certain strength in her vain little nature: she would have borne anything rather than be laughed at, or pointed at with any other feeling than admiration; she would have pressed her own nails into her tender flesh rather than people should know a secret she did not want them to know.

What fluctuations there were in her busy thoughts and feelings, while Mr Irwine was pronouncing the solemn "Absolution" in her deaf ears, and through all the tones of petition that followed! Anger lay very close to disappointment, and soon won the victory over the conjectures her small ingenuity could devise to account for Arthur's absence on the supposition that he really wanted to come, really wanted to see her again. And by the time she rose from her knees mechanically, because all the rest were rising, the colour had returned to her cheeks even with a heightened glow, for she was framing little indignant speeches to herself, saying she hated Arthur for giving her this pain - she would like him to suffer too. Yet while this selfish tumult was going on in her soul, her eyes were bent down on her prayer-book, and the eyelids with their dark fringe looked as lovely as ever. Adam Bede thought so, as he glanced at her for a moment on rising from his knees.

But Adam's thoughts of Hetty did not deafen him to the service; they rather blended with all the other deep feelings for which the church service was a channel to him this afternoon, as a certain consciousness of our entire past and our imagined future blends itself with all our moments of keen sensibility. And to Adam the church service was the best channel he could have found for his mingled regret, yearning, and resignation; its interchange of beseeching cries for help, with outbursts of faith and praise - its recurrent responses and the familiar rhythm of its collects, seemed to speak for him as no other form of worship could have done; as, to those early Christians who had worshipped from their childhood upward in catacombs, the torch-light and shadows must have seemed nearer the Divine presence than the heathenish daylight of the street. The secret of our emotions never lies in the bare object, but in its subtle relations to our own past: no wonder the secret escapes the unsympathising observer, who might as well put on his spectacles to discern odours.

THE OPENING VERSICLES AND RESPONSES

4. 'O Lord, open thou our lips', sang the resonant operatic tenor of Canon Sylvester, newly returned from Italy, and indeed, thought Ian, it might almost be La Scala itself.

'And our mouths shall show forth thy praise', responded Theodora in her pleasant baritone. Seated in her accustomed place at the back of the choir stalls, she allowed her eye to wander up to the high altar and the lancet window of the east end before descending again to the Canons' stalls and the Bishop's throne. Thank Heavens it's all over, she thought happily, and we can resume normal life, that is, Choral Evensong. Then she thought of the Bishop who had lost a son and who could not bear it.

'O Lord, make haste to help us,' the choir answered Canon Sylvester's petition. Ian, a row in front of Theodora, thought of Williams and Mrs. Thrigg and the silly collection of half-wits who had come to hate the ordinariness of virtue, the sober and godly life of the Anglican collects, and wanted excitements of a darker kind. What a lot of help we all of us do seem to need.

THE PSALMS AND OLD TESTAMENT LESSON

5. How dignified, how stately, how elegant, with ranks of tapers wavering gold against a dim background, while boys' voices lift the psalm *Audite hæc, omnes* high above the pealing organ to the high embowed roof, to linger and wander there among ten thousand cells. Through the windows richly light, slant crimson, violet and deep blue rays of October evening sunshine; it touches the round heads and white surplices of little singing boys; it glints on the altar, dimming the tall, flickering flames, gleaming on the heads of thoughtful clergymen who listen to the quire's chant. *For he shall carry nothing away with him when he dieth: neither shall his pomp follow him. For while he lived he counted himself an happy man: and so long as thus doest well unto thyself, men will speak good of thee. He shall follow the generation of his fathers: and shall never see light. Man being in honour hath no understanding: but is compared unto the beasts that perish. . . .*

The soft and melancholy chants dies on a falling lilt. The clergy, quire and people sit down in deep oak seats, all but the lector, who rustles to the lectern, adjusts his pince-nez, and says gently, "*Here beginneth the first verse of the sixth chapter of the Book of Micah. Hear ye now what the Lord saith: Arise, contend thou before the mountains, and let the hills hear thy voice. . . .*"

The musical Eton-and-Cambridge monotone, just not parsonically pitched, strolls on, relating the Lord's controversy in the mountains with his people. I turn the pages of my Prayer Book, read the charming rubrics, read the Preface, of 1662, so gentlemanlike, so suavely urbane. *It hath been the wisdom of the Church of England, ever since the first compiling of her Publick Liturgy, to keep the mean between the two extremes. . . .*

And then, Of Ceremonies, why some be abolished and some retained. . . . *And moreover, they be neither dark nor dumb ceremonies, but are so set forth, that every man may understand what they do mean, and to what use they do serve. . . . And in these our doings we condemn no other Nations, nor prescribe anything but to our own people only: For we think it is convenient that every Country should use such Ceremonies as they shall think best to the setting forth of God's honour and glory, and to the reducing of the people to a most perfect and godly living. . . .*

Meanwhile, the Eton-and-Cambridge voice is gently putting searching inquiries, becoming reluctantly menacing. *Are there yet,* it asks, *the treasures of wickedness in the house of the wicked, and the scant measure that is abominable? Shall I count them pure with the wicked balances, and with the bag of deceitful weights? Therefore also will I make thee sick in smiting thee, in making thee desolate because of thy sins. Thou shalt eat, but not be satisfied. . . . Thou shalt sow, but thou shalt not reap; thou shalt tread the olives, but thou shalt not drink wine. . . . That I should make thee a desolation, and the inhabitants thereof a hissing. . . .*

It has grown too violent, this mountain controversy. *Here endeth the first Lesson,* and so to the Magnificat. One feels that it was time.

These violent Hebrews: they break in strangely, with hot Eastern declamation and gesture, into our tranquil Anglican service, our so ordered and so decent Common Prayer. A desolation and a hissing: those are not threats that our kindly clergy like to quote, even against those of their flock who have abominable scant measures and wicked balances. Milton railed against "the oppressions of a simonious, decimating clergy," but, thought they cannot help (since they must live) being decimating, they are no longer so simonious, and are a kindly race.

As to these services, which they long since so gracefully adapted, so fitly, beautifully, and ceremoniously translated and assembled, they are, as Sir John Suckling pointed out three centuries ago, fit for the attendance of even the fastidious Cato, who was disgusted by those of his own age and country. "Then," complained the shocked Sir John, "the Ceremonies of *Liber Pater* and *Ceres*, how obscene! and those Days which were set apart for the Honour of the Gods, celebrated with such shews as *Cato* himself was ashamed to be present at. On the contrary, our Services are such, as not only *Cato*, but God himself may be there."

Or so, at least, we hope. No doubt the Romans hoped too that Liber Pater and Ceres were present with them at worship, and that their lectisternia were enjoyed by the reclining and feasting deities. Be that as it may, and whatever the gods may think of it (and one must endeavour not to fall into arrogance in this matter of divine attendance at our worship), for my part I greatly admire and enjoy the Anglican order.

Though of course there is, from time to time, a sermon. . . . But it seems that this cannot, in any Church, be helped.

Bertie Wooster and Jeeves show that their creator had a considerable knowledge of the Old Testament, Jael and Jezebel being used regularly, for example, to describe aunts and cousins. In the following passage, however, his genealogy is sadly at fault, and, whilst many extraordinary names can be found in the historical books, Jazzbo is not one of them.

6. It is always unpleasant not to be on speaking terms with an old friend. To be cooped up alone in a mouldy village pub with an old friend with whom one has ceased to converse is simply rotten. And this is especially so if the day happens to be a Sunday.

Maiden Eggesford, like so many of our rural hamlets, is not at its best and brightest on a Sunday. When you have walked down the main street and looked at the Jubilee Watering-Trough, there is nothing much to do except go home and then come out again and walk down the main street once more and take another look at the Jubilee Watering-Trough. It will give you some rough idea of the state to which Barmy Fotheringay-Phipps had been reduced by the end of the next day when I tell you that the sound of the church bells ringing for evensong brought him out of the Goose and Grasshopper as if he had heard a fire-engine. The thought that at last something was going to happen in Maiden Eggesford in which the Jubilee Watering-Trough *motif* was not stressed, stirred him strangely. He was in his pew in three jumps. And as the service got under way he began to feel curious emotions going on in his bosom.

There is something about evening church in a village in the summer-time that affects the most hard-boiled. They had left the door open, and through it came the scent of lime trees and wall-flowers and the distant hum of bees fooling about. And gradually there poured over Barmy a wave of sentiment. As he sat and listened to the First Lesson he became a changed man.

The Lesson was one of those chapters of the Old Testament all about how

Abimelech begat Jazzbo and Jazzbo begat Zachariah. And, what with the beauty of the words and the peace of his surroundings, Barmy suddenly began to become conscious of a great remorse.

He had not done the square thing, he told himself, by dear old Pongo. Here was a chap, notoriously one of the best, as sound an egg as ever donned a heliotrope sock, and he was deliberately chiselling him out of the girl he loved. He was doing the dirty on a fellow whom he had been pally with since their Eton jacket days - a bloke who time and again had shared with him his last bar of almond-rock. Was this right? Was this just? Would Abimelech have behaved like that to Jazzbo or - for the matter of that - Jazzbo to Zachariah? The answer, he could not disguise it from himself, was in the negative.

THE MAGNIFICAT AND THE NUNC DIMITTIS

7. We went to hear Father Stanton preach at St Barnabas. The service was at 8 o'clock and the evening light was setting behind the lofty Campanile as we entered. The large Church was almost full, the great congregation singing like one man. The clergy and choir entered with a procession, incense bearers and a great gilt cross, the thurifers and acolytes being in short white surplices over scarlet cassocks and the last priest in the procession wearing a biretta and a chasuble stiff with gold. The Magnificat seemed to be the central point in the service and at the words "For behold from henceforth all generations shall call me blessed" the black biretta and golden chasuble (named Shuttleworth) advanced, was "censed" by the thurifer, then took the censer from him and censed the cross, the banners, the lights and the altar, till the Church was all in a fume. At least so Mayhew said. I myself could not see exactly what was done though I knew some ceremony was going on. It appeared to me to be pure Mariolatry.

8. Later came Evensong, which was as different from Matins as a tryst from a Trafalgar Square rally. The atmosphere was gentler, moonier, more private; the service was considered to be voluntary. We choirboys, of course, were compelled to go, but for the rest they went who would.

The church at night, in the dark of the churchyard, was just a strip of red-fired windows. Inside, the oil-lamps and motionless candles narrowed the place with shadows. The display of the morning was absent now; the nave was intimate, and sleepy. Only a few solitary worshippers were present this time, each cloaked in a separate absorption: a Miss Bagnall, Widow White, the church-cleaning woman, a widower, and the postman at the back. The service was almost a reverie, our hymns nocturnal and quiet, the psalms traditional and never varying so that one could sing them without a book. The scattered faithful, half-obscured by darkness, sang them as though to themselves. "Lord, now lettest Thou Thy servant depart in peace . . . ." It was sung, eyes closed, in trembling tones. It could not have been sung in the morning.

9. I was always glad to emerge from Morning Service, but I really looked forward to Evensong. The church door stood open, and from the trees and fields there drifted in a rich mingling of sounds and smells: the lush, evening scent of grasses

and wild flowers; the domestic sounds of small birds settling down to sleep. The long, hot day was done, and all life accepted its inevitable close. Even the humans showed no strain, assumed no other worldly expressions, no holy, hollow voices. The world was disappearing into shadow, and all that was left was cupped within the soft light of the church. The church itself was wrapped around by all the leaves and lanes of Worcestershire, and Worcestershire was wrapped around by all of England. Into this sheltering bowl there dropped the *Nunc Dimittis*, so serene and simple that it reached out beyond the grey stone walls, beyond the dusky churchyard where a blackbird sang; it reached out all the way to my mother in the distant north and told me how far from her I was.

Lord, now lettest Thou thy servant depart in peace - I could get so far, and then a deep emotion, a compound both of happiness and sorrow, welled up in me and stopped my voice. It was more than simple grief at being parted from my mother, though that was part of it; it was sorrow, sorrow so poignant that it was close to joy, for the beauty, the exact rightness, of this passing moment.

VERSICLES AND RESPONSES

10. I ran up to ask our friend if she were going to church, and would take us. She consented, and I went back in triumph to Fatima. As there was no time to lose, we dressed quickly enough; so that I was rather surprised, when we went down, to find the Irish gentleman, with his face restored to its usual good humour, standing by our friend, and holding her Prayer Book as well as his own. The young lady did not speak, but, cheerfully remarking that we had plenty of time before us, he took our books also, and we all set forth.

"I remember that walk so well, Ida! The hot, sweet summer afternoon - the dusty plants by the pathway - the clematis in the hedges (I put a bit into my Prayer Book, which was there for years) - the grasshoppers and flies that our dresses caught up from the long grass, and which reappeared as we sat during the sermon.

"The old gentleman was in his pew, but his glance was almost benevolent as, in good time, we took our places. We (literally) *followed* his example with much heartiness in the responses; and, if he looked over into our pew during prayers (and from his position he could hardly avoid it), he must have seen that even the Irishman had rejected compromises, and that we all knelt together.

THE COLLECTS

11. There was no answer at the Vicarage and all the windows were dark. And then Dalgleish remembered from his first visit to the Church that the noticeboard had shown Evensong at 4 on Thursdays. Father Barnes would presumably be in church. And so it proved. The great north door was unbolted and when he turned the heavy iron handle and pushed it open, he was met by the expected waft of incense and saw that the lights were on in the Lady Chapel and that Father Barnes robed only in his surplice and scarf, was leading the responses. The congregation was larger than Dalgleish had expected and the mutter of voices came to him clearly in a gentle disjointed murmur. He seated himself in the front row just inside the door and sat to listen in patience to Evensong, that most neglected and

aesthetically satisfying portion of the Anglican liturgy. For the first time since he had known it the church was being used for the purpose for which it had been built. . . .

The service was short; there was no address and no singing; and within minutes Father Barnes' voice, as if from a far distance but very clear, perhaps because the words were so familiar, was speaking the Third Collect for aid against all perils: "Lighten our darkness we beseech Thee, O Lord; And by Thy great mercy defend us from all perils and dangers of this night for the love of Thine only Son, our Saviour Jesus Christ.

The congregation murmured their amens, got to their feet and began to disperse.

John, a Welsh Baptist minister, has English friends staying with him.
12. He was obviously cheered by Arthur's promising to go over to Towyn to hear him preach on the Sunday evening. One good listener made all the difference to a preacher, he said.

Mrs Hughes would not have been seen in a chapel at any price, but I had no such scruples and went off happily with Arthur and John to Towyn.

"You may find it rather tiresome to sit through the whole thing in Welsh," said John as we paced along, "but I'll do what I always do when I know there is an English stranger in the congregation, I'll put in one prayer in English."

"How jolly it must be," said I, "to be able to turn from one language to another like that. Very effective sometimes, surely?"

John laughed and told me the story of the Welsh preacher in an English country church who said in the middle of his sermon, "How far more impressive is this passage in the original Hebrew. Listen." He then rolled out in his richest Welsh tones, "If there is a Welshman present will he kindly keep it to himself that I am talking Welsh and not Hebrew." In such a way, John admitted, a second language could be very impressive.

This anecdote put an idea into my head. We reached the ugly little chapel up a side street of Towyn, and it was already fairly crowded when Arthur and I took our seats, and John disappeared behind somewhere. When he began to preach my idea took shape. His face was a fine one, inspiring in itself. His voice, rising and falling as he warmed to his theme, had a magnetic influence on his congregation. Since I had no notion what he was talking about my idea of imagining it to be the Sermon on the Mount was easy to carry out. I pictured its first delivery in Aramaic, to the eager people on the hill-side. When the congregation sat up a little in their interested attention, or one gave a sympathetic groan, I imagined that they had just been startled by the injunction to hit a man back good and hard by offering the other cheek.

Instead of being bored I was sorry when the sermon came to an end. Then some prayers "from the bosom" followed, and right in the midst of them fell on my entranced ears my favourite collect "Lighten our darkness". Although I had heard these words countless times, with what a fresh beauty they struck me in those strange surroundings, and my heart warmed to John for his kindness.

Why are the Clergy . . .?
13. Why are the clergy of the Church of England
   Always altering the words of the prayers in the Prayer Book?

Cranmer's touch was surer than theirs, do they not respect him?
For instance last night in church I heard
(I italicize the interpolation)
"The Lord bless you and keep you *and all who are dear unto you*"
As the blessing is a congregational blessing and meant to be
This is questionable on theological grounds
But is it not offensive to the ear and also ludicrous?
That "unto" is a particularly ripe piece of idiocy
Oh how offensive it is. I suppose we shall have next
"Lighten our darkness we beseech thee oh Lord *and the darkness of
all who are dear unto us.*"
It seems a pity. Does Charity object to objection?
Then I cry, and not for the first time to that smooth face
Charity, have pity.

THE ANTHEM

The 29th December
14. There was scarce a score of persons in the Cathedral beside the Dean and some of his clergy, and the choristers, young and old, that performed the beautiful evening prayer. But Mr Tusher was one of the officiants, and read from the eagle in an authoritative voice, and a great black periwig: and in the stalls, still in her black widow's hood, sat Esmond's dear mistress, her son by her side, very much grown, and indeed a noble-looking youth, with his mother's eyes, and his father's curling brown hair, that fell over his *point de Venise* - a pretty picture such as Vandyke might have painted. Monsieur Rigaud's portrait of my Lord Viscount, done at Paris afterwards, gives but a French version of his manly, frank, English face. When he looked up there were two sapphire beams out of his eyes such as no painter's palette has the colour to match, I think. On this day there was not much chance of seeing that particular beauty of my young Lord's countenance; for the truth is, he kept his eyes shut for the most past, and, the anthem being rather long, was asleep.

But the music ceasing, my Lord woke up, looking about him, and his eyes lighting on Mr Esmond, who was sitting opposite him, gazing with no small tenderness and melancholy upon two persons who had so much of his heart for so many years, Lord Castlewood, with a start, pulled at his mother's sleeve (her face had scarce been lifted from her book), and said, "Look mother!" so loud, that Esmond could hear on the other side of the church, and the old Dean on his throned stall. Lady Castlewood looked for an instant as her son bade her, and held up a warning finger to Frank; Esmond felt his whole face flush, and his heart throbbing, as that dear lady beheld him once more. The rest of the prayers were speedily over: Mr Esmond did not hear them; nor did his mistress, very likely, whose hood went more closely over her face, and who never lifted her head again until the service was over, the blessing given, and Mr Dean, and his procession of ecclesiastics, out of the inner chapel.

Young Castlewood came clambering over the stalls before the clergy were fairly gone, and running up to Esmond, eagerly embraced him. "My dear, dearest old Harry!" he said, "are you come back? Have you been to the wars? You'll take me with you when you go again? Why didn't you write to us? Come to mother!"

[Henry Esmond and Lady Castlewood now meet after a year's separation. She has quarrelled with him, believing him responsible for her husband's death, but in the interval has learnt how wrong she was.]

"You had spared me many a bitter night, had you told me sooner," Mr Esmond said.

"I know it, I know it," she answered, in a tone of such sweet humility, as made Esmond repent that he should ever have dared to reproach her. "I know how wicked my heart has been; and I have suffered too, my dear. I confessed to Mr Atterbury - I must not tell any more. He - I said I would not write to you or go to you - and it was better even that, having parted, we should part. But I knew you would come back - I own that. That is no one's fault. And to-day, Henry, in the anthem, when they sang it, "When the Lord turned the captivity of Zion, we were like them that dream," I thought, yes, like them that dream - them that dream. And then it went, "They that sow in tears shall reap in joy; and he that goeth forth and weepeth, shall doubtless come again with rejoicing, bringing his sheaves with him"; I looked up from the book, and saw you. I was not surprised when I saw you. I knew you would come, my dear, and saw the gold sunshine round your head."

She smiled an almost wild smile as she looked up at him. The moon was up by this time, glittering keen in the frosty sky. He could see, for the first time now clearly, her sweet careworn face.

"Do you know what day it is?" she continued. "It is the 29th of December - it is your birthday! But last year we did not drink it - no, no. My Lord was cold, and my Harry was likely to die: and my brain was in a fever; and we had no wine. But now - now you are come again, bringing your sheaves with you, my dear." She burst into a wild flood of weeping as she spoke; she laughed and sobbed on the young man's heart, crying out wildly, "bringing your sheaves with you - your sheaves with you."

THE PRAYERS - FOR THE CLERGY AND PEOPLE

15. Maurice repeated the Collect for the day, and heard them all listening, their listening breaths poured out upon the tense air of the evening.

" .... and because through the weakness of our mortal nature we can do no good thing without Thee, grant us the help of Thy grace, that in keeping Thy commandments we may please Thee, both in will and deed. . . ."

He knew what they were thinking: Weakness of his mortal nature is just about right.

Johnson-Black and his wife sat bolt upright in their pew, their eyes tight shut, their hands brought down in prayer. He did not kneel because of his stomach-trouble, and she sat up to keep him company. The Kitsons slid half-off their seats, knees almost, but not quite, to the hassock. The Hannaways knelt properly and comfortably, as if they were taking a little nap. The Fawcetts rejected hassocks, and knelt rigidly on stone. In the front pew, Kate made her slight formal genuflection, but had forced the boys to thump down by pushing at their shoulders.

There was a larger congregation than was usual at Evensong, and Maurice fancied some of them had come for the kill. The moment that he finished the Collect he wished he could repeat it to them, for he had spoken mechanically, without thought except for himself.

He did manage, later, to make the prayer for the Clergy and People in a firm and minatory voice. He and the people, he felt, needed help, they no less than he. During the hymn preceding the sermon he saw that David was pale, singing out straight ahead of him without his customary quick glance of love at Lucy Simnett, who had been waiting for it. Throughout the whole church there was a feeling of wrongness. As he settled in his stall, he thought to himself that he would fight it by the defiance of silence, the defiance of his refusal to take action of any kind.

THE PRAYER OF ST CHRYSOSTOM

16. Mr Herrick, on Midsummer Day, 1647, seditiously, defiantly, and for the last time, for by Sunday he would be an outed minister, read the Evening Service from the Book of Common Prayer, including the Collect for the Feast of St John the Baptist. He was supported in this parting act of rebellion by a congregation of three. One was his maid, Prudence Baldwin, whom he had desired regularly to attend church with him on week-day feasts, that there might be two, even if seldom three, gathered together, to form the quorum suggested by St Chrysostom as a desirable condition for Divine benevolence. Prudence sat and knelt upright, making the responses in a defiant, not-to-be-brow-beaten voice. She was leaving the vicarage when her master did; she was not going to stay on to serve Mr John Syms, the weaver to Buckfastleigh, in his usurpation of the vicar's office, even though she would have, she supposed, to sit under him and hear him pray and preach in his wild Directory way. John Syms, indeed! As if *he* could have anything to say that would do a body any good.

There is a rubric at the end of the Catechism to the intent that "the Curate of every Parish shall diligently upon Sundays and Holy Days after the second lesson at Evening Prayer openly in the Church instruct and examine so many children of his Parish sent unto him, as he shall think convenient, in some part of this catechism."

Had this rubric continued to be observed today, congregations would have been more able to give a good account of their faith. As it is, they are left to the vagarious decisions of their parsons when they choose a subject for the sermon.

THE SERMON

17. The summer Sunday was drawing to a close. Twilight had fallen on the little garden of the Angler's Rest, and the air was fragrant with the sweet scent of jasmine and tobacco plant. Stars were peeping out. Blackbirds sang drowsily in the shrubberies. Bats wheeled through the shadows, and a gentle breeze played fitfully among the hollyhocks. It was, in short, as a customer who had looked in for a gin and tonic rather happily put it, a nice evening.

Nevertheless, to Mr Mulliner and the group assembled in the bar parlour of the inn there was a sense of something missing. It was due to the fact that Miss Postlethwaite, the efficient barmaid, was absent. Some forty minutes had elapsed before she arrived and took over from the pot-boy. When she did so, the quiet splendour of her costume and the devout manner in which she pulled the beer handle told their own story.

"You've been to church," said a penetrating Sherry and Angostura.

Miss Postlethwaite said Yes, she had, and it had been lovely.

"Beautiful in every sense of the word," said Miss Postlethwaite, filling an order for a pint of bitter. "I do adore evening service in the summer. It sort of does something to you, what I mean. All that stilly hush and what not."

"The vicar preached the sermon, I suppose?" said Mr Mulliner.

"Yes," said Miss Postlethwaite, adding that it had been extremely moving.

Mr Mulliner took a thoughtful sip of his hot Scotch and lemon.

"The old, old story," he said, a touch of sadness in his voice. "I do not know if you gentlemen were aware of it, but in the rural districts of England vicars always preach the evening sermon during the summer months, and this causes a great deal of discontent to seethe among curates. It exasperates the young fellows, and one can understand their feelings. As Miss Postlethwaite rightly says, there is something about the atmosphere of evensong in a village church that induces a receptive frame of mind in a congregation, and a preacher, preaching under such conditions, can scarcely fail to grip and stir. The curates withheld from so preaching, naturally feel that they are being ground beneath the heel of an iron monopoly and chiselled out of their big chance."

[Before other members of the bar parlour can interrupt, Mr Mulliner embarks on the tale of how one of his infinite number of relations, Anselm, Curate of Rising Mattock, does indeed get his big chance, for the Vicar, endeavouring to apprehend a burglar in the night, receives a black eye.]

"Bitter," said the vicar. "Bitter."

"I beg your pardon?" said Anselm.

He turned. His superior of the cloth was standing before the mirror, regarding himself in it with a rueful stare.

"Bitter!" he repeated. "I was thinking," he explained, "of the one I had planned to deliver at evensong to-morrow. A pippin, Mulliner, in the deepest and truest sense a pippin. I am not exaggerating when I say that I would have had them tearing up the pews. And now that dream is ended. I cannot possibly appear in the pulpit with a shiner like this. It would put wrong ideas into the heads of the congregation - always, in these rural communities, so prone to place the worst construction on such disfigurements. To-morrow, Mulliner, I shall be confined to my bed with a slight chill, and you will conduct both matins and evensong. Bitter!" said the Rev. Sidney Gooch. "Bitter!"

Anselm did not speak. His heart was too full for words.

In Anselm's deportment and behaviour on the following morning there was nothing to indicate that his soul was a maelstrom of seething emotions. Most curates who find themselves unexpectedly allowed to preach on Sunday evening in the summer time are like dogs let off the chain. They leap. They bound. They sing snatches of the more rollicking psalms. They rush about saying "Good morning, good morning," to everybody and patting children on the head. Not so Anselm. He knew that only by conserving his nervous energies would he be able to give of his best when the great moment came.

To those of the congregation who were still awake in the later stages of the service his sermon at Matins seemed dull and colourless. And so it was. He had no intention of frittering away eloquence on a morning sermon. He deliberately held himself back, concentrating every fibre of his being on the address which he was to deliver in the evening.

He had had it by him for months. Every curate throughout the English countryside keeps tucked away among his effects a special sermon designed to prevent him being caught short, if suddenly called upon to preach at evensong. And all through the afternoon he remained closeted in his room, working upon it. He pruned. He polished. He searched the Thesaurus for the telling adjective. By the time the church bells began to ring out over the fields and spinneys of Rising Mattock in the quiet gloaming, his masterpiece was perfected to the last comma.

Feeling more like a volcano than a curate, Anselm Mulliner pinned together the sheets of manuscript and set forth.

The conditions could not have been happier. By the end of the pre-sermon hymn the twilight was far advanced, and through the door of the little church there poured the scent of trees and flowers. All was still, save for the distant tinkling of sheep bells and the drowsy calling of rooks among the elms. With quiet confidence Anselm mounted the pulpit steps. He had been sucking throat pastilles all day and saying "Mi-mi" to himself in an undertone throughout the service, and he knew that he would be in good voice.

For an instant he paused and gazed about him. He was rejoiced to see that he was playing to absolute capacity. Every pew was full. There, in the squire's high-backed stall, was Sir Leopold Jellaby, O.B.E., with Myrtle at his side. There among the choir, looking indescribably foul in a surplice, sat Joe Beamish. There, in their respective places, were the butcher, the baker, the candlestick-maker and all the others who made up the personnel of the congregation. With a little sigh of rapture, Anselm cleared his throat and gave out the simple text of Brotherly Love.

18. I am convinced (said he to a friend) I ought to be present at divine service more frequently than I am; but the provocations given by ignorant and affected preachers too often disturb the mental calm which otherwise would succeed to prayer. I am apt to whisper to myself on such occasions - How can this illiterate fellow dream of fixing attention, after we have been listening to the sublimest truths, conveyed in the most chaste and exalted language, throughout a Liturgy which must be regarded as the genuine offspring of piety impregnated by wisdom?

The custom has grown up to end Evensong with The Blessing which Aaron and his sons were told to give the children of Israel in Numbers Ch. 6 verses 22-27.

19. When Stanley Spencer, the artist, was in hospital and Jack Westropp, his Vicar, visited him, Westropp's habit of reciting a Blessing before he left each night pleased Stanley, because he liked the beauty of the words. For the Blessing was the great one from Numbers 6[25], "The Lord bless thee and keep thee: The Lord make his face to shine upon thee, and be gracious unto thee: The Lord lift up his countenance upon thee, and give thee peace." Stanley was excited to feel that this great Blessing had come all the way from Aaron, its beauty having made it indestructible and endowed it with a potency which remained unabated, so that now in Cliveden hospital, thousands of years later, it spread its peace as it had in Aaron's day.

"Here endeth the order of Evening Prayer throughout the year."

REFERENCES

1. W.R. Matthews, *Memories and Meanings*, Hodder & Stoughton 1969, p. 216.
2. Susan Goodyear, *Cathedral Close*, Evergreen Books 1941, p. 173.
3. George Eliot, *Adam Bede*, Blackwood 1859, Church Ch. 18.
4. D.M. Greenwood, *Clerical Errors*, Headline 1991, Ch. 11.
5. Rose Macaulay, *Personal Pleasures*, Victor Gollancz 1949, Church Going: Anglican.
6. P.G. Wodehouse, *Young Men in Spats*, Herbert Jenkins 1936, Ch. 2 Tried in the furnace.
7. *The Diary of the Revd Francis Kilvert*, ed. William Plomer, Jonathan Cape 1940, May 1876.
8. Laurie Lee, *Cider with Rosie*, Hogarth Press 1959.
9. Anthony Quayle, *A Time to Speak*, Barrie & Jenkins 1990, Ch. 4.
10. J.H. Ewing, *Mrs Overtheway's Remembrances*, op. cit., Ch: The Snoring Ghost.
11. P.D. James, *A Taste for Death*, Faber & Faber 1986, p. 385.
12. M.V. Hughes, *A London Girl of the 1880's*, O.U.P. 1946, Ch. 12. A dwfn yw tonnau Dyfi.
13. Stevie Smith, *The Collected Poems*, Allen Lane 1975.
14. W.M. Thackeray, *The History of Henry Esmond*, Harper 1852, Book 2 Ch. 20.
15. Pamela Hansford Johnson, *The Humbler Creation*, op. cit., Ch. 41.
16. Rose Macaulay, *They Were Defeated*, Collins 1932, Postscript p. 373.
17. P.G. Wodehouse, *Eggs, Beans and Crumpets*, Herbert Jenkins 1940, Anselm gets his chance.
18. *Johnsonian Miscellanies*, ed. G. Birkbeck Hill, O.U.P. 1897, Anecdotes by George Stevens.
19. *The Diaries of Maurice Collis*, ed. Louise Collis, Wm Heinemann 1976, July 1960.

CHAPTER 3
Interlude: Parallel Patterns

Top and tail Mattins and Evensong, and we find we are left with a history lesson, but a special kind of lesson about a special history. In the Christian understanding the history is that of God working through his chosen people for the sake of all mankind. Thus, the service begins with psalms, hymns first sung centuries before Christ by the chosen people, the Jews; and they are followed by a reading from the Old Testament, which tells a part of their history and in it of their relationship with God. Then, in Mattins, comes the Te Deum, which bursts into the praise of Christ, whose coming into the world is the climax of this history; and, at Evensong, the Magnificat, which is not, *vide* Kilvert, in praise of Mary, but, because it is Mary's song of rejoicing because she knows she is to bear the Christ child, likewise directs our attention to the supreme moment of his coming. The second lesson tells of his words and deeds or of those of the Apostles, the first of his new chosen people, i.e. believers in Jesus Christ from any nation. The Benedictus, rejoicing in Christ's coming, ends on a forward look: he has come "to give light to them that sit in darkness", that is to all mankind. So, too, at Evensong, the emphasis of the Nunc Dimittis falls on Christ being "a light to lighten the Gentiles" - history is still being made, for all are meant to become God's chosen people through Him - their own searching, and their own discovery of God, fulfilled in him. (Alas! this message is often betrayed by the messengers - but that is another story. Contrariwise, they also learn from those to whom they are sent: what better posture for private prayer than the perfect posture taught by Hindu sages?).

History lessons can be boring, but these services are more than lessons about the past. We find God still speaking through the Scriptures, and, as we share in the psalms and canticles, we enter into the history, not simply as passive spectators, but sharing in the emotions of those who first sang, - the psalmists and Jewish worshippers, Mary, Zacharias and Simeon, and the unknown early Christian author of the Te Deum, so that the history lesson becomes our present praise and thanksgiving for God's mighty acts. The Creed sums these up in brief.

The "top" of Morning and Evening Prayer is the proper preparation for the worship of God by penitence; the "tail", as important as the body, is the prayers of the Church.

(See diagram overleaf).

Mattins	**Evensong**

Top: Opening Sentences, Invitation, Confession, Absolution and Lord's Prayer.
Opening Versicles and Responses.

Body:
Psalms
Old Testament Lesson

Te Deum	Magnificat
(or Benedicite)	(or Cantate Domino Ps. 98)

New Testament Lesson

Benedictus	Nunc Dimittis
(or Jubilate Deo Ps. 100)	(or Deus Misereatur Ps. 67)

Creed

Tail:
Lord's Prayer
Versicles and Responses
Collect for the Day
Collect for Peace

Collect for Grace	Collect for Aid against all perils

Prayers for the Queen etc.
The Prayer of St John Chrysostom
The Grace

Two points:

1. As can be seen from the diagram, alternatives for the canticles are provided in both Morning and Evening Prayer, all of them being psalms apart from the Benedicite, which is based on the Song of the Three Children, a part of the Book of Daniel in the Apocrypha. The psalm alternatives were added to the Prayer Book in the more Puritanical edition of 1552, perhaps in order to distance the services further from those in the old Latin Breviary. They are less fitting than the canticles, but are open to the same interpretation.

2. The names given to the psalms and canticles are the first word or two of their opening sentences in the original Latin. Canticle (a little song) is the name used for the songs that are not from the Book of Psalms in the Old Testament. The Magnificat, Benedictus and Nunc Dimittis are from the opening chapters of the Gospel according to St Luke.

CHAPTER 4
Quicunque Vult, Commonly Called the Creed of St Athanasius

To be sung or said at Morning Prayer on major festivals, instead of the Apostles' Creed.

1. But in Raveloe village the bells rang merrily, and the church was fuller than all through the rest of the year, with red faces among the abundant dark green boughs - faces prepared for a longer service than usual by an advance breakfast of toast and all. Those green boughs, the hymns and anthem never heard but at Christmas - even the Athanasian Creed, which was discriminated from the others only as being longer and of exceptional virtue, since it was only read on rare occasions - brought a vague exulting sense, for which the grown men could as little have found words as the children, that something great and mysterious had been done for them in heaven above, and in earth below, which they were appropriating by their presence. And then the red faces made their way through the black biting frost to their own homes feeling themselves free for the rest of the day to eat, drink and be merry, and using that Christian freedom without diffidence.

2. It had been settled on Christmas Eve that the three Coningsbys would go to the village church on Christmas day. . . .

Nancy managed to keep Sybil between herself and her father as they filed into a pew, and sat down between her and a pillar with a sense of protection. Nothing unusual was likely to happen for the next hour or two, unless it was the Vicar's new setting of the Athanasian Creed. Aaron Lee had remarked that the man was a musical enthusiast, doing the best he could with the voices at his disposal, assisted by a few friends whom he had down at Christmas.

This Christmas, it seemed, he was attempting a little music which he himself had composed. Nancy was quite willing that he should - nothing seemed more remote from excitement or mystery than the chant of the Athanasian Creed. During the drive down her father had commented disapprovingly on the Church's use of that creed. Sybil had asked why he disliked it. Mr Coningsby had asked if she thought it Christian; and Sybil said she didn't see anything very un-Christian about it - not if you remembered the hypothesis of Christianity.

"And what," Mr Coningsby said, as if this riddle were entirely unanswerable, "what do you call the hypothesis of Christianity?"

"The Deity of Love and the Incarnation of Love?" Sybil suggested, adding, "Of course, whether you agree with it is another thing."

"Certainly I agree with Christianity," Mr Coningsby said. "Perhaps I shouldn't put it quite like that. It's a difficult thing to define. But I don't see how the damnatory clauses -"

However, there they reached the church. . . .

A door opened; the congregation stirred; a voice from the vestry said: "Hymn 61. 'Christians, awake,' Hymn 61." Everyone awoke, found the place, and stood up. The choir started at once on the hymn and the procession. Nancy docilely sent her voice along with them.

Christians, awake, salute the happy morn,

Whereon the Saviour of the world was born:

Rise to a -

Her voice ceased; the words stared up at her. The choir and the congregation finished the line -

adore the mystery of love.

"The mystery of love." But what else was in her heart? The Christmas associations of the verse had fallen away; there was the direct detached cry, bidding her do precisely and only what she was burning to do. "Rise to adore the mystery of love." What on earth were they doing, singing about the mystery of love in church? They couldn't possibly be meaning it. Or were they meaning it and had she misunderstood the whole thing?

She looked back at the hymn and hastily read it - it was really a very commonplace hymn, a very poor copy of verses. Only that one commanding rhythm still surged through her surrendered soul - "Rise to adore the mystery of love." But now everyone else was shutting up hymn-books and turning to prayer-books; she took one more glance at the words, and did the same. . . . . . .

She was still rather overwhelmed when they came to the Athanasian Creed, and it may have been because of her own general chaos that even that despised formulary took part in the general break-up which seemed to be proceeding within her. All the first part went on in its usual way; she knew nothing about musical setting of creeds, so she couldn't tell what to think of this one. The men and the boys of the choir exchanged metaphysical confidences; they dared each other, in a kind of rapture - which, she supposed, was the setting - to deny the Trinity or the Unity; they pointed out, almost mischievously, that though they were compelled to say one thing, yet they were forbidden to say something else exactly like it; they went into particulars about an entirely impossible relationship, and concluded with an explanation that something wasn't true which the wildest dream of any man but the compiler of the creed could hardly have begun to imagine. All this Nancy half-ignored.

But the second part - and it was of course the setting - for one verse held her. It was of course the setting, the chance that sent one boy's voice sounding exquisitely through the church. But the words which conveyed that beauty sounded to her full of sudden significance. The mingled voices of men and boys were proclaiming the nature of Christ - "God and man is one in Christ"; then the boys fell silent, and the men went on "One, not by conversion of the Godhead into flesh, but by taking of the manhood into God." On the assertion they ceased, and the boys rushed joyously in, "One altogether, not" they looked at the idea and tossed it airily away - "*not* by confusion of substance, but by unity" - they were silent, all but one, and that fresh perfection proclaimed the full consummation, each syllable rounded, prolonged, exact - "by unity of person".

It caught the young listening creature; the enigmatic phrase quivered with beautiful significance. Sybil at her side somehow answered to it; she herself perhaps - she herself in love. Something beyond understanding but not beyond achievement showed itself, and then the choir were plunging through the swift record of the Christhood on earth, and once more the attribution of eternal glory rose and fell - "is now," "is now - and ever shall be". Then they were all kneeling down and the vicar was praying in ritual utterance of imperial titles for "our sovereign lord King George".

3. For some three weeks the Archdeacon was in retirement, *[having been mugged]* broken only by the useful fidelity of Mrs Lucksparrow and the intrusive charity of Mr Batesby, who, having arrived at the Rectory for one reason, was naturally asked to remain for another. As soon as the invalid was allowed to receive visitors, Mr Batesby carried the hint of the New Testament, "I was sick and ye visited me" to an extreme which made nonsense of the equally authoritative injunction to be "wise as serpents." He was encouraged by the feeling which both the doctor and Mrs Lucksparrow had that it was fortunate another member of the profession should be at hand, and by the success with which the Archdeacon, dizzy and yet equable, concealed his own feelings when his visitor, chatting of Prayer Book Revision, parish councils, and Tithe Acts, imported to them a high eternal flavour which savoured of Deity Itself. Each day after he had gone the Archdeacon found himself inclined to brood on the profound wisdom of that phrase in the Athanasian Creed which teaches the faithful that "not by conversion of the Godhead into flesh, but by taking of the manhood into God" are salvation and the Divine End achieved. That the subjects of their conversation should be taken into God was normal and proper; what else, the Archdeacon wondered, could one do with parish councils? But his goodwill could not refrain from feeling that to Mr Batesby they were opportunities for converting the Godhead rather firmly and finally into flesh. "The dear flesh," he murmured, thinking ruefully of the way his own had been treated.

4. It was now nearly one o'clock, and it was quite possible that Tom, as well as herself, might be on the way to Grange Lane; but Lucilla, who, as she said, made a point of never going against the prejudices of society, made up her mind to remain sweetly unconscious of the hour of luncheon, unless some lady came to keep her company. But then Miss Marjoribanks was always lucky, as she said. A quarter of an hour before Tom applied for admission, Miss Bury came to pay Lucilla a visit. She had been visiting in her district all the morning, and was very easily persuaded to repose herself a little; and then, naturally, she was anxious about her young friend's spiritual condition, and the effect upon her mind of a year's residence abroad. She was asking whether Lucilla had not seen something soul-degrading and dishonouring to religion in all the mummeries of Popery; and Miss Marjoribanks, who was perfectly orthodox, had replied to the question in the most satisfactory manner; when Tom made his appearance, looking rather sheepish and reluctant, and followed by the "somebody amusing" whom Lucilla had commissioned him to bring. He had struggled against his fate, poor fellow! but when

it happens to be a man's instinct to do what he is told, he can no more resist it than if it was a criminal impulse. Tom entered with his amusing companion, who had been chosen with care, and was very uninviting to look at; and by and by Miss Bury, with the most puzzled of looks, found herself listening to gossip about the theatres and all kinds of profane subjects. "I think they are going to hang that fellow that killed the tailor," said the amusing man; "that will stir you up a little in Carlingford, I should suppose. It is as good as a play for a country town. Of course, there will be a party that will get up a memorial, and prove that a man so kind-hearted never existed out of paradise; and there will be another party who will prove him to be insane; and then at the end all the blackguards within a hundred miles will crowd into Carlingford, and the fellow will be hanged, as he deserves to be; but I assure you it's a famous amusement for a country town."

"Sir," said Miss Bury, with a tremulous voice, for her feeling had overcome her, "when you speak of amusement, does it ever occur to you what will become of his miserable soul?"

"I assure you, wretches of that description have no souls," said the young barrister, "or else, of course, I would not permit myself to speak so freely. It is a conclusion I have come to not rashly, but after many opportunities of observing," the young man went on with solemnity; "on the whole, my opinion is that this is the great difference between one portion of mankind and the other: that description of being, you may take my word for it, has no soul."

"I never take anybody's word for what is so plainly stated in the Holy Scriptures," said Miss Bury; "I never heard any one utter such a terrible idea. I am sure I don't want to defend a - a murderer," cried the Rector's sister, with agitation: "but I have heard of persons in that unfortunate position coming to a heavenly frame of mind, and giving every evidence of being truly converted. The law may take their lives, but it is an awful thing - a truly dreadful thing," said Miss Bury, trembling all over, "to try to take away their soul."

"Oh, nonsense, Lucilla. By Jove! he does not mean that, you know," said Tom, interposing to relieve his friend.

"Do you believe in Jove, Mr Thomas Marjoribanks," said Miss Bury, looking him in an alarming manner full in the face.

The unfortunate Tom grew red and then he grew green under this question and that awful look. "No, Miss Bury, I can't say I do," he answered humbly; and the amusing man was so much less brotherly than Tom that he burst into unsympathetic laughter. As for Lucilla, it was the first real check she had sustained in the beginning of her career. There could not have been a more unfortunate *contre-temps*, and there is no telling how disastrous the effect might have been, had not her courage and coolness, not to say her orthodoxy, been equal to the occasion. She gave her cousin a look which was still more terrible than Miss Bury's, and then she took affairs into her own hands.

"It is dreadful sometimes to see what straits people are put to, to keep up the conversation," said Lucilla; "Tom in particular, for I think he has a pleasure in talking nonsense. But you must not suppose I am of that opinion. I remember quite well there was a dreadful man once here in jail for something, and Mr Bury made him the most beautiful character! Every creature has a soul. I am sure we say so in the Creed every day of our lives, and especially in that long creed where so many people perish everlastingly. So far from laughing, it is quite dreadful to think of it," said Lucilla. "It is one of my principles never to laugh about anything that has to do with religion. I always think it my duty to speak with respect. It has such a bad effect upon some minds. Miss Bury, if you will not take anything more, I think we had better go upstairs."

To think that Tom, whose luck, as usual, had betrayed him to such an unlooked-for extent, should have been on the point of following to the drawing-room, was more than Miss Marjoribanks could comprehend; but fortunately his companion had more sense, and took his leave, taking his conductor with him.

REFERENCES

1. George Eliot, *Silas Marner*, Wm Blackwood 1861.
2. Charles Williams, *The Greater Trumps*, Faber & Faber Ltd 1964, Ch. 8 Christmas Day in the Country.
3. Charles Williams, *War in Heaven*, Faber & Faber 1947, Ch. 5 The Chemist's Shop.
4. Mrs Oliphant, *Miss Marjoribanks*, Wm Blackwood & Sons 1866, Ch. 7.

secrct thy people o lord

Let the Priests, the Ministers of the
LORD, weepe before the Porch, and
the Altar, and let them say, Spare
thy people O LORD.etc. Ioel 2.17.

CHAPTER 5
The Litany

To be sung or said after Morning Prayer upon Sundays, Wednesdays and Fridays.

A 13 year-old boy returns from holiday to find that the first services of the new church at Tooting are to be held in a tent.

1. The figure of the new vicar arrested my eye immediately. An old man, wearing the red hood of Oxford, was looking out over the congregation with a certain coldness of regard which does not seem in retrospect to have betokened any coldness of heart, but he glanced at the faces before him as if he were possessed of the experience and wisdom of the ages. I have always thought his appearance an epitome of all the milder popes. . . .

There he sat that morning in the tent church, and only he of all of us knew how majestic a building was going to take its place on that field. Nothing would be done that would not bear the mark of his own exquisite and discriminating taste. His name was John Otter Stephens, and he had come from a country rectory at Blankney, in Lincolnshire, which was Harry Chaplin's parish.

He had brought with him a particularly handsome curate, who has since, I see from Crockford, broadened into a rural dean. The curate's part of the service was read beautifully enough; but it was when the older man read the Litany that, young as I was, I apprehended that here there was something new to me, but at the same time so ancient that it seemed weighted with the faith and the imploration of the ages. The voice was strong but rather dry, and the breath was quite obviously being made to carry all its sound. The earnestness was, if possible, deepened by a controlling mind giving the wonderful sentences all the solemnity that intention could afford them:

By *thine Agony and bloody Sweat; by thy Cross and Passion;* . . . (a long pause) . . . *by thy precious Death and Burial;* . . . (then a triumphant quickening of the voice) *by thy glorious Resurrection and Ascension;* (and then quickly and fully) *and by the coming of the Holy Ghost, Good Lord, deliver us.*

All the proceedings had my absorbed attention. I observed the little altar, and the brass cross and temporary candlesticks. Nothing was done as it was done in our chapel. There was no familiarity with the Almighty. The ancient set words were read with all the preciseness of a ritual, but a ritual infused with what Walton would call a primitive piety; and the Anglican Morning Prayer became a great mystery. The voice of the man who, I thought at first, looked a little coldly at us became melted at prayer to sweetness and moved by a depth of feeling that never lessened or grew merely expected in the years that were to come. The Litany, as read that summer morning, became the world supplicating at the foot of the cross. It was the voice of the ages approaching the Deity; more exactly, it was approaching the mystery of the Trinity. Within that canvas tent I felt for the first time all that was impressive, pure unalloyed, in the ethos of the Church of England. The hour is still moving and real to me.

In a half lyrical mood I walked home, hugging my experience to my bosom. I was not to go much more to chapel. I could never again regard the services of religion with the unexperience in which I had walked up the hill that morning.

2. Aunt read none of her country's historic literature but only the popular novels of the day, the half-penny *Daily Express*, and the gossiping weeklies like *M.A.P.* (Mainly About People). Thus, except for Hilliard's *[the Vicar]* superb rendering of the Bible and of the Elizabethan and Jacobean language in Collects and Prayers at Matins and Evensong, so noble in diction, balance, and rhythm, little of true literature would have come my way in childhood. I loathed the Sundays when the Litany extended Matins almost beyond bearing, but I began to hear, dimly and as it were distantly, the beauty of its suffrages. "That it may please thee to strengthen such as do stand, and to comfort and help the weak-hearted; and to raise up them that fall, and finally to beat down Satan under our feet. . . . That it may please thee to preserve all that travel by land or by water, all women labouring of child, all sick persons and young children; and to show thy pity on all prisoners and captives."

Oh, yes, if I was listening and not day-dreaming on my knees, a little of the magic broke through.

Mr Wentworth takes a weekday service at the little mission church of St Roque's.
3. The little dangers that harassed his personal footsteps had not yet awakened so much as an anxiety in his mind. He opened his prayer book with a consciousness of the good of it which comes to men only now and then. At Oxford, in his day, Mr Wentworth had entertained his doubts like others, and like most people was aware that there were a great many things in heaven and earth totally unexplainable by any philosophy. But he had always been more of a man than a thinker, even before he became a high Anglican; and being still much in earnest about most things he had to do with, he found great comfort just at this moment, amid all his perplexities, in *the litany* he was saying. He was so absorbed in it, and so full of that appeal out of all trouble and miseries to the God who cannot be indifferent to his creatures, that he was almost at the last Amen before he distinguished that voice, which of all voices was most dear to him.

George Herbert is visited during his last illness.
4. Mr Duncan found him weak, and at that time lying on a bed; but at his seeing Mr Duncan he raised himself vigorously, saluted him, and with some earnestness inquired the health of his brother Farrer; of which Mr Duncan satisfied him, and after some discourse of Mr Farrer's holy life, and the manner of his constant serving God, he said to Mr Duncan, - "Sir, I see by your habit that you are a priest, and I desire you to pray with me:" which being granted, Mr Duncan asked him, "What prayers?" To which Mr Herbert's answer was, "O sir! the prayers of my mother,

the Church of England: no other prayers are equal to them! But at this time I beg of you to pray only the Litany, for I am weak and faint:" and Mr Duncan did so.

April 1773
5. On the 9th April, being Good Friday, I breakfasted with him on tea and cross buns. *Doctor* Levet, as Frank called him, making the tea. He carried me with him to the church of St Clement Danes, where he had his seat; and his behaviour was, as I had imagined to myself, solemnly devout. I never shall forget the tremulous earnestness with which he pronounced the aweful petition in the Litany: "In the hour of death, and at the day of judgement, good Lord deliver us."

This last prayer for deliverance is followed by the 'That-it-may-please-Thees', as Marian calls them.
6. The hot weather of July had crept upon them unawares, and the atmosphere of the flat vale hung heavy as an opiate óver the dairy-folk, the cows, and the trees. Hot steaming rains fell frequently, making the grass where the cows fed yet more rank, and hindering the late haymaking in the other meads.

It was Sunday morning; the milking was done; the outdoor milkers had gone home. Tess and the other three were dressing themselves rapidly, the whole bevy having agreed to go together to Mellstock Church, which lay some three or four miles distant from the dairy-house. She had now been two months at Talbothays, and this was her first excursion.

All the preceding afternoon and night heavy thunderstorms had hissed down upon the meads, and washed some of the hay into the river; but this morning the sun shone out all the more brilliantly for the deluge, and the air was balmy and clear.

The crooked lane leading from their own parish to Mellstock ran along the lowest levels in a portion of its length, and when the girls reached the most depressed spot they found that the result of the rain had been to flood the lane over-shoe to a distance of some fifty yards. This would have been no serious hindrance on a week-day; they would have clicked through it in their high pattens and boots quite unconcerned; but on this day of vanity, this Sun's-day, when flesh went forth to coquet with flesh while hypocritically affecting business with spiritual things; on this occasion for wearing their white stockings and thin shoes, and their pink, white, and lilac gowns, on which every mud spot would be visible, the pool was an awkward impediment. They could hear the church-bell calling - as yet nearly a mile off.

"Who would have expected such a rise in the river in summer-time!" said Marian, from the top of the roadside bank on which they had climbed, and were maintaining a precarious footing in the hope of creeping along its slope till they were past the pool.

"We can't get there anyhow, without walking right through it, or else going round the Turnpike way; and that would make us so very late!" said Retty, pausing hopelessly.

"And I do colour up so hot, walking into church late, and all the people staring round," said Marian, "that I hardly cool down again till we get into the That-it-may-please-Thees."

After attending the Litany in Magdalen College chapel, C S Lewis was heard to comment on the first four of these.

7. On Fridays our chapel service consisted of the Litany, which in the B.C.P. contains 3 substantial suffrages for the sovereign and another for his family. As we came into common room one Friday, Lewis commented, "The Litany makes one feel as if the Royal Family were not pulling their weight."

8. The leaders of the Church know their own flock. We are not qualified by their experience to judge the needs of a modern congregation, but it is surprising that it should ever have been thought necessary to add, in time of war, special petitions to the Litany. It is wonderfully comprehensive. One would venture to say that there is no human need, spiritual or temporal, that is not remembered in it. The word "all" rings through it like a bell. "All that are in danger . . . all that travel by land or by water . . . all sick persons and young children . . . all prisoners and captives . . . all that are desolate and oppressed." Nothing and no one is forgotten. Everyone in the congregation may hear prayed for that one being on earth who lies nearest his heart. And the supreme consolation of history is there, for "we have heard with our ears, and our fathers have declared unto us, the noble works that thou didst in their days, and in the old time before them . . . O Lord, arise, help us, and deliver us for thine honour." It is all said. It was written yesterday, to-day and to-morrow. As the necessities of men change, and from youth to age or from generation to generation their joys and sufferings alter their forms and names, the words of the Litany open to include them.

The 'Railway children' meet and befriend a Russian refugee, who had been condemned to the mines in Siberia. As their Mother learns his history, she tells the children, and asks them to pray for all prisoners; and that includes, though they do not know it, their own wrongly imprisoned father.

9. 'And at last he got to the mines, and he was condemned to stay there for life - for life, just for writing a good, noble, splendid book.'

'How did he get away?'

'When the war came, some of the Russian prisoners were allowed to volunteer as soldiers. And he volunteered. But he deserted at the first chance he got and -'

'But that's very cowardly, isn't it,' - said Peter - 'to desert? Especially when it's war.'

'Do you think he owed anything to a country that had done *that* to him? If he did, he owed more to his wife and children. He didn't know what had become of them.'

'Oh,' cried Bobbie, 'he had *them* to think about and be miserable about *too*, then, all the time he was in prison?'

'Yes, he had them to think about and be miserable about all the time he was in prison. For anything he knew they might have been sent to prison, too. They did those things in Russia. But while he was in the mines some friends managed to get a message to him that his wife and children had escaped and come to England. So when he deserted he came here to look for them.'

'Had he got their address?' said practical Peter.

'No; just England. He was going to London, and he thought he had to change at our station, and then he found he'd lost his ticket and his purse.'

'Oh, *do* you think he'll find them? - I mean his wife and children, not the ticket and things.'

'I hope so. Oh, I hope and pray that he'll find his wife and children again.'

Even Phyllis now perceived that Mother's voice was very unsteady.

'Why, Mother,' she said, 'how very sorry you seem to be for him!'

Mother didn't answer for a minute. Then she just said, 'Yes,' and then she seemed to be thinking. The children were quiet.

Presently she said, 'Dears, when you say your prayers, I think you might ask God to show His pity upon all prisoners and captives.'

'To show His pity,' Bobbie repeated slowly, 'upon all prisoners and captives. Is that right, Mother?'

'Yes,' said Mother, 'upon all prisoners and captives. All prisoners and captives.'

REFERENCES

1. Eric Bligh, *Tooting Corner*, op. cit., Ch. The Solemn Exercise.
2. Ernest Raymond, *The Story of My Days*, Cassell and Cy Ltd 1968, Ch. 3.
3. Mrs Oliphant, *The Perpetual Curate*, Wm Blackwood 1864, Ch. 24.
4. Isaac Walton, *The Life of George Herbert*, R. Marriot 1670.
5. James Boswell, *The Life of Samuel Johnson*, (1701) Everyman Library, J.M. Dent & Sons 1906.
6. Thomas Hardy, *Tess of the D'Urbervilles*, op. cit., Ch. The Rally.
7. *C.S. Lewis at the Breakfast Table and Other Reminiscences*, ed. James T. Como, Collins 1980, p. 92 Adam Fox.
8. Charles Morgan, *Reflections in a Mirror*, (2nd Series) Macmillan 1946, The Village Church.
9. E. Nesbit, *The Railway Children*, Darton & Co. 1906, Ch. 5 Wells Gardner.

CHAPTER 6
Prayers and Thanksgivings:
The General Thanksgiving

1. My maternal grandfather whom I never saw, must have been an interesting person too; and something of an historical type if not an historical character. He had been one of the old Wesleyan lay-preachers and was thus involved in public controversy, a characteristic which has descended to his grandchild. He was also one of the leaders of the early Teetotal movement; a characteristic which has not. But I am quite sure there was a great deal in him, beyond anything that is implied in mere public speaking or teetotalism. I am quite sure of it, because of two casual remarks he made; which are indeed the only two remarks I ever heard of him making. Once, when his sons were declaiming against mode and convention in the manner of all liberal youth, he said abruptly, "Ah, they talk a lot about fashion; but fashion is civilisation." And in the other case, the same rising generation was lightly tossing about that pessimism which is only possible in the happy time of youth. They were criticising the General Thanksgiving in the Prayer-Book, and remarking that a good many people have very little reason to be thankful for their creation. And the old man, who was then so old that he hardly ever spoke at all, said suddenly out of his silence, "I should thank God for my creation if I knew I was a lost soul."

2. We chatted on for several minutes, for I could not bear to bring the call to an end. When at length I had rung off, I remained sitting beside the telephone in a confusion of joy, surprise and excitement. Clearly Karin must be as eager and impatient to be with me as I with her. . . .

Tears filled my eyes and after a few moments, seeking an outlet for my passionate sense of gratitude and happiness, I began murmuring, half aloud, the words of the General Thanksgiving.

" — give thee most humble and hearty thanks for all thy goodness and loving kindness to us and to all men. We bless thee for our creation, preservation and all the blessings of this life; but above all, for thine inestimable love. . . ."

Frank Wentworth, the Perpetual Curate, his honour now vindicated and his appointment as Rector of Carlingford confirmed, takes the service at his mission church of St Roque's.

3. Such was the conversation which opened this memorable Sunday to Mr Wentworth. Opposite to him, again occupying the seat where his wife should have

been, had he possessed one, were the three Miss Wentworths, his respected aunts, to whose opinion, however, the Curate did not feel himself bound to defer very greatly in present circumstances; and a large and curious congregation ranged behind them, almost as much concerned to see how Mr Wentworth would conduct himself in this moment of triumph, as they had been in the moment of his humiliation. It is, however, needless to inform the friends of the Perpetual Curate that the anxious community gained very little by their curiosity. It was not the custom of the young Anglican to carry his personal feelings, either of one kind or another, into the pulpit with him, much less into the reading-desk, where he was the interpreter not of his own sentiments or emotions, but of common prayer and universal worship. Mr Wentworth did not even throw a little additional warmth into his utterance of the *General Thanksgiving*, as he might have done had he been a more effusive man; but on the contrary, read it with a more than ordinary calmness, and preached to the excited people one of those terse little unimpassioned sermons of his, from which it was utterly impossible to divine whether he was in the depths of despair or at the summit and crown of happiness. People who had been used to discover a great many of old Mr Bury's personal peculiarities in his sermons, and who, of recent days, had found many allusions which it was easy to interpret in the discourses of Mr Morgan, retired altogether baffled from the clear and succinct brevity of the Curate of St Roque's. He was that day in particular so terse as to be almost epigrammatic, not using a word more than was necessary, and displaying that power of saying a great deal more than at the first moment he appeared to say, in which Mr Wentworth's admirers specially prided themselves.

Theodore Wedel, brought up a Mennonite, joins for the first time in the General Thanksgiving.

4. My first "Prayer Book Sunday," then. The little Episcopal church in our Kansas town needed an organist. I volunteered as a candidate and was accepted. A kindly choir-mother gave me a week's training in "responses, canticles, and chants." Then came the first Sunday's initiation into the Book of Common Prayer.

Bewilderment, of course. Kneeling and standing in place of the monotonous sitting posture. Read prayers. A *book* of prayers, no less, in the worshippers' own hands. No worrying on the part of the man in the pew as to whether the minister would receive inspiration for *his* prayer, or whether it would ever end (the *book* had terminal facilities). The shock of what externally looked like Romanist sacerdotalism - a priest (a very bad word to a Mennonite brought up on the *Mirror of Martyrs*) in the sanctuary, with strange popish vestments.

But - and this was a catastrophic but - there arrived also a sudden illumination that I was experiencing something rich and strange, something which satisfied a long felt, though never consciously realized, hunger and need. I was participating in "common" prayer! The "sacerdotalism" of the sanctuary was, in a way, an illusion. The priest was servant of the worshipping congregation, not its master. He was voicing petitions and thanksgivings singly, yes, but the *book* from which he read was a common possession. And then came the corporately spoken General Thanksgiving. Except for the Lord's Prayer, this was the first prayer uttered in chorus by a congregation (the General Confession an earlier analogue to be sure) that I had ever heard.

REFERENCES

1. G.K. Chesterton, *Autobiography*, Sheed & Ward 1936, Ch. 1.
2. Richard Adams, *The Girl in a Swing*, Allen Lane (Penguin Books) 1980.
3. Mrs Oliphant, *The Perpetual Curate*, op. cit.
4. *Modern Canterbury Pilgrims,* ed. the Dean of New York, A.R. Mowbray & Co 1956, Essay by Theodore Wedel.

In the Nett which they hid is their
own Foot taken Ps 9. 15.

Our soule is escaped as a Bird out of
the snare of the Fowlers, the snare
is broken, and wee are
escaped psal: 124. 7

S.

CHAPTER 7
The Collects, Epistles and Gospels

To be used throughout the year.

1. A schoolboy came into view, with a bag slung over his shoulder containing his dinner, and a book in his hand. He passed by the gate, and, without looking up, continued murmuring words in tones quite loud enough to reach her ears.

"'O Lord, O Lord, O Lord, O Lord, O Lord": - that I know out o' book. "Give us, give us, give us give": - that I know. "Grace that, grace that, grace that, grace that" - that I know.' Other words followed to the same effect. The boy was of the dunce class apparently; the book was a prayer book, and this was his way of learning the collect.

2. Sunday mornings at home were the usual rush - chaos in the kitchen, shrill orders to wash, and everyone's eyes on the clock. We polished our hair with grease and water, and scrubbed ourselves under the pump. Being Sunday, there was a pound of large sausages for breakfast, fried black and bursting with fat. One dipped them in pepper and ate them in haste, an open prayer-book propped up by the plate.

"Heavens alive, you'll be late, our lad."

Gobble, mumble, and choke.

"What *are* you up to? Get a move on do."

"Leave off - I'm learning the Collect."

"What's that you say?"

"I-Gotta-Learn-Me-Collect!"

"Hurry up and learn it then."

"I can't hurry up! Not if you keep on! . . ."

But it was really not difficult at all; ten inscrutable lines absorbed between mouthfuls, and usually on the run. Up the bank, down the road, the greasy prayer-book in one hand, the remains of the sausage in the other: "Almighty and Most Merciful Father, who alone worketh Great Marvels. . . ." In five minutes it was all in my head.

At Sunday School Miss Bagnall, polishing her nose, said: "The Collect - now who will oblige. . . ." I would jump to my feet and gabble, word perfect, the half page of sonorous syllables. It came in through the eyes and out through the mouth, and left no trace of its passing. Except that I can never read a Collect today without tasting a crisp burnt sausage. . . .

3. The front door closed. I passed a hand across the brow.

"Tell me all, Jeeves," I said.

"Sir?"

"I say, tell me all. I am fogged."

"It is quite simple, sir. I ventured to take the liberty, on my own responsibility, of putting into operation the alternative scheme which, if you remember, I wished to outline to you."

"What was it?"

"It occurred to me, sir, that it would be most judicious for me to call at the back door and desire an interview with Miss Mapleton. This, I fancied, would enable me, while the maid had gone to convey my request to Miss Mapleton, to introduce the young lady into the house unobserved."

"And did you?"

"Yes, sir. She proceeded up the back stairs and is now safely in bed."

I frowned. The thought of the kid Clementina jarred upon me.

"She is, is she?" I said. "A murrain on her, Jeeves, and may she be stood in the corner next Sunday for not knowing her Collect.

Thus earlier generations learnt the collects by heart. For many it was, no doubt, parrot fashion, "in through the eyes and out through the mouth"; but the virtue of learning by heart is being recognised again today, for it provides a treasury in our minds, made all the more secure by being used; and the Collects are a precious part of that store.

4. Perhaps Thomas Cranmer's highest achievements were his Collects which are so crystal clear in their meaning and which are couched in words which express so deep a sense of the Divine Majesty of God the Father Almighty. Almost all we know and all we need to know about the meaning of true religion is surely contained in the Collect for the twelfth Sunday after Trinity:

Almighty and everlasting God, who art always more ready to hear than we to pray, and art wont to give more than either we desire or deserve: Pour down upon us the abundance of thy mercy; forgiving us those things whereof our conscience is afraid, and giving us those good things we are not worthy to ask, but through the merits and mediation of Jesus Christ, thy Son, our Lord.

5. By the way, *Collect*. The Oxford Dictionary (referring back to the Latin *collecta*) says "in late Latin (Jerome) an assembly or meeting. In Medieval Latin in the Liturgical sense (which was the first in English)." The Gregorian Sacramentary (late 6th century: I suppose), it goes on, has "*oratio ad collectam,*"[1] and sometimes merely "*collecta,*" as the title of any prayer said at a station where the people were *collected* in order to proceed together to church for Mass. It meant simply a prayer at the collection or gathering of people. *Earlier* than this, in the *Gallican* liturgies, "*collecta*" was used as the title of a prayer (after the Mass) which was a collecting or summing up of thoughts suggested by the *capitula*[2] for the day. Thence the word, as an equivalent for *oratio*, passed into medieval French and English missals and breviaries, and thence again into our P.B.

[1] "Prayer at the gathering of people."

[2] A *capitulum* was a short lesson from the Bible suited to the Office of the day.

6. "For my part," said Coggan, "I'm staunch Church of England."

"Ay, and faith, so be I," said Mark Clark.

"I won't say much for myself; I don't wish to," Coggan continued, with that tendency to talk on principles which is characteristic of the barley corn. "But I've never changed a single doctrine: I've stuck like a plaster to the old faith I was born in. Yes; there's this to be said for the Church, a man can belong to the Church and bide in his cheerful old inn, and never trouble or worry his mind about doctrines at all. But to be a meetinger, you must go to chapel in all winds and weathers, and make yerself as frantic as a skit. Not but that chapel members be clever chaps enough in their way. They can lift up beautiful prayers out of their own heads, all about their families and shipwracks in the newspaper."

"They can - they can," said Mark Clark with corroborative feeling, "but we Churchmen, you see, must have it all printed aforehand, or, dang it all, we should no more know what to say to a great gaffer like the Lord than babies unborn."

Having the prayers "all printed aforehand" has its justification.

7. In praying by the precomposed forms of our Common Prayer, which have been so often heard, understood, and approved by us, our wills are wholly at liberty to accompany the minister in offering them up. For our attention is not now engaged to hear them, nor our understanding to interpret them, nor our judgement to approve of them. All these things are done to our hand, and at the time of offering we have nothing to do, but only to offer them up with all our heart, with all our mind, and with all our strength. Wherefore let all the *sectarists* know assuredly, that it is in the prayers of our Church that we are enabled to pray with the Spirit. Why? because we are assured beforehand, that in these we *pray with the understanding* also.

Especially when they are explained.

8. The texts for all his future sermons - which God knows were not many - were constantly taken out of the gospel for the day; and he did as constantly declare why the Church did appoint that portion of scripture to be that day read; and in what manner the collect for every Sunday does refer to the gospel, or to the epistle then read to them; and, that they might pray with understanding, he did usually take occasion to explain, not only the collect for every particular Sunday, but the reasons of all the other collects and responses in our Church service; and make it appear to them that the whole service of the Church was a reasonable, and therefore an acceptable sacrifice to God. . . .

He informed them also when the priest did pray only for the congregation, and not for himself; and when they did only pray for him; as namely, after the repetition of the creed before he proceeds to pray the Lord's Prayer, or any of the appointed collects, the priest is directed to kneel down and pray for them, saying, "The Lord be with you;" and when they pray for him, saying, "And with thy spirit;" and then they join together in the following collects: and he assured them, that when there is such mutual love, and such joint prayers offered for each other, then the holy angels look down from heaven, and are ready to carry such charitable desires to God Almighty, and He as ready to receive them; and that a Christian congregation calling thus upon God with one heart, and one voice, and in one reverent and humble posture, looks as beautifully as Jerusalem, that is at peace with itself.

An Oxford don, who found that he could no longer believe and who reluctantly relinquished his churchgoing, recalls the years when he was a choirboy in Cornwall.

9. The sacrifice was made; yet the nostalgia remains, as it remained all his days with Thomas Hardy. Nothing can touch me like the phrases and liturgical scraps that bring back that vanished world of my childhood, a world of security and faith, now dissolved like a 'dream remembered on waking'. It is all very natural: for so many years the alternation of the seasons was marked for me by the seasons of the Church: the changes in the altar-frontals meant more to me than the changes from flower to berry, from honeysuckle to hips and haws. There was the purple of Advent and Lent, the white of the great festivals of the Church - Easter Day and Christmas and Trinity Sunday - the red of Whitsuntide, green for the ordinary occasions of the year. There were the events of the Church Calendar, the sequence of Epiphany, Septuagesima, Sexagesima, Quinquagesima and Lent. There was the distribution of palms on Palm Sunday, the desolation and gloom of the Holy Week, Good Friday with the altar stripped of its ornaments, ourselves in black cassocks singing the Passion. There were the processions, the sweet-smelling flowers in the flower-decorated church on Easter Day, Whit Sunday, Trinity Sunday, the fruit and vegetables of harvest festival. Then there was the long hiatus, an ecclesiastical desert, or those interminable Sundays after Trinity, up to the Twenty-Seventh, in which nothing seemed to happen, and August came down on us and the congregation thinned out and people went away for their holidays and even the organist went for a fortnight on his. With autumn and the colours coming out in the hedges, they came back again and things at church began to liven up. And on Sunday evenings I would go down the road with my cousin, Kate Courtenay, her husband away at the War, or the friendly, good-natured girl at the farm, for I was growing older and more staid and serious, no longer a boy; together we went down the familiar land of which we knew every turn, every tree, every bush, to the sound of the church-bells ringing us to church. Though they are silent now, I hear them still.

There can be a 27th Sunday after Trinity Sunday, but there is no Collect, Epistle and Gospel of that name. The last is the 25th Sunday after Trinity and this is kept for the Sunday next before Advent, known as Stir Up Sunday because of the opening words of the Collect, which are an unintentional reminder to mix the Christmas pudding. The gap is filled, when necessary, with Sundays omitted after the Epiphany.

Kate, now Lady Caergwent, wakes up from nightmares to greet her cousins and her former guardian, the Revd Mr Wardour, under whose tutelage, gentler than Aunt Barbara's, she had been happier.

10. That was the way Lady Caergwent spent her hour. She had been kidnapped and murdered a good many times before there was a buzz in the street, her senses came back, and she sprang out on the stairs to meet her cousins, calling herself quite well again. And then they had a very peaceful, pleasant time; she was one of them again, when, as of old, Mr Wardour came into the drawing-room, and she stood up with

Charles, Sylvia, and little Lily, who was now old enough for the Catechism, and then the Collect, and a hymn. Yes, she had Collect and hymn ready too, and some of the Gospel; Aunt Barbara always heard her say them on Sunday, besides some very difficult questions, not at all like what Mr Wardour asked out of his own head.

Kate was a little afraid he would make his teaching turn on submitting to rulers; it was an Epistle that would have given him a good opportunity, for it was the Fourth Epiphany Sunday, brought in at the end of the Sundays after Trinity. If he made his teaching personal, something within her wondered if she could bear it, and was ready to turn angry and defiant.

Another choirboy remembers the church year "following the plough". Lammas Day (the day that celebrated the beginning of harvest) is in the Calendar on the 1st of August. Rogation Sunday is in the Table of Moveable Feasts, and the following three Rogation Days are included in the Days of Fasting and Abstinence. On these days prayer is made for God's blessing on the crops. Whilst these and Plough Sunday (the 1st Sunday after the Epiphany) were kept, none had a special Collect, Epistle and Gospel. The 1928 revision of the Prayer Book provided them for the Rogation Days and also for a Thanksgiving for Harvest. A nineteenth-century vicar, Hawker of Morvenstow, is credited with introducing the latter service.

11. From our seats in the choir we watched the year turn: Christmas, Easter, Whitsun, Rogation Sunday and prayers for rain, the Church following the plough very close. Harvest Festival perhaps was the one we liked best, the one that came nearest home. Then how heavily and abundantly was our small church loaded; the cream of the valley was used to decorate it. Everyone brought of his best from field and garden; and to enter the church on Harvest morning was like crawling head first into a horn of plenty, a bursting granary, a vegetable stall, a grotto of bright flowers. The normally bare walls sprouted leaves and fruits, the altar great stooks of wheat, and ornamental loaves as big as cartwheels stood parked by the communion rails. Bunches of grapes, from the Squire's own vines, hung blue from the lips of the pulpit. Gigantic and useless marrows abounded, leeks and onions festooned the pews, there were eggs and butter on the lectern shelves, the windows were heaped with apples, and the fat round pillars which divided the church were skirted with oats and barley.

Almost everyone in the congregation had some hand in these things. Square-rumped farmers and ploughmen in chokers, old gardeners and poultry-keepers, they nodded and pointed and prodded each other to draw attention to what they had brought. The Church was older than its one foundation, was as old as man's life on earth. The seed of these fruits, and the seed of these men, still came from the same one bowl; confined to this valley and renewing itself here, it went back to the days of the Ice. Pride, placation, and the continuity of growth were what we had come to praise. And even where we sang, 'All is safely gathered in', knowing full well that some of Farmer Lusty's oats still lay rotting in the fields, the discrepancy didn't seem important.

I remember one particular Harvest Festival which perfectly summed up this feeling. I was not old enough then to be in the choir, and I was sitting beside Tony, who was three. It was his first Harvest Festival, but he'd heard much about it and his expectations were huge. The choir, with banners, was fidgeting in the doorway, ready to start its procession. Tony gazed with glittering eyes around him, sniffing the juicy splendours. Then, in a moment of silence, just before the organ crashed into the hymn, he asked loudly, "Is there going to be drums?"

It was a natural question, innocent and true. For neither drums, nor cymbals, nor trumpets of brass would have seemed out of place at that time.

At sundry times and in divers manners.

THE COLLECT FOR SEXAGESIMA SUNDAY AND A POST COMMUNION COLLECT

12. Lady Clara Boulding was to open the garden party officially at half-past two and as she had now arrived, there seemed no reason why she should not get on with it at once. But the crowd was obviously waiting for something. Agatha Hoccleve, who was standing by her husband, nudged him and said in an agitated and audible whisper, "Henry, a *prayer*."

The Archdeacon started. He had been wondering whether Lady Clara would give some definite contribution to the church-roof fund as well as buying things at the stalls. He cleared his throat.

"Let us ask for God's blessing on our endeavours," he said, in a loud voice which quite startled some people.

Belinda looked down at the grass and then at Agatha's neat suède shoes, so much more suited to the occasion than her own.

The Archdeacon began to recite a prayer. *O Lord God, who seest that we put not our trust in anything that we do, mercifully grant that by Thy Power we may be defended against all adversity. . . .*

Harriet looked at Belinda and frowned. The Archdeacon always chose such unsuitable prayers. *Prevent us O Lord in all our doings*, was the obviously correct one for such an occasion. These little departures from convention always annoyed her.

Belinda, on the other hand, was thinking loyally, what an excellent choice! It strikes just the right note of humility. When Henry prays for defence from adversity, he must mean too much confidence in our own powers. One knew that pride often came before a fall. Or perhaps he was not referring to the garden party specifically, but taking in the larger sphere of life outside it . . . here Belinda's thoughts became confused and a doubt crept into her mind, which was quickly and loyally pushed back. For it could not be that dear Henry had just said the first prayer that came into his head. . . .

There was a short pause. Count Bianco replaced his panama hat and everyone began to move, relieved to be normal once more.

THE COLLECT FOR EASTER DAY

13. But above all, I will be sure to live well, because the virtuous life of a clergyman is the most powerful eloquence to persuade all that see it to reverence and love, and at least to desire to live like him. And this I will do, because I know we live in an age that hath more need of good examples than precepts. And I beseech that God,

who hath honoured me so much as to call me to serve him at his altar, that *as by his special grace he hath put into my heart these good desires* and resolutions; *so He will*, by his assisting grace, give me ghostly strength *to bring the same to good effect*. And I beseech him, that my humble and charitable life may so win upon others, as to bring glory to my Jesus, whom I have this day taken to be my master and governor; and I am so proud of his service, that I will always observe, and obey, and do his will; and always call him, Jesus my Master; and I will always contemn my birth, or any title or dignity that can be conferred upon me, when I shall compare them with my title of being a priest, and serving at the altar of Jesus my Master."

THE COLLECT FOR THE 12TH SUNDAY AFTER TRINITY

14. I now became a successful writer. And the good fortune worked backwards as well as forwards because a successful book re-animates past books as well as casting a rosy glow over future ones. They are read and in the course of time became a habit with one's readers. I did not want to be a rich woman, and hoped I would never succeed in living as one. But the resolve meant that I had to learn to administer what came to me, and the mistakes I made in learning were at times catastrophic; - and to think that I had at one time, at our leanest period, actually prayed for money! Desiring, of course, only a modest competence.

"The prayer I must pray for you," a friend told me, when she had finished laughing at my complaints on my good fortune, "is the collect for the *12th Sunday after Trinity*" -

"Almighty and everlasting God who . . . art wont to give more than either we desire or deserve. . . ."

THE COLLECT FOR THE 19TH SUNDAY AFTER TRINITY

15. The one Toc H member who was to become known throughout the Christian world was an irreverent young man who had the unbelievable name of Gonville Aubie ffrench-Beytagh. He was born in Shanghai in 1912 and in 1933 came to South Africa on the Chinese quota. He was an agnostic and had no time for the church, but said daily the Collect for the *Nineteenth Sunday after Trinity*:

O God, forasmuch as without thee we are not able to please thee: mercifully grant that thy Holy Spirit may in all things direct and rule our hearts: through Jesus Christ our Lord. Amen.

He had promised an old governess to do this, and he kept his promise, but he declared it was not religion. Though not a Christian he joined Toc H and he believed that one's life is wasted if not used in the service of others. When it was time for prayers he shed his irreverence. What happened next, though startling, was not totally out of pattern.

On a dark night in 1936 he was walking through the Braamfontein subway on his way home. He was set upon by thugs who knocked him on the head, broke his jaw, and left him for dead. When he came to himself in a bed in Johannesburg General Hospital, the first person he saw was myself. His injuries were very serious, and his long stay in the hospital gave him time to reflect on the nature and destiny of man, and the nature and destiny of himself. When he recovered he went to live in the Toc H House in Johannesburg, under the leadership of Tom Savage. Then he wrote to Bishop Clayton asking for advice as to whether he should enter the priesthood.

THE COLLECT FOR THE 20TH SUNDAY AFTER TRINITY

Tom, a beater, has been shot by accident.

16. "It has penetrated the brain. I shall be called home. It grows dark. A prayer, I beg you, Sir at the last. You and I Sir, we may not be always on the same side of things, you are a gentleman and I have always been a poor man but we share one thing Sir, we share a God. Say a prayer from me, Sir, before I go!". . .

"Give me a prayer, Sir. Don't deny me that. It's your way to pray - 'tis you that orders up the prayers in church, the Vicar only prays what prayers you tell him to, even I know that that hardly crosses the doorstep of the Church from year to year. Say a prayer, Sir; I'll say Amen."

"If that's what you want, Tom." Sir Randolph put his hand on Tom's shoulder, cleared his throat and repeated last Sunday's collect at high speed - in fact, such was his embarrassment, he more or less gabbled it.

"Oh almighty and most merciful God of thy bountiful goodness keep us we beseech Thee from all things that may hurt us, that we being ready in body and soul, may cheerfully accomplish those things that thou wouldest have done, through Jesus Christ Our Lord. Amen."

"Amen", echoed Tom loudly, "Amen, I say. Amen, Amen."

FOR ST MARK THE EVANGELIST

17. Cordelia wasn't sure what made her decide to stop at Bury and walk for ten minutes in the Abbey gardens. But she felt she couldn't face the drive back to Cambridge without calming her spirits and the glimpse of grass and flowers through the great Norman doorway was irresistible. She parked the Mini on Angel Hill, then walked through the gardens to the river bank. There she sat for five minutes in the sun. She remembered that there was money spent on petrol to be recorded in her notebook and felt for it in her bag. Her hand brought out the white prayer book. She sat quietly thinking. Suppose she had been Mrs Callender and had wanted to leave a message, a message which Mark would find and other searchers might miss. Where would she place it? The answer now seemed childishly simple. Surely somewhere on the page with the collect, gospel and epistle for St Mark's Day. He had been born on April 25th. He had been named after the Saint. Quickly she found the place. In the bright sunlight reflected from the water she saw what a quick rustle through the pages had missed. There against Cranmer's gentle petition for grace to withstand the blasts of false doctrine was a small pattern of hieroglyphics so faint that the mark on the paper was little more than a smudge. She saw that it was a group of letters and figures.

E M C   A A   14.1.52

At the beginning of the Prayer Book are tables of lessons to be read at Morning and Evening Prayer. One is for Sundays and Holy Days, and, as it now stands, is the revised lectionary of 1871. The first lesson at Mattins for the 21st Sunday after Trinity is the 3rd chapter of the Book of Daniel, which

will be read on a Sunday between the 11th October and the 14th November according to the date of Easter.

18. His thoughts were further away than usual this Sunday as he sat by his grandmother in the front pew. The low winter sun lit up the red throat of the green whale in the window close by, into which Jonah, as long as he could remember, had been taking a header without getting any further. But for the first time in his life he scarcely noticed it. What it was that was puzzling and perplexing him he could not tell, until the Psalms were finished, and the clergyman, with white curly hair and musical voice, stood by the Bible that rested on the eagle's back, and gave out the first lesson.

"Here beginneth the third chapter of the book of the Prophet Daniel:- Nebuchadnezzar the King . . . ."

Then it all flashed upon him. It was "Shadrach, Meshach and Abed-Nego Sunday," when, as his Father had often told him, the woodcock are due.

In turning to an earlier edition of the BCP lectionary a critic writing of Defoe's Gullivers' Travels finds in the Table of Moveable Feasts and the Proper Lessons for Morning and Evening Prayer an explanation of the dates in Gullivers' Travels. "They are," he writes, "Swift's fanciful way of offering us Christian hope."
19. It is surely reasonable for Swift to have assumed that his English readers would have been aware that the dates had a significance in the lectionary of the Church of England. Although few of Swift's contemporaries would have read the "Proper Lessons at Morning and Evening Prayer" with their families, as Swift did with his when he was Dean, they would at least have been aware that each date in the year had designated lessons. . . .

There are only two dates at the opening of Book III, both in the first sentence of the third paragraph. The second of these dates, 11th April, in 1707 was Good Friday. Psalm 88, which is to be read at Evening Prayer on Good Friday, makes it clear this is the Church's commemoration of Christ's harrowing of hell. The Good Friday service is a perfect ironic antiphony for Gulliver's private harrowing of hell.

Earlier editions of the Prayer Book also had annexed to them, with Collect, Epistle and Gospel, and Lessons for Morning and Evening Prayer, A Form of Prayer with Thanksgiving to be used yearly upon the 5th day of November for the happy deliverance of the King and the three Estates of the Realm from the traitorous and bloody intended massacre by gunpowder, and A Form of Common Prayer to be used yearly upon the 30th day of January, being the day of the Martyrdom of King Charles the first.

20. Mr Jones having spent three hours in reading and kissing the aforesaid letter, and being, at last, in a state of good spirits, from the last mentioned considerations, he agreed to carry an appointment, which he had before made, into execution. This was, to attend Mrs Miller, and her younger daughter, into the gallery at the play-house, and to admit Mr Partridge as one of the company. For as Jones had really that taste for humour which many affect, he expected to enjoy much entertainment in the criticisms of Partridge, from whom he expected the simple dictates of nature,

unimproved, indeed, but likewise unadulterated, by art.

In the first row then of the first gallery did Mr Jones, Mrs Miller, her youngest daughter, and Partridge, take their places. Partridge immediately declared it was the finest place he had ever been in. When the first music was played, he said, "It was a wonder how so many fiddlers could play at one time, without putting one another out." While the fellow was lighting the upper candles, he cried out to Mrs Miller, "Look, look, madam, the very picture of the man in the end of the common-prayer book before the gunpowder-treason service." Nor could he help observing, with a sigh, when all the candles were lighted, "That here were candles enough burnt in one night, to keep an honest poor family for a whole twelve-month."

21. As soon as Adams came into the room, Mr Barnabas introduced him to the stranger, who was, he told him, a bookseller, and would be as likely to deal with him for his sermons as any man whatever. Adams, saluting the stranger, answered Barnabas, that he was very much obliged to him; that nothing could be more convenient, for he had no other business to the great city, and was heartily desirous of returning with the young man, who was just recovered of his misfortune. He then snapt his fingers (as was usual with him), and took two or three turns about the room in an extasy. And to induce the bookseller to be as expeditious as possible, as likewise to offer him a better price for his commodity, he assured them their meeting was extremely lucky to himself; for that he had the most pressing occasion for money at that time, his own being almost spent, and having a friend then in the same inn, who was just recovered from some wounds he had received from robbers, and was in a most indigent condition. "So that nothing," says he, "could be so opportune for the supplying both our necessities as my making an immediate bargain with you."

As soon as he had seated himself, the stranger began in these words: "Sir, I do not care absolutely to deny engaging in what my friend Mr Barnabas recommends; but sermons are mere drugs. The trade is so vastly stocked with them, that really, unless now it was a sermon preached on the 30th of January; or we could say in the title-page, published at the earnest request of the congregation, or the inhabitants; but, truly, for a dry piece of sermons, I had rather be excused; especially as my hands are so full at present. However, sir, as Mr Barnabas mentioned them to me, I will, if you please, take the manuscript with me to town, and send you my opinion of it in a very short time."

REFERENCES

1. Thomas Hardy, *Far from the Madding Crowd*, op. cit., Ch. 44.
2. Laurie Lee, *Cider with Rosie*, op. cit.
3. P.G. Wodehouse, *Very Good Jeeves*, Herbert Jenkins 1930, Jeeves and the Kid Clementina.
4. H.C. Davis, *Twelve Good Men and True*, BBC Publications 1981.
5. Rose Macaulay, *Letters to a Friend*, op. cit., 15 May 1952.
6. Thomas Hardy, *Far from the Madding Crowd,* op. cit., Ch.42.
7. Thomas Bisse, *The Beauty of Holinesse in the Common Prayer*; as set forth in 4 Sermons preached at the Rolls Chapel 1716.
8. Isaac Walton, *Lives*, op. cit.

9. A.L. Rowse, *A Cornish Childhood*, Jonathan Cape 1942, Church.
10. C.M. Yonge, *Countess Kate*, 1862, 1948 ed. Faber & Faber.
11. Laurie Lee, *Cider with Rosie*, op. cit., Last Days.
12. Barbara Pym, *Some Tame Gazelle*, Jonathan Cape 1956.
13. Isaac Walton, *Lives*, op. cit.
14. Elizabeth Goudge, *The Joy of Snow*, Hodder & Stoughton 1974, p. 232.
15. Alan Paton, *Towards the Mountain*, Penguin Books Ltd 1986, Ch. 26.
16. Isabel Colegate, *The Shooting Party*, Hamish Hamilton 1980, p. 167f.
17. P.D. James, *An Unsuitable Job for a Woman*, Faber& Faber 1972, Ch. 4.
18. Sir Digby Pigott, *The Changeling*, Witherby & Co 1908.
19. L.J. Morrissey, *Gulliver's Progress*, Archon Books 1978.
20. Henry Fielding, *The History of Tom Jones*, Andrew Millar 1749.
21. Henry Fielding, *The Adventures of Joseph Andrews*, op. cit.

CHAPTER 8
Holy Communion

And the priest ... shall say the Lord's Prayer, with the Collect following. Then shall the priest rehearse distinctly all the ten Commandments.

1. It was a perfect July morning, the town hall clock sharp against a clear, blue sky, the Roary Water fallen silent for Sunday and a few chub bubbling the surface as they rose below the towpath under the further bank. I parked the car and we walked round the tower and in at the southwest door.

I had been right about the likelihood of there being few people at the service. There were about fifteen - none with whom I was acquainted, though one or two I recognized as regular attenders. The verger - who always whispered, whether anything was going on or not - was directing people into the chancel, and we went up and took our places. The sun, shining through the east window, was dappling the floor with coloured light - red, blue and green; the centurion's cloak, the Virgin's robe, the grass on which the soldiers crouched, rolling their dice. I recalled some architect once telling me that the reason he liked trees round buildings was that the sun in leaves had the effect of bringing light down to the ground. This was the same, I thought, watching the dim-edged, glowing patches on the tiles as I looked up from a short prayer of thanks for our prosperity and happiness. A minute or two later the clock struck eight and Tony entered from the vestry.

It was Tony's way to say the initial Lord's Prayer very quietly, his back to the congregation, as though commending himself to God before beginning the Communion service itself. Having completed this, he would turn round and speak the Collect facing his parishioners, and thus by implication on their behalf.

'Almighty God, unto whom all hearts be open, all desires known, and from whom no secrets are hid. . . .'

Had I any secrets? I wondered. There is nothing covered that shall not be revealed; and whatsoever ye have spoken in darkness shall be heard in the light. I could think of nothing I was concealing from anyone - nothing, anyway, which they ought by rights to know. Could Karin? What a secret person she was, I reflected; indeed, one might say an adept at concealment. I, who had been married to her for six weeks, still did not know her place of birth, her parentage or anything about her past life; and this did not bother me in the least. The beautiful and good, I thought, are privileged to bend workaday rules. 'Trust me,' says the master to the disciple. 'It's not possible for me to explain to you as yet the full meaning of all you're going to learn, or the delight you're going to derive from it. For the moment you have to learn these - let's say - Greek verbs, so that one day you'll be able to read Homer - a joy I can't communicate to you now. You've simply got to trust me.' In effect, this was what Christ said to us; and what Karin had said to me. And what had I not learned, and gained, from trusting her? I was a new man. If she had secrets, I was well content to leave them between her and God.

I emerged from these thoughts to realize that I was not joining, as I ought, in the responses to the Ten Commandments (which Tony always read in full, as appointed). I found the place.

'Honour thy father and thy mother; that thy days may be long in the land which the Lord thy God giveth thee.'

'Lord, have mercy upon us, and incline our hearts to keep this law.'

'Thou shalt do no murder.'

'Lord, have mercy upon us, and incline our hearts to keep this law.'

Well, my heart was inclined right enough; and I didn't want to commit adultery, or steal, or bear false witness either. Had I ever, in fact, been faced with the temptation to commit a grave sin for personal gain? I couldn't remember it. I was lucky. 'It's easy enough,' I remembered my housemaster once saying, 'to feel enthusiastic about religion, until the time when you come up against real and actual temptation.' Yes, I was lucky all right. 'It's lovers who can afford to be generous.'

2. 1849. Every year shows me more and more the utter deceitfulness of the heart: "who can know it!" Oh, the comfort of thinking that there is One who knows it, and can therefore cleanse its most hidden chambers from their dark pollution. "O God unto whom all hearts be open" etc. is one of the sweetest things in our sweet Liturgy, to me, and it is wonderful what confidence it has often given me.

The ten Commandments, and indeed all the other commandments of the Law in the Old Testament, are contained, according to Jesus, in the two great Commandments: "Thou shalt love the Lord thy God with all thy heart, mind, soul and strength; and thy neighbour as thyself." This summary began to come into use in the eighteenth century, and was officially sanctioned in the 1928 Revision of the Prayer Book.

3. One incident during our early days at Cuffley stands out vividly in my memory. On another Sunday morning I found myself one of a congregation of about a dozen. Instead of the Vicar, a visiting clergyman, a youngish man, appeared. I have attended countless Communion Services, of every description, from the highly ornate and choral to the severely simple. But never have I known one so impressive as that. The Ten Commandments gave place to the Two. Everything was read as if fresh-minted. There was no trace of over-expression or 'feeling', but the man seemed to be meaning every word he uttered, and a long experience tells me this cannot be put on. I have no idea who this man was, nor what his doctrine may have been about the real presence, but it was the first and only time that I have felt the spirit of it.

Then shall follow the Collect for the Queen.

Kingston, Chaplain at a Hill Station in India in the late nineteenth century, is an Anglo-Catholic, using the ceremonial of the Roman Catholic church, which incites extreme Protestants to barrack the service. However, he is faithful to the words of the Prayer Book, and, after the Ten Commandments, says the Collect for the Queen.

4. When the choir, manifestly demoralised by the noise from outside, had sung the last Kyrie, Kingston turned back to the altar and began the Collect for the Queen. Almighty and everlasting God, we are taught by the holy Word, that the hearts of Kings are in thy rule and governance, and that thou dost dispose and turn them as it seemeth best to thy godly wisdom: We humbly beseech thee so to dispose and govern the heart of Victoria thy Servant, our Queen and Governor, that, in all her thoughts, words, and works, she may ever seek thy honour and glory, and study to preserve thy people committed to her charge, in wealth, peace and godliness: Grant this, O merciful Father, for thy dear Son's sake, Jesus Christ our Lord. Amen.

This Collect had a sobering effect, not only on the restive members of the congregation but on the noisy mob outside who appeared to have some means of following the progress of the service within. They remained quiet too, during the Epistle and the Gospel both of which Kingston read in a normal speaking tone. McNab dared to hope that the interruptions were now over.

The Collect, Epistle and Gospel are now read. And the Gospel ended, shall be sung or said the Creed. Then shall follow the Sermon.

Then shall the priest return to the Lord's Table, and begin the Offertory, saying one or more of these sentences following:

5. "He *[Levi Everdene]* got so much better, that he was quite godly in his later years, wasn't he, Jan?" asked Joseph Poorgrass. "He got himself confirmed over again in a more serious way, and took to saying 'Amen' almost as loud as the clerk, and he liked to copy comforting verses from the tombstones. He used, too, to hold the money plate at Let your Light so Shine, and stand godfather to poor little come by chance children; and he kept a missionary box upon his table to nab folk unawares when they called. . . ."

Whilst these sentences are in reading the Deacons, Church Wardens or other fit persons appointed for that purpose shall receive the Alms for the Poor. . . .

6. Monday April 14th 1825

I called upon Bacon, Junior, at Meadgates, after breakfast, the man who has been so long ill with the liver complaint, in order to give him some of the Sacrament money.

After which done, the Priest shall say,

Let us pray for the whole state of Christ's Church militant here in earth.

7. The old Prayer Book prayed that the magistrates might 'truly and indifferently administer justice'. Then the revisers thought they would make this easier by altering *indifferently* to *impartially*. A country clergyman ... asked his sexton what

he thought *indifferently* meant and got the correct answer, "It means making no difference between one chap and another." "And what," continued the parson, "do you thing impartially means?" "Ah," said the sexton after a pause, "I wouldn't know *that*."

8. Around the time of the first anniversary of his wife's death, Samuel Johnson went to Bromley where she lay buried and received the Sacrament in the church there. "I ardently applied to her the prayer for the Church Militant where the dead are mentioned and commended her again to eternal mercy, as in coming out I approached her grave."

There follow the Exhortations; one to prepare the people for the next celebration of Holy Communion, and an alternative one for when they have proved reluctant to come; the third one to be used at a celebration. They emphasise the great gift offered by God and demand that the communicant prepares most carefully to receive it. These exhortations were a necessary part of the service at a time when the laity had only been used to receiving Communion, and that in one kind, once a year, and also when Communion was only added on to the normal lengthy Sunday service monthly or even quarterly. As the service of Holy Communion came to stand by itself, said or sung, so the custom of reading the Exhortations died out. However, the increasing frequency of Communion services, especially at the most popular time for Sunday worship, perhaps invites the occasional reading of the 3rd Exhortation or at least a reminder that it is there to be read.
"amend your lives, and be in perfect charity with all men; so shall ye be meet partakers of those holy mysteries."

9. One day whilst the Arch-Bishop of Canterbury waited upon His Majesty *[King George IV]* in order to administer to him the Holy Sacrament, one of the attendants some how or other so offended His Majesty, that he sternly forbid him the Royal Presence, and then turned round to the Arch-Bishop to receive the Host; the Arch-Bishop, be it ever spoken to his praise, declined administering the same until such time as His Majesty was more calm and free from anger. His Majesty bowed with submission and reverence; sent for the servant; shook him by the hand, sincerely forgave him; and after a few moments spent in solemn devotion, received the *'living bread'* from the hands of the *'High Priest'*.

10. There was always a communion at Clyston St Fay on the first Sunday in the month. There were not many communicants, as a rule, but there was a solemn hush and stillness in the air, and over the whole parish, at that particular moment, as though something mysterious and beyond the common was taking place. This was especially the case on fine summer Sundays, after the first service was over when, on ordinary days, boys and young men lingered about the churchyard and the village road. On these first Sundays of the month no one was to be seen. At such times there was a stillness and pause, during which Nature herself seemed to hold her breath, and the yew trees, and the apple orchards, and the rows of stately elms, lay passive and silent in the sunlight glow, and seemed to own and to proclaim a Presence, which was of earth and yet divine, to await the tread of the feet of

heavenly messengers, the rustle of angelic wings, the gift of heavenly food that nourishes all conditions and ranks alike.

There was a larger congregation than was usually the case on this particular Sunday, many people from the neighbouring parishes coming in.

The Rector preached a well-known sermon. 'The Unrelenting Steward, or the Forgiveness of Wrongs.'

It was a favourite sermon, but not of equal popularity with 'The Ungrateful Son'. It was listened to, to-day, with an unusual relish. A sense of personal interest, of something real and vital, that entered into the life of each and every one, seemed to pervade the church. The well-remembered, sonorous sentence that concluded the sermon was uttered, and the congregation waited for the ascription, that they might rise in their seats, but it did not come. There was a pause, during which the Rector seemed bracing himself to an unusual effort, then he went on again, speaking now without note or book.

"I have not done. There is something more which I have to say. An event has occurred here, where so few events occur, which is by this time known to you all." *[The Rector is referring to the cruel deception practised upon his daughter, Blanche, by a priest, who, while declaring his affection for her, has been pursuing a more worldly wise profitable relationship with another woman. His engagement to her has now come to light.]*
It would take a very great preacher - I doubt whether there is one now living in England who, in the ordinary course of his calling, could do it - to produce such a hush as followed upon these words.

The Rector went on, it is possible somewhat incoherently -

"A stunning blow, dealt at that part where I am most vulnerable, of which you are all thinking, has caused in your hearts, always so kindly affectioned to me and mine, indignation and grief. From the depth of my heart, the heart of a stricken man, I thank you for this last token of your affection and regard. But I have preached to you now for a lengthened time - long, that is, in relation to the short space given us to work in here - of many high and difficult things. I have enforced, as was my duty, many duties upon you; woe be to me if, when my turn comes, I do not, at least, recognise my share in the obligation - if I do not, at least, make an effort to practise what I have preached. In this solemn asseveration, therefore, before God and before you all, I purge my conscience of all bitterness and offence against any man, however deeply he may have injured me; and I go to that Holy Table, and I hope many of us will go to-day, in perfect charity and forgiveness, remembering what black and deep offences God, for Christ's sake, has forgiven me."

It was the custom of the Rector on Communion morning, after the sermon was over, to move up very slowly towards the Communion Table, that he might give the principal part of the congregation who wished to leave time to do so. He did so now, but he need not have delayed; no one stirred.

The English peasant is slow, but there are moments, and those of not such infrequent occurrence as some may be disposed to think, in which he rises to an instinctive sympathy, in which I do not think that he can be beaten by any race or people upon earth.

Such a moment occurred now. 'And I hope many of us will go to-day,' - these words decided the action of the people of Clyston St Fay. Mrs Churchwarden Wike, acting upon some impulse which she never explained, even to her most intimate friends, put her hand upon her children to keep them in their places, and this intimation was instinctively followed throughout the whole church. No one stirred. The children - their young eyes alight with gazing upon mysteries of which they had only heard before - sat still in their places, their hands clasped before them. Many herdsmen and farmboys, hewers of wood and drawers of water - the Gibeonites of Nature's tyranny - who never would have thought of approaching that awful table, on this day, struck and overpowered by the pervading feeling, remained at gaze.

Mr Churchwarden Wike, very red in the face, and somewhat dim about the eyes, rose in his seat, and, in the company with his fellow-warden, proceeded to collect the alms in two large silver basins, marked 'J.Y. (John Yarde), Rector, 1689.'

It was usually a very simple matter, and occupied a very short time, but to-day it taxed the efforts of the wardens considerably, and a very remarkable collection of coins, to the curious in such matters, was that presented to the Rector at the altar that day.

The Rector read the prayer for the whole state of Christ's Church Militant here on earth, *the exhortation to those minded to come to the Holy Communion of the Body and Blood of our Saviour Christ*, the comfortable words addressed to such, and that marvellous prayer, the supremest effort of divine genius, that conceives and hopes that the sinful and leprous flesh is made clean by the divine food; and then, after the prayer of consecration and his own communicating, he made a pause.

It may strike many, doubtless, in these days, with astonishment and even disgust, but it is nevertheless a fact, that no one would have dreamt of communicating at Clyston St Fay before the Rector's daughter had gone up.

Blanche rose in her seat. Perfectly pale, but without the slightest apparent effort or tremor, she passed up the old chancel, between the foliated scrolls of the memorials of dead rectors upon the walls, and knelt before her father in the angle of the rails. There never has been such a Communion at Clyston St Fay either before or since.

The priest now calls the people to make the General Confession.

11. '. . . *and make your humble confession to Almighty God.* . . .' She listened while Canon Jones abjured his congregation to unburden their sins. Thank heaven the cathedral would stick to the old Book of Common Prayer so long as Gilbert was Dean. She didn't at all care for the uninspired language of the modern alternative book.

12. In 1934, at the age of thirty-one, I was very uncritical of Tubby. Now in 1946, at lunch with him, I was repelled by the boisterous bonhomie, which conveyed, and I think was meant to convey, that the relationship between us was deep and precious.

I attended a quiet communion at All Hallows by the Tower at which Tubby celebrated. There he was a different man. When he came to the words

We do earnestly repent,

And are heartily sorry for these our misdoings;

The remembrance of them is grievous unto us,
The burden of them is intolerable.

he spoke them with a great and unfeigned humility, almost with pain. We should always do that, but we do not. I came to the conclusion that somewhere, somehow, something had gone wrong. And I came to the further conclusion that - to him - his sin was that he had not fulfilled the promise of those inspired days at the Old House in Poperinghe, and his incomparable ministry to men who were going, many of them, to certain death. And I have no doubt that the praise of men had come between him and his Creator. The booming voice, the bonhomie were meant to hide it all, but in the chapel he hid nothing, for was he not prostrating himself before One from whom no secrets are hid? Who am I indeed, and who is anyone else, to have judged him at all?

13. She *[Mrs Babcock]* had grown up terrorized by the prospect of hellfire and damnation from sermons every Sunday at the Southern Baptist Church. The austere Anglican Book of Common Prayer had been balm to her cowering spirit. The Episcopal approach was really more her style: "We acknowledge and bewail our manifold sins and wickedness, which we, from time to time, most grievously have committed, by thought, word, and deed, against thy Divine Majesty, provoking most justly thy wrath and indignation against us. We do earnestly repent, and are heartily sorry for these our misdoings; the remembrance of them is grievous unto us; the burden of them is intolerable. . . ."

After the Confession and Absolution "then shall the priest say" the Comfortable Words

14. My father loved the Anglican prayer-book, the music of its words, the beauty of its ceremonies, the magic of its mysteries, and he strove to create at St Chad's a reflection of this music and beauty and magic. His thoughtful voice as he read the services still echoes in my inner ear. I hear him speaking the 'comfortable words' of Jesus, 'Come unto me all that travail and are heavy laden, and I will refresh you,' and the climax of the prologue of the Gospel of John. 'And the Word was made flesh, and dwelt among us (and we beheld his glory, the glory of the only-begotten of the Father) full of grace and truth.' When he was a very old man and read this passage in church his voice would break with emotion.

After which the Priest shall proceed, saying,
Lift up your hearts. . . .

15. The sunlight - the very sun itself - was moving on through the upright form before the altar, and darkness and light together were pouring through it, and with them all things that were. He saw, standing at the very edge of that channel, the small figure of Adrian, and then he himself had passed the boy and was entering upon the final stage of the Way. Everything was veiled; the voice of the priest-king was the sound of creation's movement; he awaited the exodus that was to be.

Everything was veiled, but not so entirely that he did not hear from somewhere behind him, in space or in experience, the Duke's voice saying, "Et cum spiritu tuo," or a call from in front, "Lift up your hearts," or again, from behind, Barbara's voice crying, "We lift them up unto the Lord," or, in a higher and more tremendous summons, "Let us give thanks unto our Lord God," and, amid the tumult of song that broke out, Lionel's own voice joining in the answer, "It is meet and right so to do."

"It is very meet, right. . . ." the priest-king said; the three heard it, and heard no more intelligible words. They saw Adrian moving up and about; they saw his grave and happy face as he turned to some motion of his Lord's; they saw him go back and sit down again on his hassock, cuddling his knees, glance down at his mother, and turn to watch the event. For now the unknown sounds were pealing steadily on; all separate beings, save where the hands of the lovers lingered in a final clasp, were concentrated on that high motionless Figure - motionless, for in Him all motions awaited His movement to be loosed, and still He did not move. All sound ceased; all things entered into an intense suspension of being; nothing was anywhere at all but He.

16. On a Sunday in late March there occurred another of those small unforgettable happenings Mark had grown to expect. The snow was gone. Day after day the rain had fallen patiently. When Mark shook up the fire in the big round stove and rang the church bell, he noticed that the leaden sky, which had overhung the village all winter long, seemed less dark and gloomy. During the communion service, just as he spoke the old, old words, "Therefore, with Angels and Archangels and with all the company of heaven," bright light suddenly filled the church and all the bowed heads lifted to see the sun glistening on the snows that crowned Whoop-Szo, and it seemed to Mark that he felt the burden of the winter lift as from a common shoulder, and heard the sign of gratitude rise from a common heart.

When the service was over, the tribe poured slowly from the church, lingering in little groups on the path by the Cedar man at the foot of the great totem.

"How thin we are," said old Peter. "We are like the bear when he leaves his den, and stands blinking in the light."

They all agreed, nodding that the cruel winter had been hard on them all.

There follows the Prayer of Humble Access and the Prayer of Consecration. "Then shall the Minister first receive the Communion in both kinds himself..."

17. Another powerful asset of English - including (what is by no means irrelevant to ordinary speech and writing) a rhetorical asset - is the peculiarly flexible English relative pronoun. How brilliantly Cranmer exploited this and how ruthlessly his revisers have dispensed with it is strikingly illustrated by the prayer of consecration in the Holy Communion ("commonly called the Mass," 1548), which in Common Prayer consists of one continuous vast sentence, made possible by the relative pronoun: "Almighty God, our heavenly father, *who* of thy tender mercy . . . *who* made there by his one oblation. . . . HEAR US and GRANT . . . *who* in the same night that he was betrayed. . . . Amen." Quite deliberately the revisers have destroyed this architectural structure and replaced it with a series of separate independent sentences, in the belief presumably that English speakers and hearers no longer understand and appreciate relative pronouns - have, in other words, become de-Latinized and linguistically uneducated. Only draftsmen who were themselves in that condition could have dared in the *Te Deum* to replace the correct English

equivalent "we praise thee, O God" with the horrific mistranslation "You are God, and we praise you."

18. The squat church stood on the hill's brow. Looking back Peplow could see Minden's plan: roofs, streets, the bronze horseman above the Square, the road to the station, the stream and the broken mill, the featureless plain. He casually wondered when the first lorries bringing in the paraphernalia of the fairground would arrive. He thought of the appalling disaster of Herbert Ruskin propped in his wheelchair, of Ted Bellenger beginning his last day, the day that, already, was scarcely going as he had planned it.

Turning away from both view and thoughts, his trouser leg was caught by a bramble runner and bending to loosen it, he became aware of the appalling state of the churchyard, a wilderness of self-sown elderberries, leaning stones, broken jam jars, matted grass and nettles. Then he heard the low murmur of voices and turned back towards the open door of the church.

It seemed empty, an arcade of thick pillars rising from the stone-flagged floor, a stunted chancel arch and, above it, Dives writhing in faded vermilion flames, stretching agonised arms to a half-obliterated Lazarus cradled in a heaven of peeling paint. Entering quietly, he knelt behind the only other communicants, two elderly women. A small boy, the acolyte, knelt in the sanctuary; the Priest faced the east window.

Listening intently, he followed the murmuring voice: "'This is my blood of the New Testament . . . which is shed for you and for many . . . for the remission of sins. . . . Do this as oft as ye shall drink it . . . in remembrance of Me.'"

The Priest raised the chalice and drank.

Following the women, he too rose and knelt at the rail. The wafer was put into his hands, and afterwards, the cup to his lips. He involuntarily shuddered, the hair rising on his neck - was this an absolution?

The insistent murmur went on: "'Drink this in remembrance . . . that Christ's blood was shed for thee . . . and be thankful.'"

Head bent, the taste of wine in his mouth, it suddenly seemed quite natural that tomorrow, at this time, someone else would be kneeling in his place and that he would be dead.

19. Alethea knelt in her seat in front of the Canons, and looking forward to the High Altar and the glowing window behind it, conscious of the presence of the little community in which she was to live, she was moved by a service so new to her, and so strongly different from the conventional 'staying behind' of her Cambridge days. She thought to herself, "it is here I shall find what it is, that Spirit which eludes me, the mysterious something that binds these others together. Perhaps this morning - now - I shall make it mine and then I shall be able to live here with content, and work like them and feel it good."

Her thoughts faded into a prayer that it might be so. Canon Trent was celebrating and his beautiful voice reached the farthest corners of the Choir and with such gentleness that each felt the words were said by one who stood close by.

Then when he had knelt before the altar and taken the bread and wine himself, he turned to face the congregation, and holding the paten high he murmured something, some invitation to them to approach. For a moment there was silence and no one moved, and in that moment the storm outside broke, there was a sound of a rustling mighty wind; and in the cathedral others, besides Alethea, became conscious of a Presence. . . .

Many felt their Communion that first day of Lent had given them a vision they had not known before.

"Then shall the Priest say the Lord's Prayer, the people repeating after him every Petition."
"After shall be said as followeth". . . .

20. CRANMER [*writing*]: . . . here we offer and present unto thee, O Lord, ourselves, our souls and bodies, to be a reasonable, holy, and lively sacrifice unto thee; humbly beseeching thee, that all we who are partakers of this holy Communion, may be fulfilled with thy grace and heavenly benediction. And although we be unworthy, through our manifold sins, to offer unto thee any sacrifice, yet we beseech thee to accept this our bounden duty and service; not weighing our merits, but pardoning our offences, through Jesus Christ our Lord; by whom and with whom, in the unity of the Holy Ghost,
THE SINGERS: all honour and glory be unto Thee, O Father Almighty, world without end. Amen.
THE SKELETON: Many a master hath made device,
    in words, of incomparable sacrifice,
    but woe, woe,
    to any who see not where the words go:
    it were better they had said but *yes* or *no*.
CRANMER [*writing*]: We praise thee, we bless thee, we worship thee, we glorify thee. . . .
THE SKELETON [*leaping up*]: We praise thee,
THE SINGERS [*joining with the* SKELETON]: we bless thee, we worship thee, we glorify thee, we give thanks to thee for thy great glory, O Lord God, heavenly King, God the Father Almighty.
CRANMER [*writing*]: The peace of God which passeth all understanding . . . .
THE SINGERS: Keep your hearts and minds in the knowledge and love of God.

In the 1662 Book of Common Prayer the Gloria comes at the end of the service, and fittingly.

21. We may no longer talk of "our incomparable liturgy": yet I sometimes wonder whether our forefathers, for most of whom Comparative Liturgiology was a comparatively unknown science were not for that reason the better situated to appreciate the construction of our own Prayer Book Services and to grasp what they are meant to teach. Thus, it was plain to them why the Gloria must come where it does in the Order of the Ministration of Holy Communion, because they were unconscious that it occupies a different position in a different rite; and equally they could see the perfect appropriateness of the Prayer of Humble Access following immediately upon the Sanctus, and the priest kneeling for it, because they were not distracted by the totally irrelevant consideration that there is no Prayer of Humble

Access in the Roman Church. The palmary criteria of a liturgy are whether it makes sense or not (ie. whether it has a logical coherence), and what kind of sense it makes when measured by the standard of the Bible. Cranmer's work measures up to these criteria well.

Researching for a biography of Vice Admiral the Revd A.R.W. Woods, the author has an appointment with Prebendary Inglis at 12.30 in a London city church, where he held Holy Communion every Thursday at noon.

22. It was a church I did not know and to be certain of being punctual, I arrived early. I went into the church. It was a Palladian affair in the 18th Century style, very light and gay with various marbles. There were 3 people in the church, the priest, the verger and a young man.

I knelt and pretended to pray.

I thought, this was how Alex must have felt officiating in his empty chapel and the still emptier church in Dock Street, trying to console himself with "where two or three are gathered together in my name" while the heavy traffic thundered down to the docks.

It was 27 years since I had heard the Order for Holy Communion. I had forgotten the beauty of its language. As the still familiar words came back to me, spoken bravely by the priest, it occurred to me that it might all be nonsense but it was a *magnificent* waste of time and it did not matter if there were only one or two people in the congregation, provided that the churches were open. The very fact that in this busy city where at the moment almost everybody was engrossed in commerce, there was a priest celebrating the Lord's Supper to a legitimate congregation of one was magnificent.

At that moment the door of the church opened and a young woman, good-looking and well-dressed, but clearly worried about something, came in and knelt down to pray.

I found myself struggling with the Gloria, "Glory be . . . Father Almighty." It was merely an exercise in memory, how much one could remember after all these years.

"O Lord, the only begotten son Jesu Christ, O Lord God, Lamb of God, Son of the Father, that takest away the sins of the world, have mercy upon us. . . ." I couldn't go on even for the priest's sake. The idea of Jesus taking away the sins of the world was impossible.

I looked at the girl, who seemed absolutely engrossed in her prayer. The priest raised his hands in benediction. "The peace of God which passeth all understanding. . . ."

That was no good for me. "But I hope it's some use to you," I thought, "because you're a jolly worried young woman."

By the conclusion of his researches the author had returned to his long lost faith.

REFERENCES

1. Richard Adams, *The Girl in a Swing*, op. cit., Ch. 22.
2. M.V.G. Havergal, *Memorials of Frances Ridley Havergal*, James Nisbet and Co. 1880, p. 53.

3. M.V. Hughes, *A London Family between the Wars*, O.U.P. 1940, Ch. 4.
4. J.G. Farrell, *The Hill Station*, Weidenfeld & Nicholson 1981.
5. Thomas Hardy, *Far from the Madding Crowd,* op. cit., Ch. 8.
6. John Skinner, *Journal of a Somerset Rector 1803-34,* ed. Howard & Peter Coombs, Kingsmead Press, 1930.
7. C.S. Lewis, *First and Second Things*, Fount Paperbacks 1986, Ch. 11.
8. Christopher Hibbert, *The Personal History of Samuel Johnson*, Longman 1971.
9. 'The Last Moments of our late beloved Sovereign George IV' Elliot 1830 quoted in *English Church Life* by J. Wickham Legg, Appendix to Ch. 2, Longman & Green 1914.
10. J.H. Shorthouse, *Blanche, Lady Falaise*, Macmillan 1891, Part 1 Ch. X.
11. David Williams, *Murder in Advent*, Macmillan 1985, Ch. 20.
12. Alan Paton, *Towards the Mountain*, op. cit., Ch. 29.
13. Lisa Alther, *Kinflicks*, Alfred A. Knopf New York 1976, p. 90.
14. Escott Reid, *Radical Mandarin*, University of Toronto Press 1989, Ch. 8.
15. Charles Williams, *War in Heaven*, op. cit., Ch. 8.
16. Margaret Craven, *I Heard the Owl call my Name*, George G. Harrap & Co 1968, Ch. 19.
17. Enoch Powell, 'Further Thoughts: Grammar and Syntax', essay in *The State of the Language* eds C. Ricks & L. Michaels, Faber & Faber 1990.
18. J.L. Carr, *A Day in Summer,* Hogarth Press 1986, pp. 16, 17.
19. Susan Goodyear, *Cathedral Close*, op. cit. page 51.
20. Charles Williams, *Thomas Cranmer of Canterbury,* O.U.P. 1936. (First produced in the Chapter House, Canterbury).
21. C.H. Smyth, *The Genius of the Church of England*, S.P.C.K. 1947.
22. A. Calder-Marshall, *No Earthly Command*, Rupert Hart Davis 1957, Ch. 14.

CHAPTER 9
Interlude: 1662 And All That

All that went before was considerable. We take for granted that in church priest and people share together in a common prayer. However, before 1549 men and women would have regarded church as a place where they went under obligation, whilst simply continuing their private devotions. The choir offices, which were to form the basis of Mattins and Evensong, were for the clergy; and the Mass which the laity attended was celebrated at the 'holy end' in Latin by the priest whilst the people continued to pray privately, reminded by bells to look up only at the Elevation, that is when the priest lifted the consecrated wafer and chalice. Receiving Communion, in bread only, was for most of the laity an annual event. Moreover, different parts of the country used different service books. With this background in mind we can begin to appreciate the revolution brought about by Archbishop Cranmer with the publication and authorisation of the first Book of Common Prayer in English in 1549 for exclusive use throughout the realm.

This book was succeeded by a second, published in 1552, in which changes were made, especially with regard to the service of Holy Communion, distancing it further from the Latin Mass and the doctrine of transubstantiation, and placing the people's reception of Communion at the place where, in the old service, the Elevation had been: the sacrament was not for adoration, but to be partaken of - in both bread and wine.

The second Prayer Book had been in use for less than a year when Queen Mary ascended the throne. The Latin services were restored, and Cranmer died at the stake. However, six years later, with Queen Elizabeth on the throne, a new edition of the Prayer Book was authorised, and the words to be used at the administration of the Holy Communion combined those of 1549 with those of 1552, as we find them in the Prayer Book of 1662. Behind such small changes lay a battle between those who wanted more drastic reform after the Continental manner, for many 'Puritans' remained within the established church, and those who saw the church catholic as well as reformed, departing from Rome not in her essence, but in her errors.

When King James I came to the throne in 1603 the Puritans hoped for great things, presenting him on his way south from Scotland with a 'Millenary Petition', raising a number of objections to the 1559 Prayer Book. James summoned a conference at Hampton Court, where he made it clear that he was on the side of the Bishops; and the most significant change in the Prayer Book was the addition to the Catechism of teaching concerning the sacraments, with a 'high' doctrine of the Holy Communion. Plans were also made for a new translation of the Holy Bible.

The distinguished Anglican divines of the reigns of James and his successor Charles I did much to establish the particular character of the Church of England through their adherence to the Book of Common Prayer and their exposition and justification of its liturgy and doctrine. However, two years after civil war broke out, in 1644, the Book of Common Prayer was declared illegal and replaced by the Directory of Public Worship, which stated that "the liturgy used in the Church of England hath proved an offence, not only to many of the godly at home, but also to the reformed Churches abroad." As papist Queen Mary had banned the Book, so now Puritan Oliver Cromwell.

Charles II was brought to the throne by the Presbyterian party, so that the restoration of the Prayer Book was no foregone conclusion. Instead it was the achievement of those clergy who had gone into exile during the Commonwealth, who combined dedication with skilful manoeuvring. King Charles II summoned twelve Anglican bishops and twelve Presbyterian ministers to the Savoy Conference "to review the Book of Common Prayer." A new book, adjusted to the objections of the Presbyterian party and so able to comprehend their ministers with the Church of England, was the hope of those present, but the obstinate fanaticism of Richard Baxter, the leader of the Presbyterians, who remained "passionately argumentative" to the last, made any compromise impossible, with the result that in the end the Prayer Book was revised by the Bishops alone. Bishop Gunning provided the Prayer for All Sorts and Conditions of Men; Bishop Reynolds the General Thanksgiving; and Prayers to be Used at Sea and the service for Adult Baptism were added. The Authorised Version of the Bible, planned by King James I, was now used for the Epistles and Gospels, (though his labours were not acknowledged, the greater part of these was the work of William Tyndale), whilst Coverdale's translation of the Psalms was retained. There was, too, a further distancing from the Puritans: the word 'priest' was substituted for 'minister', 'church' for 'congregation'; the prayer over the bread and wine was called the Prayer of Consecration. Canon Smyth, who in his book "The Church and the Nation" provides the details of the Savoy Conference, concludes that the 1662 revision of the Prayer Book was the authentic climax of the English Reformation. "For more than a century, the liturgical development of the Church of England had oscillated slightly between radical and conservative, Reformed and Catholic, currents of opinion; and it had settled into what may be described as Central Churchmanship with a High Church tinge." It is this edition of the Prayer Book that remains in use today.

All that followed after was again considerable, although nothing reached the stage of legislation. From the arrival of King William III onwards individual clergymen and laymen and groups of like-minded men, sought to have the Prayer Book altered in order to make it acceptable to nonconformists (except Roman Catholic ones!), or more agreeable to doctrinal fashions or to changing sensibility. Ecclesiastical historians of the nineteenth century find a constant stream of publications, filled with the intention of improving the Book of Common Prayer; but all in vain, apart from the discontinuance of the special services commemorating the Gunpowder Plot and the Martyrdom of King Charles I in 1859 and the authorising of a new Lectionary in 1871.

It was elsewhere that changes came: in 1764 the Scottish Episcopal Church produced a Communion Office, and in 1790 the Protestant Episcopal Church of the United States of America its Prayer Book, based on Cranmer's 1549 Book as well as that of 1662. In the Preface it explains:

'When in the course of Divine Providence, these American States became independent with respect to civil government, their ecclesiastical independence was necessarily included; and the different religious denominations of Christians in these States were left at full and equal liberty to model and organize their respective Churches, and forms of worship, and discipline, in such manner as they might judge most convenient for their future prosperity; consistently with the constitution and laws of their country.

The attention of this Church was in the first place drawn to those alterations in the Liturgy which became necessary in the prayers for our Civil Rulers, in consequence of the Revolution. And the principal care herein was to make them conformable to what ought to be the proper end of all such prayers, namely, that "Rulers may have grace, wisdom, and understanding to execute justice, and to maintain truth"; and that the people "may lead quiet and peaceable lives, in all godliness and honesty."

But while these alterations were in review before the Convention, they could not but, with gratitude to God, embrace the happy occasion which was offered to them (uninfluenced and unrestrained by any worldly authority whatsoever) to take a further review of the Public Service, and to establish such other alterations and amendments therein as might be deemed expedient.

It seems unnecessary to enumerate all the different alterations and amendments. They will appear, and it is to be hoped, the reasons of them also, upon a comparison of this with the Book of Common Prayer of the Church of England. In which it will also appear that this Church is far from intending to depart from the Church of England in any essential point of doctrine, discipline, or worship; or further than local circumstances require.'

William Wordsworth in his Ecclesiastical Sonnet, "American Episcopacy" pays tribute to Dr William White, the chairman of the Committee for Prayer Book Revision in the Episcopal Church of the U.S.A.

Patriots informed with Apostolic light
Were they, who, when their Country had been freed,
Bowing with reverence to the ancient creed,
Fixed on the frame of England's Church their sight,
And strove in filial love to reunite
What force had severed. Thence they fetched the seed
Of Christian unity, and won a meed
Of praise from Heaven. To Thee, O saintly White,
Patriarch of a wide-spreading family,
Remotest lands and unborn times shall turn,
Whether they would restore or build - to Thee,
As one who rightly taught how zeal should burn,
As one who drew from out Faith's holiest urn
The purest stream of patient Energy.

Indeed, by 1914, the Prayer Book in its 1549, 1662 or American version had been translated into 114 languages and was in use in all corners of the globe, and the number continued to grow.

During the latter part of the nineteenth century departures from the Prayer Book had become common practice among Anglo-Catholic clergy, and in 1904 a Royal Commission on Ecclesiastical Discipline was appointed to consider these irregularities. As a result of their survey, they recommended that Letters of Business should be issued to the Convocations with instructions "to frame modifications in the existing law relating to the conduct of Divine Service . . . as may tend to secure the greater elasticity which a reasonable recognition of the comprehensiveness of the Church of England and of its present needs seems to demand."

In 1927 the Church produced its long gestated answer in the Revised Prayer Book, which was passed by a large majority in its own National Assembly. A majority voted in favour in the House of Lords, but the Bill was narrowly defeated in the Commons as a result of the Welsh and Scottish nonconformist vote excited to fears of Popery through the passionate denunciations of Sir Thomas Inskip and his friends. It was defeated again the following year; but the Bishops published the Book under their own authority and gave parishes permission to use it.

It was described as 'cumbrous' because it contained the 1662 services and the alternative orders of service: no one at that time imagined the possibility of a tome the size of the A.S.B.; and it might have been better had the alternative services been published separately for a period of experimental use. Be that as it may, despite some infelicitous expressions (O Lord Jesus Christ, who callest to thee whom thou *willest*), the 1928 Prayer Book does on the whole achieve a style that harmonises with that of 1662, as in the fine anthem and collects of Compline. Because of this, changes that are made in the forms of service appear constructive rather than destructive, conservative rather than revolutionary. Some of the changes indeed were already common practice, and more quickly became so, like the use of the summary of the Commandments and the salutation of the Gospel at the Holy Communion. The book also tried to bring within the bounds of legality those High Church parishes which preferred Cranmer's 1549 Order of Holy Communion, permitting the Prayer of Oblation to follow upon that of Consecration. A considerable number of prayers were added to be used at Morning and Evening Prayer, extending the scope of the intercessions following the Anthem. Sensitive additions and alterations were made to the Marriage Service (the second cause for which matrimony was ordained and the optional use of 'obey' by the bride, for example), and the Burial Service ('vile body' is not a correct translation of St Paul's Greek, and 'the body of our low estate' improves upon it; there is a greater choice of psalms, lessons and prayers; and there is a special form of service for the Burial of a Child). The order for the Visitation of the Sick replaces the old order, and is written more in the spirit of the Gospel than of the Old Testament. There are additional festivals, including Harvest. The Athanasian Creed remains, though no longer obligatory, and the damnatory verses, 2 and 42, may be omitted - though not 41. "And they that have done good will go into life eternal: they that have done evil into eternal fire." This "creed" is a splendid declaration of the doctrines of the Trinity and the Incarnation. In an age when heresy seemed to shake the very foundations of Christendom, the stand-no-nonsense sentiments of the damnatory clauses and verse 41 might have seemed appropriate warnings; but no longer. It would have been better simply to have omitted these. The Psalms are left in Coverdale's translation, but brackets round the verses least Christian in spirit permit them to be omitted. It would have been sensible to have made many small changes, clarifying the sense without spoiling the poetry, but this was not done.

Almost all the alternative forms of service came into common use through the parish priest's purchase of The Prayer Book as Proposed in 1928, but few churches obtained copies for the congregation, although occasional services such as the Burial service were obtained in pamphlet form. Perhaps the complication of two services side by side was thought too confusing: again, no one in 1928 imagined the possibility of A.S.B. complexity.

Despite its imperfections, the 1928 book stands in the true line of succession to its 1549 and 1662 forebears; and when we speak of Prayer Book services today, its alternative forms are accepted as being included within that nomenclature.

Here, for the time being, the history of the development of the Prayer Book ends, for the new experimental services combined in the Alternative Services Book are not true heirs of 1662. As G.J. Cuming writes in *A History of Anglican Liturgy*, "Elements of the Prayer Book are still to be found in the 1980 Book, but they have taken on the character of family heirlooms in a not wholly congenial setting. Other sources, other theologies have inspired the liturgies produced since 1965."

However, a new Liturgical Commission, in an exchange of views with the Prayer Book Society in 1992, wrote that it 'shared the view that the Book of Common Prayer and the Authorised Version of the Bible should remain in the mainstream of Anglican worship', and 'to the extent that this has not been so in the last generation', it went on, 'the Commission believes that Anglicans need to take seriously and to recover their heritage'. New service books there will be after the authorisation of the present A.S.B. expires with the century, but the Commission also shows a determination to learn from the mistakes of the A.S.B. and provide supplementary books that express the church's worship more fittingly, including for this purpose material in the 1928 Prayer Book style. The problem remains: how to implement the Commission's desire for the Prayer Book to "remain in the mainstream of Anglican worship", when the only implements to hand are the clergy, many of whom have scarcely known it, and many of whom are obstreperous.

Except in churches given to the eccentricities of the more extreme Anglo-Catholics from the late nineteenth century onward (when Bishop of London, Lord Fisher was invited to attend a High Mass at the Church of St Magnus Martyr. Asked afterwards what he thought of the service, he replied, "I cannot say that I am in favour of presbyterian congregationalism"), the ordinary member of the Church of England, were he transported in time through the past three and more centuries, whilst he might find changes of time and length of services, changes of music and singing, changes of clerical costume, would nevertheless feel at home in any church of the realm, for the words he would hear and speak would be the familiar ones of the Book of Common Prayer.

11 Samuel 22. Verse 44.

Thou haſt delivered me from the ſtrivings of my people, thou haſt kept me to be head. ──

CHAPTER 10
The Ministration of Public Baptism of Infants to be Used in the Church

1. August 9th 1832

I think the baptismal service almost perfect. What seems erroneous assumption in it to me is harmless. None of the services of the Church affect me so much as this. I never could attend a christening without tears bursting forth at the sight of the helpless innocent in a pious clergyman's arms.

2. My Baptismal Birth-day

God's child in Christ adopted, - Christ my all, -
What that earth boasts were not lost cheaply, rather
Than forfeit that blest name, by which I call
The Holy One, the Almighty God, my Father? -
Father! in Christ we live, and Christ in Thee -
Eternal Thou, and everlasting we.
The heir of heaven henceforth I fear not death:
In Christ I live! in Christ I draw the breath
Of the true life! - Let then earth, sea and sky
Make war against me! On my front I show
Their mighty master's seal. In vain they try
To end my life, that can but end its woe. -
Is that a death-bed where a Christian lies? -
Yes! but not his - 'tis Death itself there dies.

The people are to be admonished that it is most convenient that Baptism should not be administered but upon Sundays and other Holy-days, when the most number of people come together; as well for that the congregation there present may testify the receiving of them that be newly baptised into the number of Christ's Church; as also because in the Baptism of Infants every Man present may be put in remembrance of his own profession made to God in his Baptism. . . .

Mrs Tangye, the cleaner of the chapel, gives birth to twins and asks for them to be baptised by the Vicar, Mark Lidderdale.

3. So it fell out that about 3 weeks later on a Lenten grey Sunday morning Lydia and Celia Tangye were made lively members of Christ's holy church. Mark decided to let attendance at the baptism count as an attendance at Sunday School, because he thought that an object lesson in the administration of the sacrament would impress itself a good deal more than an hour's theoretical talking. Major Drumgold had been stirring up opposition to Mark's way of conducting the services, and had already written two or three times to the Bishop about the lack of respect he accorded to Morning Prayer; and, having found out that it annoyed his Vicar, he had taken to attending Morning Prayer in order to stalk out of church in the middle of Mass. Mark was glad of an opportunity to obey one of the rubrics implicitly, and he rather fancied that the Major might protest against his interrupting Morning Prayer to administer Baptism after the 2nd lesson.

[and indeed the Major is annoyed and remonstrates by letter:]
"... this morning you exceeded the bounds by introducing an immensely long Baptism in the middle of Mattins so that even though, as you know, I never stay for the 2nd service, I did not get back to Angarrack until nearly one o'clock. It was particularly annoying this morning, as my wife was anxious to take the opportunity of our having a cook to go for a walk with me. Moreover, I must remark that there is something particularly objectionable and almost irreverent in having a baptism in the middle of a public service. . . .

Yours sincerely,

Henry H. Drumgold"

And note, that there shall be for every Male-child to be baptised two Godfathers and one Godmother; and for every Female one Godfather and two Godmothers.

4. After 1920 there were fewer direct challenges, public or private, to critics and reviewers, and a less strenuous insistence upon the deliberate nonobservance of certain social and religious forms. He went to church from time to time, chiefly because he enjoyed the singing and the long-familiar rituals, but also because he remembered that the church had once been a centre of village life and felt that, in a period of immense social and political upheaval, it might still have a cohesive and 'disciplinary' role to play. 'I believe in going to church.' he told J.H. Morgan in 1922. 'It is a moral drill, and people must have something. If there is no church in a country village, there is nothing.' Asked by Mrs Hanbury of Kingston Maurward to stand as godfather to her daughter Caroline, Hardy not only agreed to do so but wrote a little poem ('To C.F.H. On her Christening-Day') for the occasion, inscribed it on parchment, and presented it in a silver box. When Robert Graves and Nancy Nicholson told him in 1921 that their children had not been baptised, he merely observed that 'his old mother had always said of baptism that at any rate there was no harm in it, and that she would not like her children to blame her in after-life for leaving any duty to them undone.' He added: 'I have usually found that what my old mother said was right.'

5. *To C. F. H. On her Christening-Day*
    Fair Caroline, I wonder what
    You think of earth as a dwelling-spot,
    And if you'd rather have come, or not?

    To-day has laid on you a name
    That, though unasked for, you will claim
    Lifelong, for love or praise or blame.

    May chance and change impose on you
    No heavier burthen than this new
    Care-chosen one your future through!

    Dear stranger here, the prayer is mine
    That your experience may combine
    Good things with glad. . . . Yes, Caroline!

Then the priest shall take the child into his hands, and shall say to the Godfathers and Godmothers: Name this child.

6. "I remember," said Mrs Overtheway, "I remember my first visit. That is, I remember the occasion when I and my sister Fatima did, for the first time in our lives, go out visiting without our mother, or any grown-up person to take care of us."

"Do you remember your mother?" asked Ida.

"Quite well, my dear, I am thankful to say. The best and kindest of mothers!"

"Was your father alive, too?" Ida asked, with a sigh.

The old lady paused, pitying the anxious little face opposite, but Ida went on eagerly:

"Please tell me what *he* was like."

"He was a good deal older than my mother, who had married very early. He was a very learned man. And I must tell you that whatever the subject might be, so long as his head was full of it, the house seemed full of it too. It influenced the conversation at meals, the habits of the household, the names of the pet animals, and even of the children. I was called Mary, in a fever of chivalrous enthusiasm for the fair and luckless Queen of Scotland, and Fatima received her name when the study of Arabic had brought about an eastern mania. My father had wished to call her Shahrazád, after the renowned sultana of the 'Arabian Nights', but when he called upon the curate to arrange for the baptism, that worthy man flatly rebelled. A long discussion ended in my father's making a list of eastern names, from which the curate selected that of Fatima as being least repugnant to the sobriety of the parish registers. So Fatima she was called, and as she grew up pale, and moon-faced, and dark-eyed, the name became her very well."

7. 'Thank you, Jeeves. You speak airily or glibly of inducing L.G. Trotter to throw off the yoke and defy his considerably better half, but are you not too . . . . dash it, I've forgotten the word.'

    'Sanguine, sir?'

'That's it. Sanguine. Brief though my acquaintance with these twain has been, I have got L.G. Trotter's number, all right. His attitude towards Ma Trotter is that of an exceptionally diffident worm towards a sinewy Plymouth Rock or Orpington. A word from her, and he curls up into a ball. So where do you get off with that simple-matter-to-override-wishes stuff?'

I thought I had him there, but no.

'If I might explain. I gather from Mr Seppings, who has had opportunities of overhearing the lady's conversation, that Mrs Trotter, being socially ambitious, is extremely anxious to see Mr Trotter knighted, madam.'

Aunt Dahlia nodded.

'Yes, that's right. She's always talking about it. She thinks it would be one in the eye for Mrs Alderman Blenkinsop.'

'Precisely, madam.'

I was rather surprised.

'Do they knight birds like him?'

'Oh, yes, sir. A gentleman of Mr Trotter's prominence in the world of publishing is always in imminent danger of receiving the accolade.'

'Danger? Don't these bozos like being knighted?'

'Not when they are of Mr Trotter's retiring disposition, sir. He would find it a very testing ordeal. It involves wearing satin knee-breeches and walking backwards with a sword between the legs, not at all the sort of thing a sensitive gentleman of regular habits would enjoy. And he shrinks, no doubt, from the prospect of being addressed for the remainder of his life as Sir Lemuel.'

'His name's not Lemuel?'

'I fear so, sir.'

'Couldn't he use is second name?'

'His second name is Gengulphus.'

'Golly, Jeeves,' I said, thinking of old Uncle Tom Portarlington, 'there is some raw work pulled at the font from time to time, is there not?'

'There is indeed, sir.'

Dipped into the water, or having had water poured upon it, in the name of the Father, Son and Holy Ghost, the child is then received "into the congregation of Christ's flock. (Here the priest shall make a cross upon the child's forehead) in token that he shall not be ashamed ... to continue Christ's faithful soldier and servant unto his life's end."

8. *The Bishop* (arguing with his brother, the General): My profession also compels me to turn my back on snobbery. You see, I have to do such a terribly democratic thing to every child that is brought to me. Without distinction of class I have to confer on it a rank so high and awful that all the grades in Debrett and Burke seem like the medals they give children in Infant Schools in comparison. I'm not allowed to make any class distinction. They are all soldiers and servants, not officers and masters.

Hotchkiss: Ah, you're quoting the Baptism service . . .

There are three services of Baptism in the Prayer Book. The second is the private Baptism of Children in houses, which is to be used when the child is

likely to die. In the urgency the service consists of the act of baptizing and a prayer of thanksgiving. Should the child live, the service is continued in church at a later date.

Tess, fearing that her child is going to die, asks her father if she might send for the parson, but her father locks the door and puts the key in his pocket. Tess finally decides to perform the baptism herself, and does it fully.

9. 'O merciful God, have pity; have pity upon my poor baby!' she cried. 'Heap as much anger as you want to upon me, and welcome; but pity the child!'

She leant against the chest of drawers, and murmured incoherent supplications for a long while, till she suddenly started up.

'Ah! perhaps baby can be saved! Perhaps it will be just the same!'

She spoke so brightly that it seemed as though her face might have shone in the gloom surrounding her.

She lit a candle, and went to a second and a third bed under the wall, where she awoke her young sisters and brothers, all of whom occupied the same room. Pulling out the washing-stand so that she could get behind it, she poured some water from a jug, and made them kneel around, putting their hands together with fingers exactly vertical. While the children, scarcely awake, awestricken at her manner, their eyes growing larger and larger, remained in this position, she took the baby from her bed - a child's child - so immature as scarce to seem a sufficient personality to endow its producer with the maternal title. Tess then stood erect with the infant on her arm beside the basin, the next sister held the Prayer-Book open before her, as the clerk at church held it before the parson, and thus the girl set about baptizing her child.

Her figure looked singularly tall and imposing as she stood in her long white nightgown, a thick cable of twisted dark hair hanging straight down her back to her waist. The kindly dimness of the weak candle abstracted from her form and features the little blemishes which sunlight might have revealed - the stubble scratches upon her wrists, and the weariness of her eyes - her high enthusiasm having a transfiguring effect upon the face which had been her undoing, showing it as a thing of immaculate beauty, with a touch of dignity which was almost regal. The little ones kneeling round, their sleepy eyes blinking and red, awaited her preparations full of a suspended wonder which their physical heaviness at that hour would not allow to become active.

The most impressed of them said:

'Be you really going to christen him, Tess?'

The girl-mother replied in a grave affirmative.

'What's his name going to be?'

She had not thought of that, but a name suggested by a phrase in the book of Genesis came into her head as she proceeded with the baptismal service, and now she pronounced it:

'Sorrow, I baptise thee in the name of the Father, and of the Son, and of the Holy Ghost.'

She sprinkled the water, and there was silence.

'Say "Amen," children.'

The tiny voices piped in obedient response 'Amen!'

Tess went on:

'We receive this child' - and so forth - 'and do sign him with the sign of the Cross.'

Here she dipped her hand into the basin, and fervently drew an immense cross upon the baby with her forefinger, continuing with the customary sentences as to his manfully fighting against sin, the world, and the devil, and being a faithful soldier and servant unto his life's end. She duly went on with the Lord's Prayer, the children lisping it after her in a thin gnat-like wail, till, at the conclusion, raising their voices to clerk's pitch, they again pipped into the silence, 'Amen!'

Then their sister, with much augmented confidence in the efficacy of this sacrament poured forth from the bottom of her heart the thanksgiving that follows, uttering it boldly and triumphantly in the stop-diapason note which her voice acquired when her heart was in her speech, and which will never be forgotten by those who knew her. The ecstasy of faith almost apotheosized her; it set upon her face a glowing irradiation, and brought a red spot into the middle of each cheek; while the miniature candleflame inverted in her eye-pupils shone like a diamond. The children gazed up at her with more and more reverence, and no longer had a will for questioning. She did not look like Sissy to them now, but as a being large, towering, and awful - a divine personage with whom they had nothing in common.

The third service is the ministration of Baptism to such as are of riper years and able to answer for themselves.

10. At this moment there was a stir of excitement as the curate appeared with his best man, a stocky, red-haired young clergyman, a typical rowing man, as Harriet whispered to Belinda.

Shortly afterwards the bride entered on the arm of the Professor of Middle English, a tall, thin man, ill at ease in his formal clothes. Belinda wondered whether Henry and Agatha were remembering their own wedding day. She had heard that people did on these occasions unless they were in a position to look forward rather than back. Count Bianco might be looking forward, but more quietly and with less rapture than a younger man. Was there anybody in the church without some romantic thought? Possibly Miss Prior, sitting with her old mother, was more interested in the bride's dress which, Belinda noticed with approval, was not white but sapphire-blue velvet, the kind of thing that would 'come in' afterwards and could if necessary be dyed and worn for years. She really looked very nice, almost pretty and not as tall as she had seemed to be at the presentation.

If I'm ever married I shall certainly have a *fully* choral ceremony,' said Harriet enthusiastically as they filed out of the church. 'Or is there a special one for those of riper years?'

Belinda said nothing because she had been crying a little and could not trust herself to speak yet.

'No, that's only baptism,' said Edith cheerfully.

11. 'And what a horrid experience you must have had,' said Lucia, 'Tea will be ready: let us go in.'

'A waste of waters,' said Elizabeth impressively, 'and a foot deep in the dining room. We had to have a boat to take our luggage away. It reminded Benjy of the worst floods on the Jamna.'

'Pon my word, it did,' said Benjy, 'and I shouldn't wonder if there's more to come. The wind keeps up, and there's the highest of the spring tides tonight. Total immersion of the Padre, perhaps. Ha! Ha! Baptism of those of Riper Years.'

'Naughty,' said Elizabeth. Certainly the Padre had been winning at Bridge all this week, but that hardly excused levity over things sacramental, and besides he had given them lunch and breakfast.

REFERENCES

1. S.T. Coleridge, *Table Talk and Omniana*, ed. H.N. Coleridge, O.U.P. 1917.
2. S.T. Coleridge, *Poems,* eds Derwent & Sara Coleridge, Edward Moxon 1852.
3. Compton Mackenzie, *The Heavenly Ladder*, Cassell & Cy 1924, Ch. The Tangye Baptism.
4. Michael Millgate, *Thomas Hardy: A Biography*, O.U.P. 1985, Ch. 26.
5. Thomas Hardy, *Collected Poems*, Macmillan 1930.
6. J.H. Ewing, *Mrs Overtheway's Remembrances*, op. cit., Ch. The Snoring Ghost.
7. P.G. Wodehouse, *Jeeves and the Feudal Spirit*, Herbert Jenkins 1954.
8. George Bernard Shaw, *Getting Married*, Constable & Cy. 1908.
9. Thomas Hardy, *Tess of the D'Urbervilles*, op. cit., Ch. 14.
10. Barbara Pym, *Some Tame Gazelle*, op. cit., Ch. 22.
11. E.F. Benson, *Lucia's Progress*, Hodder & Stoughton 1935, Ch. 11.

S. Wale delin. W. Ryland sculp.

But JESUS said, Suffer little Children, and
forbid them not to come unto me: for of such
is the kingdom of Heaven.
Matt. XLX. 14.

CHAPTER 11
A Catechism

That is to say: An Instruction to be learned of every person before he be brought to be confirmed by the bishop.

1. There is another Thing which I most earnestly recommend to you, partly as the best Antidote and Preservative against the Irreligion and wild Opinions now reigning among us; partly as a noble Instance of your Charity and Condescension towards those that most need your Help, and of your Submission to the Wisdom of the church; that is, that you apply yourselves to the *Catechising of Youth* every *Sunday* in the Afternoon: This the Canons enjoin most expressly, this my Lord's Grace recommends most earnestly, and of the doing of this, or neglecting of it, I must and shall take Account most impartially.

The Church has prepared an excellent Form to your Hands, wherein you are to instruct and examine the younger and more ignorant Sort of People; and I will not be so injurious as to think, that any here want either Reason or Conviction to persuade him, that it is a Duty indispensably necessary. If we consider who they were that first fell away from the Church, and were given over to strong Delusions, and *carried away with every Wind of Doctrine*, we shall find them to be such as had been never taught the first Principles, and the true Grounds of our Religion.

In a Word, Sirs, if you would have a Church of Men, you must set up for a Church of Children; and that you cannot expect to obtain, but by this Method; for I dare appeal to everyone's Observation here, whether they have found anything, next to the preventing, assisting, and restraining Grace of God, that has kept us from running into false and erroneous Opinions, so steadily, so effectually, as the early Prepossession of our Church Catechism, and the Care and Example of our Parents recommending it unto us.

2. During the summer and part of the autumn, he followed the good old usage of catechising the children, after the 2nd lesson in the evening service. His method was to ask a few questions in succession, and only from those who he knew were able to answer them; and after each answer he entered into a brief exposition suited to their capacity. His manner was so benevolent, and he made himself so familiar in his visits, which were at once pastoral and friendly, that no child felt alarmed at being singled out; they regarded it as a mark of distinction, and the parents were

proud of seeing them thus distinguished. This practice was discontinued in winter; because he knew that to keep a congregation in the cold is not the way either to quicken or cherish devotional feeling. Once a week during Lent he examined all the children, on a weekday; the last examination was in Easter week, after which each was sent home happy with a lovely cake, the gift of a wealthy parishioner, who by this means contributed not a little to the good effect of the pastor's diligence.

3. The chaplain has often told me that on a catechising day, when Sir Roger has been pleased with a boy that answers well, he has ordered a Bible to be given him next day for his encouragement, and sometimes accompanies it with a flitch of bacon to his mother.

The poet William Wordsworth records, "I remember my mother only in some few situations, one of which was her pinning a nosegay to my breast when I was going to say the Catechism in the church, as was customary before Easter." For it was the custom in Cockermouth that the pupils of All Saints' Sunday School should be publicly catechized, after processing from school into church with due ceremonial, churchwardens and sidesmen leading the procession, and the bells chiming.
4. *Catechising*
> From Little down to Least, in due degree,
> Around the Pastor, each in new-wrought vest,
> Each with a vernal posy at his breast,
> We stood, a trembling, earnest Company!
> With low soft murmur, like a distant bee,
> Some spake, by thought-perplexing fears betrayed;
> And some a bold unerring answer made:
> How fluttered then thy anxious heart for me,
> Belovèd Mother! Thou whose happy hand
> Had bound the flowers I wore, with faithful tie:
> Sweet flowers! at whose inaudible command
> Her countenance, phantom-like, doth re-appear:
> O lost too early for a frequent tear,
> And ill requited by this heartfelt sigh!

5. Sunday July 20th 1823
A wet morning; very few at Church in consequence. After service I heard the children their Catechism and explained the several Articles, as I did the preceding Sunday. In the evening the Church very full and the people attentive. Two classes of the collier boys attended to say their Catechism after dinner, but could not recollect what they formerly learned, and when I explained it to them they were so very ignorant or ill behaved I did not think I could in conscience give them tickets for Confirmation. I therefore dismissed the whole - in number about 14, only giving a ticket to young Clarke, the schoolmaster's son, who said his very well. There were 18 girls who passed, among them the daughter of Sarah Somet, who behaved so improperly lately, but on her promising amendment, I gave her a ticket. The impropriety, not to say the injustice of Mrs Jerrett's having dissolved the Sunday School which I established on my first coming to Camerton was never

more exemplified than on the present occasion. The boys used to say their Catechism very well, and were pretty constant in their attendance at Church; the whole object of the lady in doing away with a benefit of such essential consequence to the Parish was no other than because she thought her authority was infringed by having a school to which she did not contribute one sixpence, and which had been supported by the clergyman of the Parish at his own expense for upwards of 20 years. One need not turn to Shakespeare for a Kate, nor to Russia for a Catherine, the prototype exists at Camerton vocé persona et re.

The "ticket" seems to have been a card given to the Confirmation candidate to show that he had learnt the Catechism to the satisfaction of his parish priest and could therefore be presented to the Bishop for Confirmation. However, the Royal Commission on Historical Manuscripts has been unable to find any such certificates.

6. The first of October had come, and the cards bearing the words "Examined and approved, Herbert Somerville" were given and received.

Emmeline and Kate are two young ladies, who, as part of their charitable work, do some teaching in the village church school.

7. Still they went to the school, where they had for some time been making a point of the Church Catechism. By rewards and praises, Emmeline had obtained of her class its perfect repetition, and now, with the help of questions caught from Mr Brent's catechising in church, and with recollections of the teaching of her own earlier days, she was endeavouring to instruct the children in its meaning.

One day, however, when she was in the midst of questioning on the Catechism, she was startled by a short dry cough of disapprobation close behind her, and looking up, saw a tall thin gentleman in black, with rather grey curling hair, a long narrow face, and a solemn expression, standing near her chair.

Annoyed and confused, she found it impossible to go on. She waited a moment, expecting the stranger to apologize and depart, but as he did no such thing, she shut up her book, and with Kate, left the school very indignant, though they did not divulge the adventure for fear Frank should triumph over them.

A day or two after the Miss Shaws called upon them, and Miss Penelope, in rather a mysterious manner, asked Emmeline to take a walk in the garden with her.

"My dear Miss Berners, you will forgive me," said she. "You know how grateful we are for your assistance in the school, but you must allow me just to make one little suggestion. I am sure you mean it all most rightly, but people talk about it. Could you not dwell rather less on the Church Catechism?"

Emmeline started. "I thought," said she, "that it was one of the chief things to be taught."

"My dear, I say nothing against the Catechism itself, it is a most admirable compilation, but you know it has been made so much a badge of party, and people talk -"

"But what do they say?" asked Emmeline, in a maze of surprise, perplexity, and displeasure.

"O, my dear Miss Emmeline, people will say things, they remark on your dwelling so much on that and nothing else, and some of the children's parents are

Dissenters, and have scruples about their learning it. Indeed, I think you had better adopt some other line.

Gentle as Emmeline was, she never felt less persuadable, perhaps from a secret conviction that this must be a result of the spying of last Thursday's visitor. "What can people have to remark?" said she. "We taught the Catechism because no one else seemed to do so, and you told us we might teach what we pleased."

"Yes, yes, my dear, I am sure it is a good thing, only it has become a badge of party, and - and - there is your connection with Lord Herbert Somerville, whose views are so well known. I hope you will not be vexed with me, my dear, but I thought it would be as well just to give you a hint; I do so dread any thing of party spirit."

"If you would but tell me what Lord Herbert Somerville can possibly have to do with it," said Emmeline, growing very angry and very formal.

"Ah! my dear girl, how I envy your sweet innocence of party. I would not say a word against Lord Herbert for the world, only every one knows what a high Church, intolerant part, his family have always taken."

"I know where the intolerance is now," thought Emmeline to herself; but she let Miss Penelope go on as far as "Mr Denham -" before her schooled manners gave way, and she interrupted her by saying, "Was that Mr Denham that came and listened to me last Thursday?"

"My dear, you must not be annoyed - I am sure you have too much good sense -"

"I disliked it very much indeed," said Emmeline. "I cannot think how he could do such a thing."

"Ah! your retiring nature, which would shrink from observation, my dear; I can quite sympathize with you; but you must consider what an interest good Mr Denham takes in the school."

[When told of this conversation Kate and Emmeline's Mother and Stepfather suggest that the girls give up their teaching altogether.]

"Give it up! No, never!" said Emmeline, with a sort of would-be martyr look, as soon as she had Kate to herself.

"Never," echoed Kate, "it would be giving up our principles."

"Yes; and think of the influence it must have upon all the school, to see how important we think it, and how steadily we keep to it."

"It is not like some trumpery question-book, to be taken up one week, and thrown aside the next," said Kate; "it is something to hold fast and value."

"Yes; and we will show them our value for it," said Emmeline. "Committee, and children, and all, shall see that we think the Catechism no badge of party, but the watch-word of the English Church. I dare say this controversy about it will make the children value it all the more."

"The children are so fond of you, they will love it for your sake," said Kate; "that little Mary Parsons, her mother told Miss Shaw the other the day, she would do anything for her dear teacher, Miss Emma Line."

When the teaching of scripture replaced the catechism in many elementary schools, such change found a redoubtable and eloquent opponent in a country parson, who read a paper at Oxford criticizing "what passes as religious education," and then published it under the title "Huppim and Muppim", after the sons of Benjamin. The whole essay is a superb example of impassioned rhetoric and scathing denunciation: a veritable Philippic, but very amusing.

8. To know these worthies is a fair example of the knowledge which still passes muster as religious education. It is a good average example, because some educators are still to be found who boast that the infants under their hands have had a complete course of lessons in "the insects of the Old Testament." The very flies and lice have a hallowed buzz and a spiritual bite, when they are hatched in so august a land. . .

If we come to inquire what instruction the English Church insists upon, and how she thinks this instruction should be given, we have not only the Church Catechism to tell us the former, but also the 59th Canon (1603), and the Rubrics to guide us, as to the latter. By the Canon the Parish Priest is straitly commanded to catechize every Sunday and holy day. If he neglects this (and those who are filling the air with shrieks and wails about religious education always do neglect it) he is to be sharply reproved by the Bishop, for a second offence suspended, and for a third excommunicated. The teaching is not of Huppim, but a plain tale of what to give up, what to believe, and how to worship God; things too simple, apparently, for modern minds. What worlds of hypocrisy and fussiness we should be saved, if this simple act of canonical obedience were enforced upon our clerical anarchists! "But," say our reverend canon-smashing divines, "this canon was drawn up before the elementary education system was born, and refers to a wholly different state of society." Exactly; but if an absolutely illiterate people could learn enough in one weekly half-hour's catechizing, much more easily can a better-educated people acquire, by the same means, all that is necessary for the perfect life. This is both too easy a thought and too difficult an exertion for our aspiring clergymen. Where would then be the need of political agitation? The collection of great sums of money? And the blowing of trumpets and the banging of tom-toms? It can be effected without taxing schismatics, without wrecking the national chicken-fatting establishments, without a diocesan syllabus, and the rushing of rural deans; in a word, without all the lashing and splashing and hustling which is required in order to bring our youth into the clear light of Baasha and a knowledge of the missionary journeys.

The first question in the Catechism is "What is your name?" and the answer "N or M" standing for the name or names of each child, but a source of confusion, if, though this hardly seems possible, it is left unexplained.

Perhaps Teddy Short was inattentive.

9. In the daily scripture lesson I had memorized the Church Catechism by the age of ten including the more obscure bits on the sacraments towards the end and of course the ten commandments but I never understood why, when asked my name, I had to reply "N or M" when everybody knew I was called Teddy Short. I was also puzzled by the question: "What did thy Godfather and Godmother then for thee?" Was "then" a strange verb which I did not know, some peculiar service or rite my godparents had performed for me? But I was much too shy to run the risk of appearing to be silly by asking.

Daniel Robson tells of the occasion on his whaling adventures when he was tumbled into the sea by a whale.

10. "There were a great roar i' my ears, an' a great dizziness i' my eyes, an' t' boats'

crew kept throwing out their oars, an' a kept clutching at 'em, but a could na make out where they was, my eyes dazzled so wit' cold, an' a thought a were bound for Kingdom come, an' a tried to remember t'Creed as a might die a Christian. But all a could think on was 'What is your name? N or M'; and just as a were giving up both words an' life, they heeved me aboard."

"Who gave you this name?" Colonel Esmond, Lady Castlewood and her daughter Beatrix are talking about The Spectator and its editor, Mr Steele.
11. "How stupid your friend Mr Steele becomes!" cries Miss Beatrix. "Epsom and Tunbridge! Will he never have done with Epsom and Tunbridge, and with beaux at church, and Jocastas and Lindamiras? Why does he not call women Nelly and Betty, as their Godfathers and Godmothers did for them in their baptism?"
    "Beatrix, Beatrix!" says her mother, "speak gravely of grave things."
    "Mamma thinks the Church Catechism came from heaven, I believe," says Beatrix with a laugh, "and was brought down by a Bishop from a mountain. Oh! how I used to break my heart over it!"

12. She started taking her goddaughter Mary Anne and her younger sister Jane to the children's services at St Mary Abbots and then out to tea afterwards, and helped them to learn the Prayer Book Catechism. "Perhaps I made a mistake in telling them that the proper answer to "what did your godfathers and godmothers then for you?" was "Silver mug, spoon and fork"; this joke stuck, and I fear I shall get this answer only. I remember we used to think it funny."

After the questions about Holy Baptism, the catechist next says "Rehearse the Articles of thy Belief", and the answer is the Apostles' Creed.

Anyone who has taught Latin to schoolboys will know how a mischievous boy can whisper to his neighbour a nonsensical translation, and this boy, in his panic at being asked to translate, will blurt out the nonsense. A similar situation is recollected as farm labourers discuss the seeming apparition of the dead squire, Sir Blount Constantine.
13. "'Twas very curious; but we had likewise mentioned his name just afore, in talking of the confirmation that's shortly coming on," said Hezzy.
    "Is there soon to be a confirmation?"
    "Yes. In this parish - the first time in Welland church for twenty years. As I say, I had told 'em that he was confirmed the same year that I went up to have it done, as I have very good cause to mind. When we went to be examined, the pa'son said to me, "Rehearse the articles of thy belief." Mr Blount (as he was then) was nighest me, and he whispered, "Women and wine." "Women and wine," says I to the pa'son: and for that I was sent back till next confirmation, Sir Blount never owning that he was the rascal."

After the Creed come the Commandments and the details of "my duty towards God, and my duty towards my neighbour."

14. Though by all means, added my father (not attending to my uncle Toby) 'The son ought to pay her *[the mother]* respect,' as you may read, Yorick, at large in the

first book of the *Institutes of Justinian*, at the eleventh title and the tenth section. - I can read it as well, replied Yorick, in the Catechism.

Trim can repeat every word of it by heart, quoth my uncle Toby. - Pugh! said my father, not caring to be interrupted with Trim's saying his Catechism. He can, upon my honour, replied my uncle Toby. - Ask him, Mr Yorick, any question you please. -

- The fifth Commandment, Trim - said Yorick, speaking mildly, and with a gentle nod, as to a modest Catechumen. The corporal stood silent. - You don't ask him right, said my uncle Toby, raising his voice, and giving it rapidly like the word of command: - The fifth - cried my uncle Toby. - I must begin with the first, an' please your honour, said the corporal. -

- Yorick could not forbear smiling. - Your reverence does not consider, said the corporal, shouldering his stick like a musket, and marching into the middle of the room, to illustrate his position, - that 'tis exactly the same thing, as doing one's exercise in the field. -

'Join your right-hand to your firelock,' cried the corporal, giving the word of command, and performing the motion. -

'Poise your firelock,' cried the corporal, doing the duty still both of adjutant and private man.

'Rest you firelock'; - one motion, an' please your reverence, you see leads into another. - If his honour will begin but with the first -

The First - cried my uncle Toby, setting his hand upon his side -

15. Painfully and slowly, I was learning my catechism by heart; my Duty to my Neighbour is inseparably connected with the afternoon breeze over the hot sand, with the feeling of my heels pushing against the planking of the hut wall as I lay on my palm-branch bed. My duty to my neighbour is to love him as myself and to do unto all men as I would they should do unto me. Round about three o'clock the splashing of the waves always became a little bit louder as the breeze freshened. To love, honour, and succour my father and mother. To honour and obey the King, and all that are put in authority under him. What sort of jam for tea, I wonder? Chicken and ham paste, with luck. To submit myself to all my governors, teachers, spiritual pastors and masters. (But not Miss Simpson, or, come to that, Mademoiselle Matthéi). To order myself lowly and reverently to all my betters. (Like Mr Horan, and one's grandparents). To hurt nobody by word or deed. If I could finish this there might be time before tea to play round the children's golf course with the little mashies that my father had had made for Alethea and me in Cairo. To bear no malice nor hatred in my heart. To bear, to bear - oh goodness what comes next? Frank Tottenham can learn by heart quite easily. But he can't swim out as far as the second sandbank. To be true and just in all my dealings. But that ought to have come in before. Not to covet nor desire other men's goods, but to learn and labour truly to get mine own living. I've left out about keeping my tongue from evil-speaking, lying and slandering, and my body in temperance, soberness and chastity. Temperance means not being greedy, soberness means not getting in a fuss, chastity means not showing off. If I begin at the beginning again perhaps it will go better. *Martin Rattler* was lying at the foot of the bed and I opened the first chapter with my toes. If only one could read a book with one's toes and learn by heart with one's heart at the same time. Learning by heart was

stone-breaking labour. I finally dissolved into tears over my inability to master an outward and visible sign of an inward and spiritual grace, although it had a sort of rhyme to it.

More remembrances of my Duty to my Neighbour. Silas Marner and Dolly discuss the child Silas has found.

16. "You'll have a right to her if you're a father to her, and bring her up according. But," added Dolly, coming to a point which she had determined beforehand to touch upon, "you must bring her up like christened folk's children, and take her to church, and let her learn her catechism, as my little Aaron can say off - the 'I believe', and everything, and 'hurt nobody by word or deed' - as well as if he was the clerk. That's what you must do, Master Marner, if you'd do the right thing by the orphin child."

Kate, now a Countess, has to leave the family she has lived with and the man she has regarded as her father.

17. "We are all sorry to lose our little Kate," said Mr Wardour.

"Lose me, Papa!" cried Kate, clinging to him, as the children scarcely ever did, for he seldom made many caresses; "Oh no, never! Doesn't Caergwent Castle belong to me? Then you must all come and live with me there; and you shall have lots of big books, Papa; and we will have a pony-carriage for Mary, and ponies for Sylvia and Charlie and me, and -"

Kate either ran herself down, or saw that the melancholy look on Mr Wardour's face rather deepened than lessened, for she stopped short.

"My dear," he said, "you and I have both other duties."

"Oh, but if I built a church! I dare say there are people at Caergwent as poor as they are here. Couldn't we build a church and you mind them, Papa?"

"My little Katharine, you have yet to understand that 'the heir, so long as he is a child, differeth in nothing from a servant, but is under tutors and governors'. You will not have any power over yourself or your property till you are twenty-one."

"But you are my tutor and my governor, and my spiritual pastor and master," said Kate. "I always say so whenever Mary asks us questions about our duty to our neighbour."

"I have been so hitherto," said Mr Wardour, setting her on his knee; "but I see I must explain a good deal to you. It is the business of a court in London, that it called the Court of Chancery, to provide that proper care is taken of young heirs and heiresses and their estates, if no one have been appointed by their parents to do so; and it is this court that must settle what is to become of you."

The loquacious and pleasantly self-satisfied sailor narrator of "The Maid of Sker" remembers the last phrase of My Duty to my Neighbour.

18. Into whatever state of life it may please God to call me - though I fear there cannot be many more at this age of writing - it always will be, as it always has been, my first principle and practice to do my very utmost (which is far less than it was, since the doctor stopped my hornpipes) to be pleasant and good company.

The Catechist goes on to say "My good child, know this, that thou art not able to do these things of thyself . . . without his special grace; which thou must

learn at all times to call for by diligent prayer . . . " and the child has to say the Lord's Prayer and learn what "he desires of God in this prayer."

Finally the Catechism teaches about the sacrament of Baptism and Holy Communion, beginning with the question, "How many sacraments hath Christ ordained in his Church?"

Corporal Trim preaches his sermon in the presence of Tristram Shandy's father and his uncle Toby and of Dr Slop.

19. "Surely, you will think conscience must lead a vicious and debauched man a troublesome life; he can have no rest night or day from its reproaches.

Alas! Conscience had something else to do all this time than break in upon him; as Elijah reproached the god Baal, - this domestic god "was either talking, or pursuing, or was in a journey, or peradventure he slept and could not be awoke."

"Perhaps He was gone out in company with Honour to fight a duel: to pay off some debt at play; - or dirty annuity, the bargain of his lust; Perhaps Conscience all this time was engaged at home, talking aloud against petty larceny, and executing vengeance upon some such puny crimes as his fortune and rank of life secured him against all temptation of committing; so that he lives as merrily" - [If he was of our church, tho', quoth Dr Slop, he could not] - "sleeps as soundly in his bed; - and at last meets death as unconcernedly; - perhaps much more so, than a much better man."

[All this is impossible with us, quoth Dr Slop, turning to my father, - the case could not happen in our church. - It happens in ours, however, replied my father, but too often. - I own, quoth Dr Slop, (struck a little with my father's frank acknowledgement) - that a man in the Romish church may live as badly; - but then he cannot easily die so. - 'Tis little matter, replied my father, with an air of indifference, - how a rascal dies. - I mean, answered Dr Slop, he would be denied the benefits of the last sacraments. - Pray how many have you in all, said my uncle Toby, - for I always forget? - Seven, answered Dr Slop. - Humph! said my uncle Toby; tho' not accented as a note of acquiescence, - but as an interjection of that particular species of surprise, when a man in looking into a drawer, finds more of a thing than he expected. - Humph! replied my uncle Toby. Dr Slop, who had an ear, understood my uncle Toby as well as if he had wrote a whole volume against the seven sacraments. - Humph! replied Dr Slop, (stating my uncle Toby's argument over again to him) - Why, Sir, are there not seven cardinal virtues? - Seven mortal sins? - Seven golden candlesticks? - Seven heavens? - 'Tis more than I know, replied my uncle Toby. - Are there not seven wonders of the world? - Seven days of the creation? - Seven planets? - Seven plagues? - That there are, quoth my father with a most affected gravity. But prithee, continued he, go on with the rest of thy characters, Trim.]

REFERENCES

1. William Wynne, *The Life of Sir Leoline Jenkins*, London 1724. Address to the Clergy of the Diocese of Canterbury.
2. Robert Southey, Two Love Stories from *The Doctor*, (1847) The York Library 1904.

3. *The Spectator* No. 112 Monday July 9th 1711, Everyman Edition, J.M. Dent & Sons Ltd. 1907.

4. William Wordsworth, *Ecclesiastical Sonnets*, Ed Moxon 1850.

5. John Skinner, *Journal of a Somerset Rector,* op. cit.

6. C.M. Yonge, *The Castlebuilders,* J. & C. Mozley 1854.

7. Ibid.

8. Charles Marson, *Huppim Muppim and Ard*, Society of SS Peter & Paul 1917.

9. Edward Short, *I Knew My Place,* op. cit.

10. Mrs Gaskell, *Sylvia's Lovers*, Smith Elder & Cy 1863.

11. W.M. Thackeray, *The History of Henry Esmond,* op. cit., Book 3 Ch. 32.

12. C. Babington-Smith, *Rose Macaulay*, Collins 1972, Ch. 17.

13. Thomas Hardy, *Two on a Tower*, Macmillan 1882.

14. Laurence Sterne, *Tristram Shandy*, 1760-68, 1948 ed. John Lehmann Ltd., Book 5 Ch. 31.

15. Priscilla Napier, *A Late Beginner,* op. cit.

16. George Eliot, *Silas Marner*, op. cit., Ch. 14.

17. C. M. Yonge, *Countess Kate*, op. cit., Ch. 1.

18. R.D. Blackmore, *The Maid of Sker*, Doughty Library 1872 and Anthony Blond 1968, Ch. 13.

19. Laurence Sterne, *Tristram Shandy*, op. cit., Book 2 Ch. 17.

CHAPTER 12
The Order of Confirmation

Or Laying on of Hands upon those that are baptized and come to years of discretion.

1. So Phillis Jane Carman, one week-day afternoon, sat in the heart of St Boniface's, Hamden Hill, dressed in a white frock and a long white veil, and with neither powder on her nose nor hint of irreligious scarlet on her mouth. She sat in a square block of sixty similar white veils, for other parishes had sent their musters of candidates to this, the largest church of the neighbourhood. On the other side of the nave a drove of boys sat impounded in another square pen, but this block was smaller, male animals being notoriously more difficult to herd into church than females. They made almost as black a patch as the girls made a white one, since each boy who had a dark suit had cleaned and donned it for this solemnity. The rest of the church was bespattered with the families and friends of the candidates; and among these, some way towards the back, sat Mr and Mrs Carman, also clad in dark garments for a solemnity.

Mr Carman sat at the open end of a pew so that by inclining his head outwards he could gaze up the nave and see all that was going on. He was often at a loss to know what was going on, but he stood up when all the others stood up - usually a second or so late because taken by surprise - and he sat down when - again unexpectedly - they all sat down. When they knelt, he leaned forward with his elbows on his knees. He felt bashful about praying himself, because he remembered certain triumphs of salesmanship at his barrow's side, and now and then a margin of profit such as the Reverend Welcome could hardly approve; but he did mumble once or twice when his head was dropped towards his clasped hands, "Gawd forgive me all me sins and bless our Phil Janey."

"Do ye here in the presence of God and of this congregation. . . ."

It was the little old bishop's voice, and Mr Carman saw his Phil Janey, the smallest in her pew of older girls, leaning sideways to get a glimpse, through all them white veils, of the little old barsted where he stood on the steps before his big arm-chair. Blimey, a crumpled red face like a smiling raspberry, and looking all the redder for all them red things he'd got on. They did doll themselves up, these bishops. More like a telephone box on the prowl than anything else.

". . . acknowledging yourselves bound to believe and to do all those things which your godfathers and godmothers then undertook for you?"

"I do."

All the kids had said it in one big murmur. Kind'a got you. Gave you a lump in the throat. Didn't hear our Phil Janey, but suppose she'd said it all right. Anyhow too late now because the old bish had just said something - "Our help is in the name of the Lord" - and all the kids were answering something and - "Oh, gawd help us! - they're all kneeling down again."

Mr Carman leaned forward and put a hand before his eyes. But one of his eyes, the acuter one, continued to study the proceedings over the top of his hand.

Ah, now was the time. Now the kids were filing out of their pews like lags being marched out for exercise. Mr Carman sat back again and watched, leaning out into the nave. Reverend Welcome was forming them up in pairs so that two could kneel side by side in front of the old bishop's chair. See, they were kneeling there, and the old tomato was putting his mitts on their heads. There was Phil Janey, coupled up with an enormous long girl like a blooming great hollyhock rather the worse for wear. If that girl was the same age as Phil Janey, she was twice her height, and they didn't half look a pair walking up towards the bishop. Mr Carman, leaning outwards to see his Phil Janey done, turned and grimaced at Mrs Carman. "Crikey!" he whispered. "Look at our Phil Janey and her mate. The long and the short of it, not 'ahf. Kind'a Mutt and Jeff.

Mrs Carman hissed, "*Tsh!*" rebukingly, but leaned over, herself, to see better.

Now Phil Janey and the maypole were kneeling before the bishop, and he'd got a hand on each of their nuts, so that one hand was rather high and the other rather low like the hands of that there organist when he was fair blowing out the tune.

"Defend, O Lord, this thy child - and this thy child - with thy heavenly grace that they may continue thine for ever. . . . "

Mr Carman, having heard other people say the Amen to this constantly repeated prayer, said it himself now that it was his daughter that was being done, but he said it rather too loud and too late so that Mrs Carman laid an anxious hand on his knee, chiding him for speaking out of his turn. But he only grimaced triumphantly at her as if he'd just publicly distinguished himself, and winked. After all, why shouldn't he pray for Phil Janey? He wanted their Phil Janey to be good even if *he* wasn't. It was the best, all said and done, for a girl.

And here was little Phil Janey coming back to her place with her head down, properly blessed by the old bishop, and presumably good now. And on the whole he was glad; real glad; and that was a fact. He'd tell the Reverend Welcome so after the service; he'd say, "I'm glad I gave my little gurl to you", both because it was the truth and because it sounded well and would please a gentleman who was always friendly and sometimes useful.

What, another hymn? Mr Carman struggled to his feet with the rest and, recognizing the hymn as a lively one which he'd sung often enough out of sheer boredom after the sergeants had marched him muttering to Church Parade, or after the screws had shepherded him, still muttering, into the chapel at the Moor, he reaffirmed his right to pray by singing it with a lustihood that turned a few heads in his direction, and bent Mrs Carman's in doubt and embarrassment. He let it go with a will, quite pleased with the quality of his voice, and winking now and then at the reproachful Mrs Carman:

Soldiers of Christ, arise,
And put your armour on.

2. Everything was ready for the confirmation. The women of the church were there, in their white dresses, each with the green cloth about her neck. Those men that were not away, and who belonged to this church, were there in their Sunday clothes, which means their working clothes, patched and cleaned and brushed. The children for the confirmation were there, the girls in their white dresses and caps, the boys in their school-going clothes, patched and cleaned and brushed. Women were busy in the house, helping the wife of the umfundisi, for after the confirmation there would be a simple meal, of tea boiled till the leaves had no more tea left in them, and of heavy homely cakes made of the meal of the maize. It was simple food, but it was to be eaten together.

And over the great valley the storm clouds were gathering again in the heavy oppressive heat, so that one did not know whether to be glad or sorry. The great dark shadows sailed over the red earth, and up the bare red hills to the tops. The people looked at the sky, and at the road by which the Bishop would come, and did not know whether to be glad or sorry. For it was certain that before this sun had set, the lightening would strike amongst the hills, and the thunder would echo amongst them. . . .

They stood there talking quietly and soberly till the Bishop came.

It was dark in the church for the confirmation, so that they had to light the lamps. The great heavy clouds swept over the valley, and the lightning flashed over the red desolate hills, where the earth had torn away like flesh. The thunder roared over the valleys of old men and old women, of mothers and children. The men are away, the young men and the girls are away, and the soil cannot keep them any more. And some of the children are there in the church being confirmed, and after a while they too will go away, for the soil cannot keep them any more.

It was dark there in the church, and the rain came down through the roof. The pools formed on the floor, and the people moved here and there, to get away from the rain. Some of the white dresses were wet, and a girl shivered there with the cold, because this occasion was solemn for her, and she did not dare to move out of the rain. And the voice of the Bishop said, Defend, O Lord, this Thy child with Thy heavenly grace, that he may continue Thine for ever, and daily increase in Thy Holy Spirit more and more, till he come unto Thy everlasting Kingdom. And this he said to each child that came, and confirmed them all.

After the confirmation they crowded into the house, for the simple food that was to be taken. Kumalo had to ask those who were not that day confirmed, or who were not parents of those confirmed, to stay in the church, for it was still raining heavily, though the lightning and the thunder had passed. Yet the house was full to overflowing; the people were in the kitchen, and in the room where Kumalo did his accounts, and in the room where they ate, and in the room where they slept, even in the room of the young demonstrator.

3. In such silence they went home. The sisters went to their own room, and still in silence knelt together. Constance came in, and herself arranged their white veils, kissing each of them. With her and their uncle they walked to Church, and were placed among the many maidens, with white covered heads, and grave, modest faces.

And now the time is come. The demand is made, to be answered once and for ever, whether they renew the vow of their Baptism, and take on themselves the promise they never can unsay, engaging in their own persons to fulfil the *perfect law.*

"I do."

Multitudes of clear young trembling voices make answer in one note. "I do." Wavering, unstable Emmeline, unreflecting, easily-led Katherine, how can you dare to bind yourselves to such an awful covenant with Him who is Justice itself?

Hear the answer.

"Our help is in the name of the Lord:
Who hath made heaven and earth."

And now their brother in his white robe stands at the entrance of the Chancel, and signs to them, and his face seems, in one look of love and earnest hope, to sum up all that he has striven so long to infuse into them.

They kneel on that Altar step where they never have before approached, and the Apostolic hand is on their heads; the blessing is spoken, that unspeakable Gift imparted, that, unless they fall away, will increase daily more and more, till they come to the everlasting kingdom.

Many who today fly from "wearing their heart on their sleeve" in religious matters will find the Victorian novel's solemn emotion alien. That it was shared and expressed unselfconsciously by sincere Christians in that age is shown by this extract from a young lady's diary about her confirmation at Worcester Cathedral on July 17th 1854.

4. On reaching our seat very near the rails, I sank on my knees, and for the first time today the thought of "whose I am" burst upon me, and I prayed "my God, oh my *own* Father, Thou blessed Jesus my *own* Saviour, Thou Holy Spirit my *own* Comforter," and I stopped. It scarcely seemed right for me to use the language of such strong assurance as this, but yet I did not retract. The Litany only was chanted, and tho' my thoughts would have fain flown with each petition heavenward, yet every little thing seemed *trebly* a distraction, and the chanting was too often the subject of my thoughts. My heart beat very fast, and my breath almost seemed to stop, while the solemn question was being put by the Bishop. Never I think did I feel my own weakness and utter helplessness so much. I hardly dared answer; but "the Lord is my strength" was graciously suggested to me, and then the words came quickly from (I trust) my very heart; "Lord, I cannot without Thee, but oh, with Thy almighty help, - I Do."

I believe that the solemnity of what had just been uttered, with its exceeding comprehensiveness, were realized by me as far as my mind could grasp it. I thought a good deal of the words "now unto Him that is able to keep you from Falling"; and that was my chief comfort. We were the first to go up, and I was the 4th or 5th on whom the bishop laid his hands. At first, the thought came as to who was kneeling next to me, but then the next moment I felt alone, unconscious of my fellow candidates, of the many eyes fixed upon us, and the many thoughts of and prayers for me, alone with God and His chief minister. My feelings when his hands were placed on my head (and there was solemnity and earnestness in the very touch and manner) I cannot describe, they were too confused; but when the words "Defend, O Lord, this Thy child with Thy heavenly grace, that she may continue Thine for ever, and daily increase in Thy Holy Spirit more and more, until she come unto Thy everlasting Kingdom," were solemnly pronounced, if ever my heart followed a prayer it did then, if ever it thrilled with earnest longing not unmixed with joy, it did at the words "Thine for ever." We returned to our seats, and for some time I wept, why I hardly know, it was not grief, nor anxiety, nor exactly joy. About an hour and a quarter elapsed before all the candidates had been up to the rails. Each time that the "Amen" was chanted in a more distant part of the Cathedral, after the "Defend" had been pronounced, it seemed as tho' a choir of angels had come down to witness, and pour out from their pure spirits a deep and felt "Amen".

The bishop pronounced the closing blessing so very impressively that it was like soothing balm to me, and the thought came "why should I doubt that my soul will indeed receive the blessing which God's minister is thus giving?"

5. *Confirmation*

The Young-ones gathered in from hill and dale,
With holiday delight on every brow:
'Tis past away; far other thoughts prevail;
For they are taking the baptismal Vow
Upon their conscious selves; their own lips speak
The solemn promise. Strongest sinews fail,
And many a blooming, many a lovely, cheek
Under the holy fear of God turns pale;
While on each head his lawn-robed servant lays
An apostolic hand, and with each prayer seals
The Covenant. The Omnipotent will raise
Their feeble Souls; and bear with *his* regrets,
Who, looking round the fair assemblage, feels
That ere the Sun goes down their childhood sets.

A most unwilling candidate!

6. Thursday, April Eve. Read to old Price the keeper and then walked to Hay across the fields.

In Hadley's shop I met Dewing who told me of a most extraordinary misfortune that befell Pope the curate of Cusop yesterday at the Whitney Confirmation. He had one candidate Miss Stokes, a farmer's daughter, and they went together by train. Pope went in a cutaway coat very short, with his dog, and took no gown. The train was very late. He came very late into church and sat down on a bench with the girl cheek by jowl. When it came to his turn to present his candidate he was told by the Rector (Henry Dew) or someone in authority to explain why he came so late. The Bishop of Hereford (Atlay) has a new fashion of confirming only two persons at a time, kneeling at the rails. The Bishop had marked two young people come in very late and when they came up to the rails he thought from Pope's youthful appearance and from his having no gown that he was a young farmer candidate and brother of the girl. He spoke to them severely and told them to come on and kneel down for they were extremely late. Pope tried to explain that he was a clergyman and that the girl was his candidate but the Bishop was overbearing and imperious and either did not hear or did not attend, seeming to think he was dealing with a refractory ill-conditioned youth. "I know, I know," he said. "Come at once, kneel down, kneel down." Poor Pope resisted a long time and had a long battle with the Bishop, but at last unhappily he was overborne in the struggle, lost his head, gave way, knelt down and was *confirmed* there and then, and no one seems to have interfered to save him, though Mr Palmer of Eardisley and others were sitting close by and the whole Church was in a titter. It is a most unfortunate thing and will never be forgotten and it will be unhappily a joke against Pope all his life. The Bishop was told of his mistake afterwards and apologized to Pope, though rather shortly and cavalierly. He said, what was quite true, that Pope ought to have come in his gown. But there was a little fault on all sides for if the Bishop had been a little less hasty, rough and overbearing in his manner things might have been explained, and the bystanding clergy were certainly very much to blame for not stepping forward and preventing such a farce. I fear poor Pope will be very much vexed, hurt and dispirited about it.

REFERENCES

1. Ernest Raymond, *The Witness of Canon Welcome*, Cassell & Cy 1950, Ch. 9.
2. Alan Paton, *Cry the Beloved Country*, Jonathan Cape 1948, Ch. 5.
3. C. M. Yonge, *The Castlebuilders*, op. cit., The end of the story.
4. M.V.G. Havergal, *Memorials of Frances Ridley Havergal*, op. cit.
5. William Wordsworth, *Ecclesiastical Sonnets*, op. cit.
6. *The Diary of the Revd Francis Kilvert,* ed. William Plomer, op. cit., March 1870.

CHAPTER 13
Interlude: Found in Possession

The Prayer Book is very often a Godparent's gift to the newly confirmed.
"And the Common Prayer Book is well styled the best companion, being doubtless superior to any other forms that have been made or can be made *for the closet as well as the sanctuary."*

Ginny visits her Mother in hospital.
1. Carefully Ginny opened the table drawer, thinking of her promise to her Mother years ago to put her out of her misery, and hoping to find huge bottles crammed with pain killing tablets and capsules of all kinds that she could slip to her Mother, if that was what the situation required. But there were no bottles, only a worn Bible and an Anglican prayer book.

Candia McWilliam writes of the books at her bedside in "Who's reading whom?"
2. Hilaire Belloc's The Bad Child's Book of Beasts; and a Collected Larkin and the Book of Common Prayer, both always there.

As Allan Quartermain carried his Prayer Book on his travels in Rider Haggard's novels, so also did William Howard Russell, the first great War Correspondent of The Times.
3. The day before he left home, Mary gave him a Book of Common Prayer (now in the possession of Russell's great granddaughter, Mrs Simonds). A small stout volume with a metal edge and clasp. Russell carried it with him throughout the Crimean campaign and on all his subsequent travels.

Frank in The Castlebuilders, when he and his friends are caught by the tide, takes his little Prayer Book from his waistcoat pocket. Mr St John, the curate in charge, also keeps one upon his person. His daughters, Cicely and Mab have returned home to help him on the death of their stepmother, though Mab wishes to go away again to train as an artist.
4. 'Papa, it is not that. Supposing that we are best at home' (Mab said this with the corners of her mouth going down, for it was not her own opinion), 'yet there are other things to consider. We should be earning something - '

Mr St John got up almost impatiently for him. 'I have never been left to want,' he said. 'I have been young, and now I am old, but I have never seen the righteous forsaken, nor his seed begging their bread. Providence will raise up friends for the children; and we have always had plenty. If there is enough for me, there is enough for you.'

And he went out of the room as nearly angry as it was possible for his mild nature to be. Cicely and Mab once more looked at each other wondering. 'Papa is crazy, I think,' said Mab, who was the most self-assertive; But Cicely only heaved a sigh, and went out to the hall to brush his hat for him, as she remembered her mother used to do. Mr St John liked this kind of tendance. 'You are a good girl, Cicely; you are just such another as your mother,' he said, as he took the hat from her; and Cicely divined that the late Mrs St John had not shown him this attention, which I think pleased her on the whole.

'But, papa, I am afraid Mab was right,' she said. 'You must think it over, and think what is best for Mab.'

'Why should she be different from you?' said Mr St John, feeling in his breast pocket for the familiar prayer-book which lay there. It was more important to him to make sure it was safe, than to decide what to do with his child.

A midshipman picks one up by chance.

5. The next day, rather a singular circumstance occurred. One of the midshipmen was mast-headed by the second lieutentant, for not waiting on deck until he was relieved. He was down below when he was sent for, and expecting to be punished from what the quarter-master told him, he thrust the first book into his jacket-pocket which he could lay his hand on, to amuse himself at the mast-head, and then ran on deck. As he surmised, he was immediately ordered aloft. He had not been there more than five minutes when a sudden squall carried away the main-top gallant mast, and away he went flying over to leeward (for the wind had shifted, and the yards were now braced up). Had he gone overboard, as he could not swim, he would in all probability have been drowned; but the book in his pocket brought him up in the jaws of the fore-brace block, where he hung until taken out by the main-topmen. Now it so happened that it was a prayer-book which he had laid hold of in his hurry, and those who were superstitious declared it was all owing to his having taken a religious book with him. I did not think so, as any other book would have answered the purpose quite as well: still the midshipman himself thought so, and it was productive of good, as he was a sad scamp, and behaved much better afterwards.

"Wherefore above all things, let this custom of the people's joining in reading the Psalms be everywhere kept up (For this engages the parishioners *to furnish themselves and their children with Common Prayer books, and to use them at church.")*

Mrs Overtheway records that, getting ready for church, "Miss Lucy lost her Prayer Book, and it was not till another five minutes had gone that she remembered having left it in the church the Sunday before." No doubt a forgotten Prayer Book was one of the items that accounted for Sydney Smith's "Screeching Gate".
6. A mile beyond the church is the gate to Foston Rectory. A well kept drive, winding through park·like grounds, leads up to the house; halfway between the turnpike road and the parsonage a second gate is passed, which bears the curious name of the "Screeching Gate". Sydney Smith, it need scarcely be said, gave it that name, and it received it not on account of any infirmity of its own, but because

of an infirmity apparent in his wife and daughters. The master of the house had learnt by experience that on Sundays, when on his way with his family to church, one or other of the ladies was certain to cry out at this stage of the journey that she had forgotten this or that, and to run back in sudden haste to the house to secure it, and so the "Screeching Gate" received its name.

Certainly it was common practice until recent times for many churchgoers to bring their prayer book, often bound up with Hymns A & M, to church with them and to take it home. Eileen Baillie describes her embarrassment and fears, when as a small girl, she is allowed to leave the church after the Offertory at the Sung Eucharist.

7. The sermon finished, we rose for the offertory hymn, my collection-penny gripped despairingly in a sticky palm. Once it had been dropped into the sidesman's little bag, there was no going back. My mother's hand propelled me gently towards the aisle. Normally a tremendous ritualist, I enjoyed bowing to the altar, but now it became a mere perfunctory bob. I was out of the pew, alone in the vast wastes of the middle aisle, which appeared to elongate itself into an endless vista with the west door as an impossibly distant haven. (Perhaps this is one of the reasons why, since attaining independence, I have always preferred to sit at the very back of the church). My trembling legs could not carry me fast enough between the serried ranks of the congregation, all, it seemed, staring at me with curious or accusing eyes, as much to say: 'So *that* little girl can't last the service out!' In reality, of course, they scarcely gave a passing glance to the Vicar's youngest daughter, in button boots and bonnet, scuttering out of the church like a terrified rabbit.

Once outside, the worst was still to come. Clutching desperately my prayer-book and Hymns A. & M., with thumping heart I traversed the enormous stretch of pavement until I came at last to the fatal gate. The relief when I had got inside was immense. No early settler pursued to the very walls of a frontier fort by Red Indians could have felt a greater sense of deliverance from peril as the gates of the stockade closed fast behind him. Now I had only to run up the front-door steps and ring the bell.

Perhaps some just carried them.

8. A solemn friend of my Grandfather used to go for walks on Sunday, carrying a prayer-book, without the least intention of going to church. And he calmly defended it by saying, with uplifted hand: "I do it, Chessie, as an example to others." The man who did that was obviously a Dickens character. And I am disposed to think that, in being a Dickens character, he was in many ways rather preferable to many modern characters. Few modern men, however false, would dare to be so brazen. And I am not sure he was not really a more genuine fellow than the modern man who says vaguely that he has doubts or hates sermons, when he only wants to go and play golf. Hypocrisy itself was more sincere. Anyway, it was more courageous.

The Prayer Books provided in churches seem to diminish in number when there is an incumbent using modern services; and a return to the old ways brings an appeal for people once again to bring their Prayer Book with them!

9. When the Marquess of Hartington was asked what was the proudest day of his life, he replied that it was when his finest pig won first prize at Skipton Fair. My only similar success is that, after ten glum years, I was instrumental in restoring the Book of Common Prayer to Evensong in my parish church. As the local paper put it: 'The decision was taken because some church members have expressed reservations in recent months about the use of the yellow booklet for all services.'

How did I win my equivalent of the pig at Skipton Fair? The answer, crudely, is blackmail, the one consummate gift still pursued and respected by the Church of England. The church needed a new roof. After the unease of years, plus a few stickers on cars and the feigned threat of unrenewed covenants, the murmurers found the tongues that had been taken from them.

It's only a beginning and it's not first prize. Doubtless I shall have to take my own King James Bible if I am again asked to read the lesson. The local newspaper notes that, 'The Vicar hopes that churchgoers will revive the practice of taking their own prayer books to service in case there are not enough to go round!'

REFERENCES

1. Lisa Alther, *Kinflicks*, op. cit.
2. *The Sunday Times* 28th May 1989.
3. Alan Hankinson, *Man of Wars*, Heinemann Educational Books 1982.
4. Mrs Oliphant, *The Curate in Charge*, Wm Blackwood & Sons 1875, ch.6.
5. Captain Marryat, *Peter Simple*, (1834) Everyman Library, J.M. Dent 1907.
6. Stuart J. Reid, *The Life and Times of Sydney Smith*, Sampson Low, Marston & Cy 1896.
7. Eileen Baillie, *Shabby Paradise*, Hutchinson 1958.
8. G.K. Chesterton, *Autobiography*, op. cit.
9. John Osborne, 'Great Sighs of Today', in *The Spectator* 22nd December 1984.

CHAPTER 14
The Form of Solemnization of Matrimony

The printed service begins with rubrics (directions for the conduct of service, originally printed in red) concerning the publication of the Banns.

1. Mr Marsden entertained me with some reminiscences of his own. "A public house in the village, haven't we?" he said. "We just have, and they keep a fearful noise there sometimes. Then I put my head out of my bedroom window and holla to them and they fly like the wind. When I was curate of Llangorse," he said, "the vicar of Talgarth was ill and I had to procure an assistant curate. So I wrote to Llewellyn, now Dean of St David's - then Principal of Lampeter - to send me a man who wanted a title for orders and could speak Welsh and English. Llewellyn wrote that he had the very man for me, *doctus utriusque linguae*. The man came. I saw his Welsh was very shaky.

Once he was publishing Banns. He meant to say, "Why these two persons may not lawfully be joined together in holy Matrimony". But what he did say was, "Why these two backsides may not lawfully be joined together in Holy Matrimony." Everyone in Church hid their faces. When we came out of Church I said, "Well, you *have* done it now." "What?" said he. I told him. "God forbid," said he. "It is true," I said.

Fairway tells his neighbours how he heard Tamsin Yeobright's aunt forbid her banns in church.

2. 'I not only happened to be there,' said Fairway, with a fresh collection of emphasis, 'but I was sitting in the same pew as Mis'ess Yeobright. And though you may not see it as such, it fairly made my blood run cold to hear her. Yes, it is a curious thing; but it made my blood run cold, for I was close at her elbow.' The speaker looked round upon the bystanders, now drawing closer to hear him, with his lips gathered tighter than ever in the rigorousness of his descriptive moderation.

' 'Tis a serious job to have things happen to 'ee there,' said a woman behind.

'"Ye are to declare it," was the parson's words,' Fairway continued. 'And then up stood a woman at my side - a-touching of me. "Well, be damned if there isn't Mis'ess Yeobright a-standing up," I said to myself. Yes, neighbours, though I was in the temple of prayer that's what I said. 'Tis against my conscience to curse and swear in company, and I hope any woman here will overlook it. Still what I did say I did say, and 'twould be a lie if I didn't own it.'

'So 'twould, neighbour Fairway.'

'"Be damned if there isn't Mis'ess Yeobright a-standing up," I said,' the narrator repeated, giving out the bad word with the same passionless severity of face as before, which proved how entirely necessity and not gusto had to do with the iteration. 'And the next thing I heard was, "I forbid the banns," from her. "I'll speak to you after the service," said the parson, in quite a homely way - yes, turning all at once into a common man no holier than you or I. Ah, her face was pale! Maybe you can call to mind that monument in Weatherbury church - the cross-legged soldier that have had his arm knocked away by the school-children? Well, he would about have matched that woman's face, when she said, "I forbid the banns."'

The audience cleared their throats and tossed a few stalks into the fire, not because these deeds were urgent, but to give themselves time to weigh the moral of the story.

'I'm sure when I heard they'd been forbid I felt as glad as if anybody had gied me sixpence,' said an earnest voice - that of Olly Dowden, a woman who lived by making heath brooms, or besoms. Her nature was to be civil to enemies as well as to friends, and grateful to all the world for letting her remain alive.

'And now the maid have married him just the same,' said Humphrey.

'After that Mis'ess Yeobright came round and was quite agreeable,' Fairway resumed, with an unheeding air, to show that his words were no appendage to Humphrey's, but the result of independent reflection.

Licences are dispensations from the necessity of banns, issued by the Bishop through his surrogate. They make it possible for a marriage to take place outside the parish and without publicity.

A garrulous old sailor tells of his Captain's wedding.
3. Among poor Heaviside's many weak qualities, one of the most conspicuous was a resolute curiosity. This compelled him to open a great part of the breadth of his nature to the legitimate, or otherwise, affairs of his fellow-creatures.

And being an orthodox champion of wedlock (from the moment he left his wife and children, without any power to draw on him), he helped all the rest of the world in this way, as a host recommends his hot pickles.

Therefore he had been chosen, by very bad taste upon somebody's part, and an utter forgetfulness of me, to be up at our Captain's snap of a wedding, and to say 'Amen' to it. What could be worse than a huddle of this kind, and a broad scattering afterwards? If they had only invited me, both sense and honesty would have been there; as well as a man not to be upset by things, however female.

For from what Heaviside told me, it seems that the Captain and his fair Isabel, before our present cruise began, had resolved that no one should ever be able legally to sever them. But one special term of the compact was that the outer world should have no acquaintance with things that happened between them. In other words, that they should leave their excellent friends and relatives all in the dark about this matter, as well as save the poor Captain's oath, by quitting each other immediately. It is to the utmost extent beyond my own experience to deny, that this is the wisest of all arrangements (if there can be anything wise) after the deed of wedlock; for what can equal severance in the saving of disagreement? However, they had not the wisdom as yet to look at it in this light, and the one wept and the other sighed, when they parted at the churchyard gate; for the Defence must sail at 1 p.m.

The lady had been content to come and dwell in a very dirty village of the name of Gosport, so that the licence might be forthcoming from proper people when paid for. Because, of course, in her own country, nothing could have been done without ten thousand people to talk of it. And thus they were spliced, without hoisting flag; for ever spliced, both in soul and in law (which takes the lead of the other one), and yet in body severed always, till there should come fair repute.

The first spoken words are the Exhortation concerning the purposes for which matrimony was ordained.

4. Let us go on: Mrs Wadman sat in expectation my uncle Toby would do so, to almost the first pulsation of that minute, wherein silence on one side or the other, generally becomes indecent: so edging herself a little more towards him, and raising up her eyes, sub-blushing, as she did it - she took up the gauntlet - or the discourse (if you like it better) and communed with my uncle Toby, thus:

The care and disquietudes of the marriage state, quoth Mrs Wadman, are very great. I suppose so - said my uncle Toby: and therefore when a person, continued Mrs Wadman, is so much at his ease as you are - so happy, Captain Shandy, in yourself, your friends and your amusements - I wonder, what reasons can incline you to the state -

- They are written, quoth my uncle Toby, in the Common-Prayer Book.

Thus far my uncle Toby went on warily, and kept within his depth, leaving Mrs Wadman to sail upon the gulf as she pleased.

5. Lucia . . . directed her stream of consciousness to her hostess, who, as Elizabeth Mapp, had been her timorous partner in the great adventure on the kitchen table a year ago. She, at any rate, had not vegetated since their return, for she had married Major Benjamin Flint, and since he had only an Army Pension, and she was a woman of substance in every sense of the word, and owner of Mallards, it was only proper she should hyphenate her surname with his. The more satirical spirits of Tilling thought she would have preferred to retain her maiden name like Foljambe and famous actresses. At the marriage service she had certainly omitted the word "obey" when she defined what sort of wife she would make him. But the preliminary exhortation had been read in full, tho' the Padre had tactfully suggested that the portion of it relating to children need not be recited: Elizabeth desired to have it all.

After the revision of the Prayer Book in 1927, it became possible to use a slightly different form of Exhortation in place of the "old, coarse Prayer Book" one.

Lord Peter prefers to stand in the old ways, as the diary of Honoria Lucasta, Dowager Duchess of Denver, reveals.

6. *16 September* - Helen obligingly presented us with a copy of the new form of marriage service, with all the vulgar bits left out - which was asking for trouble. Peter very funny about it - said he knew all about the "procreation of children" in theory though not in practice, but that the "increase of mankind" by any other method sounded too advanced for him, and that, if he ever did indulge in such dangerous

amusements, he would, with his wife's permission, stick to the old-fashioned procedure. He also said that, as for the "gift of continence," he wouldn't have it as a gift, and had no objection to admitting as much. At this point, Helen got up and left the house, leaving P. and Harriet to wrangle over the word "obey". P. said he would consider it a breach of manners to give orders to his wife, but H. said, Oh, no - he'd give orders fast enough if the place was on fire or a tree falling down and he wanted her to stand clear. P. said, in that case they ought both to say "obey," but it would be too much jam for the reporters. Left them to fight it out. When I came back, found Peter had consented to be obeyed on condition he might "endow" and not "share" his worldly goods. Shocking victory of sentiment over principle.

Helen, Duchess of Denver, writes to her friend Lady Grummidge, about the wedding.

7. MY DEAR MARJORIE,

The bride came attended by the most incredible assortment of bridesmaids - all female dons! - and an odd, dark woman to give her away, who was supposed to be the Head of the College. I am thankful to say, considering her past history, that Harriet (as I suppose I must now call her) had enough sense of propriety not to get herself up in white satin and orange-blossom; but I could not help thinking that a plain costume would have been more suitable than cloth of gold. I can see that I shall have to speak to her presently about her clothes, but I am afraid she will be difficult. I have never seen anybody look so indecently triumphant - I suppose, in a way, she had a right to; one must admit that she has played her cards very cleverly. Peter was as white as a sheet; I thought he was going to be sick. Probably he was realising what he had let himself in for. Nobody can say that I did not do my best to open his eyes. They were married in the old, coarse Prayer-book form, and the bride said "Obey" - take this to be their idea of humour, for she looks as obstinate as a mule.

The Exhortation concludes with appeals to the congregation and then to the bridal pair to disclose any impediments.

8. And now I can recall the picture of the grey old house of God rising calm before me, of a rook wheeling round the steeple, of a ruddy morning sky beyond. I remember something, too, of the green gravemounds; and I have not forgotten either two figures of strangers straying amongst the low hillocks and reading the mementoes graven on the few mossy headstones. I noticed them, because, as they saw us, they passed round to the back of the church, and I doubted not they were going to enter by the side-aisle door and witness the ceremony. By Mr Rochester they were not observed; he was earnestly looking at my face, from which the blood had, I daresay, momentarily fled; for I felt my forehead dewy, and my cheeks and lips cold. When I rallied, which I soon did, he walked gently with me up the path to the porch.

We entered the quiet and humble temple; the priest waited in his white surplice at the lowly altar, the clerk beside him. All was still: two shadows only moved in a remote corner. My conjecture had been correct: the strangers had slipped in before us, and they now stood by the vault of the Rochesters, their backs towards us, viewing through the rails the old time-stained marble tomb, where a kneeling angel guarded the remains of Damer De Rochester, slain at Marston Moor in the time of the civil wars, and of Elizabeth, his wife.

Our place was taken at the communion rails. Hearing a cautious step behind me, I glanced over my shoulder: one of the strangers - a gentleman, evidently - was advancing up the chancel. The service began. The explanation of the intent of matrimony was gone through; and then the clergyman came a step further forward, and, bending slightly towards Mr Rochester, went on -

"I require and charge you both (as ye will answer at the dreadful day of judgment, when the secrets of all hearts shall be disclosed), that if either of you know any impediment why ye may not lawfully be joined together in matrimony, ye do now confess it; for be ye well assured that so many as are coupled together otherwise than God's word doth allow, are not joined together by God, neither is their matrimony lawful."

He paused, as the custom is. When is the pause after that sentence ever broken by reply? Not, perhaps, once in a hundred years. And the clergyman, who had not lifted his eyes from his book, and had held his breath but for a moment, was proceeding - his hand was already stretched towards Mr Rochester, as his lips unclosed to ask, "Wilt thou have this woman for thy wedded wife?" - when a distinct and near voice said -

"The marriage cannot go on: I declare the existence of an impediment."

The clergyman looked up at the speaker, and stood mute; the clerk did the same. Mr Rochester moved slightly, as if an earthquake had rolled under his feet: taking a firmer footing, and not turning his head or eyes, he said, "Proceed."

Profound silence fell when he had uttered that word, with deep but low intonation. Presently Mr Wood said -

"I cannot proceed without some investigation into what has been asserted, and evidence of its truth or falsehood."

"The ceremony is quite broken off," subjoined the voice behind us. "I am in a condition to prove my allegation: an insuperable impediment to this marriage exists."

Mr Rochester heard, but heeded not; he stood stubborn and rigid, making no movement but to possess himself of my hand. What a hot and strong grasp he had! - and how like quarried marble was his pale, firm, massive front at this moment! How his eye shone, still, watchful, and yet wild beneath!

Mr Wood seemed at a loss. "What is the nature of the impediment?" he asked. "Perhaps it may be got over - explained away?"

"Hardly," was the answer. "I have called it insuperable, and I speak advisedly."

The speaker came forward, and leaned on the rails. He continued, uttering each word distinctly, calmly, steadily, but not loudly.

"It simply consists in the existence of a previous marriage. Mr Rochester has a wife now living."

Now the wedding begins.

At the Rainbow Inn Mr Macey, the Parish Clerk tells the story of the marriage of Mr Lammeter and Miss Osgood.
9. Here Mr Macey paused; he always gave his narrative in instalments, expecting to be questioned according to precedent.

"Ay, and a particular thing happened, didn't it, Mr Macey, so as you were likely to remember that marriage?" said the landlord in a congratulatory tone.

"I should think there did, - a *very* particular thing," said Mr Macey, nodding sideways. "For Mr Drumlow - poor old gentleman, I was fond on him, tho' he'd got a bit confused in his head, what wi' age and wi' taking a drop of summat warm when the service come of a cold morning. And young Mr Lammeter, he'd have no way but he must be married in January, which, to be sure's a unreasonable time to be married in, for it isn't like a christening or a burying as you can't help; and so Mr Drumlow, poor old gentleman, I was fond on him - but when he come to put the questions, he put em' by the rule o' contrairy, like, and he says, 'Wilt thou have this man to thy wedded wife?' says he, and then he says, 'Wilt thou have this woman to thy wedded husband?' says he. But the partic'larest thing of all is, as nobody took any notice on it but me, and they answered straight off 'yes,' like as if it had been me saying 'Amen' i' the right place, without listening to what went before."

"But *you* knew what was going on well enough, didn't you, Mr Macey? You were live enough, eh?" said the butcher.

"Lord bless you!" said Mr Macey, pausing, and smiling in pity at the impotence of his hearer's imagination - "why, I was all of a tremble: it was as if I'd been a coat pulled by the two tails, like; for I couldn't stop the parson, I couldn't take upon me to do that; and yet I said to myself, I says, 'Suppose they shouldn't be fast married, 'cause the words are contrairy?' and my head went working like a mill, for I was allays uncommon for turning things over and seeing all round 'em; and I says to myself, 'Is't the meanin' or the words as makes folks fast i' wedlock?' For the parson meant right, and the bride and bridegroom meant right. But then, when I come to think on it, meanin' goes but a little way i' most things, for you may mean to stick things together and your glue may be bad, and then where are you? And so I says to mysen, 'It isn't the meanin', it's the glue.' And I was worreted as if I'd got three bells to pull at once, when we got into the vestry, and they begun to sign their names. But where's the use o' talking - you can't think what goes on in a 'cute man's inside."

"But you held in for all that, didn't you, Mr Macey?" said the landlord.

"Ay, I held in tight till I was by mysen wi' Mr Drumlow, and then I out wi' everything, but respectful, as I allays did. And he made light on it, and he says, 'Pooh, pooh, Macey, make yourself easy,' he says, 'it's neither the meaning nor the words - it's the re*ges*ter does it - that's the glue.' So you see he settled it easy; for parsons and doctors know everything by heart, like, so as they aren't worreted wi' thinking what's the rights and wrongs o' things, as I'n been many and many's the time. And sure enough the wedding turned out all right, on'y poor Mrs Lammeter - that's Miss Osgood as was - died afore the lasses were growed up; but for prosperity and everything respectable, there's no family more looked on."

Then shall the priest say "Who giveth this woman to be married to this man?"

10. Jude, will you give me away? I have nobody else who could do it so conveniently as you, being the only married relation I have here on the spot, even if my father were friendly enough to be willing, which he isn't. I hope you won't think it a trouble? I have been looking at the marriage service in the Prayer-book, and it seems to me

very humiliating that a giver-away should be required at all. According to the ceremony as there printed, my bridegroom chooses me of his own will and pleasure; but I don't choose him. Somebody *gives* me to him, like a she-ass or she-goat, or any other domestic animal. Bless your exalted views of woman, O Churchman! But I forget: I am no longer privileged to tease you. - Ever,

    'SUSANNA FLORENCE MARY BRIDEHEAD'

Jude screwed himself up to heroic key; and replied:

My dear Sue, - Of course I wish you joy! And also of course I will give you away. What I suggest is that, as you have no house of your own, you do not marry from your school friend's, but from mine. It would be more proper, I think, since I am, as you say, the person nearest related to you in this part of the world.

I don't see why you sign your letter in such a new and terribly formal way? Surely you care a bit about me still! - Ever your affectionate,

    JUDE

Then shall they give their troth to each other.

Absalom Kumalo has been sentenced to death and is in prison. His father and Father Vincent bring the girl who is with child by him so that they can be married.
11. They passed again through the great gate in the grim high wall, Father Vincent and Kumalo and Gertrude and the girl and Msimangu. The boy was brought to them, and for a moment some great hope showed in his eyes, and he stood there trembling and shaking. But Kumalo said to him gently, we are come for the marriage, and the hope died out.

- My son, here is your wife that is to be.

The boy and the girl greeted each other like strangers, each giving hands without life, not to be shaken, but to be held loosely, so that the hands fell apart easily. They did not kiss after the European fashion, but stood looking at each other without words, bound in a great constraint. But at last she asked, Are you in health? and he answered, I am greatly. And he asked, Are you in health? and she answered, I am greatly also. But beyond that there was nothing spoken between them.

Father Vincent left them, and they all stood in the same constraint. Msimangu saw that Gertrude would soon break out into wailing and moaning, and he turned his back on the others and said to her gravely and privately, Heavy things have happened, but this is a marriage, and it were better to go at once than to wail or moan in this place. When she did not answer he said sternly and coldly, Do you understand me? And she said resentfully, I understand you. He left her and went to a window in the great grim wall, and she stood sullenly silent, but he knew she would not do what it was in her mind to have done.

And Kumalo said desperately to his son, Are you in health? And the boy answered, I am greatly, Are you in health, my father? So Kumalo said, I am greatly. He longed for other things to say, but he could not find them. And indeed it was a mercy for them all, when a white man came to take them to the prison chapel.

Father Vincent was waiting there in his vestments, and he read to them from his book. Then he asked the boy if he took this woman, and he asked the girl if she took this man. And when they had answered as it is laid down in that book, for better for worse, for richer for poorer, in sickness and in health, till death did them part, he married them. Then he preached a few words to them, that they were to remain faithful, and to bring up what children there might be in the fear of God. So were they married and signed their names in the book.

After it was done, the two priests and the wife and Gertrude left father and son, and Kumalo said to him, I am glad you are married.

- I am also glad, my father.

12. At fifteen minutes to four the two brothers stepped out into the sunshine of the court. Old Morris had left a half-hour earlier so that Hastings could seat him inconspicuously in the gallery. They went in the side way and on to the vestry room where they found Bronson already with Dr Farley, the rector of Christ Church. Bronson looked bigger and more imposing than ever in his full ecclesiastical regalia. He spoke in friendly fashion to Dick, however, and there descended upon the four an intangible male oneness of spirit as they waited the final signal.

"Nervous?" Dr Farley asked Hilary, smiling.

"A little."

"I remember when I was married I shook so much I thought everyone could see," Bronson volunteered. Strange, Hilary thought, to hear Bronson confess to anything less than complete assurance, ever. He was speaking again.

"I am using the old English form of the marriage service. You are familiar with it, no doubt?"

"Yes. Oh, yes," Hilary said, his mind fixed upon Lex, leaving the house, driving through the streets, entering the vestibule, starting up the aisle.

"That is satisfactory to you, then?"

"Oh, quite. . . ."

"Dearly beloved, we are gathered together here in the sight of God, and in the face of this company. . . ."

He heard Dr Farley pronounce the familiar opening words which he himself had so often uttered for others. Now, incredible wonder, it was he, himself, who was being married. He and Lex.

As they moved forward to where Bronson waited before the altar itself, Hilary felt his throat tight and choked. Would his voice be heard? Would he, who had repeated them so often before, now fumble the final vows?

"I Hilary, take thee, Alexa. . . ."

When her voice came he felt as though all the deeps within him were breaking up. After his long, torturing uncertainty he heard now clearly, unfalteringly,

"I, Alexa, take thee, Hilary. . . ."

He had been conscious of no great deviation from the usual service until he placed the ring upon Lex's finger; then he found himself repeating after Bronson:

"With this ring I thee wed, with my body I thee worship." He had read the old form, of course, but had forgotten it. He flushed now, wondering whether Lex or the congregation at large would think the words strange. At least he could not have spoken a profounder truth.

13. In the full liturgic sense of the word, he *[Dr Dace]* worshipped her, that is, he loved and cherished, and respected and honoured her: and she would have obeyed him cheerfully as well as dutifully, if obedience could have been shown where there was ever but one will.

Then shall the priest join their right hands together and say "Those whom . . ."

14. *The General*: It would become you better, Alfred, to send that silly girl back to her husband and her duty than to talk clever and mock at your religion. "What God hath joined together let no man put asunder." Remember that.

The Bishop: Don't be afraid, Boxer. What God hath joined together no man ever shall put asunder. God will take care of that. *[To Leo]* By the way, who was it that joined you and Reginald, my dear?

Leo: It was that awful little curate that afterwards drank and travelled first class with a third class ticket, and then tried to go on the stage. But they wouldn't have him. He called himself Egerton Fotheringay.

The Bishop: Well, whom Egerton Fotheringay hath joined, let Sir Gorell Barnes put asunder by all means.

The General: I may be a silly soldier man; but I call this blasphemy.

The Bishop (gravely): Better for me to take the name of Mr. Egerton Fotheringay in earnest than for you to take a higher name in vain.

Lesbia: Can't you three brothers ever meet without quarrelling?

The Bishop (mildly): This is not quarrelling, Lesbia: it's only English family life.

After the giving and receiving of a ring and the joining of hands, the priest pronounces that the couple 'be man and wife together', and blesses them. There follows a Psalm while they go up to the altar rail for the final prayers. The rubric then says,
   "After which, if there be no sermon declaring the duties of man and wife, the minister shall read as followeth."

15. Bertha is to be married at The Sawpits. At first there was some talk of a wedding at St Ursula's, and it was to have been made an occasion of high parochial festivity. Mr Soulsby *[the Vicar]* wrote a new wedding-hymn - or, as he preferred to call it, a "sacred epithalamium" - which was to have been sung to music composed by Mrs Soulsby. The Fishers in Deep Waters were to have walked in procession behind the bridesmaids, and the bridegroom was to have been attended by a deputation of grateful shop-assistants, whose teeth he had knocked down their throats at the Parochial Club. All this would have been, to use the Vicar's favourite phrase, "very teaching"; but Bertha set her face against it with unmistakable determination. The fact is that Mr Soulsby's matrimonial ministrations are a little at a discount in Stuccovia. His taste in arranging an arch of artificial palms over the chancel gate is unequalled, and his white stole, embroidered with love-knots and arrows, is the envy of all his clerical brethren; but his oratorical instinct sometimes runs away with him, and the extempore harangues which he substitutes for the prescribed discourse about Abraham and Sarah are not always felicitous. Only the other day the Barrington-Bounderleys' eldest girl was married at St Ursula's to General Padmore - who certainly had one wife in Brompton Cemetery, even if we leave out of account his Indian experiences, of which old Lady Farringford had heard a good deal from her late husband. As this blushing bridegroom rose slowly from his

knees, rendered a little stiff,

"By pangs arthritic that infest the toe
Of libertine excess,"

the undaunted Soulsby opened his discourse: "Dear brother and sister, you are entering on a new phase of being. Strange and untried experiences lie before you. You will encounter little trials of temper, little demands for daily self-surrender, of which you have hitherto known nothing;" and, after a good deal of maundering eloquence on this infelicitous topic, ended by saying that the knot which he had just tied was tied for ever, and that General and Mrs Padmore were man and wife to all eternity.

This misplaced rhetoric roused all Selina's ire. "Did you ever hear such stuff?" she exclaimed, as the wedding guests fought their way into the porch. *"Strange and untried experiences,* indeed! Poor Hildegarde is inexperienced enough, I admit; but it must be forty years if it's an hour since that dreadful old General was first married. And as for all that nonsense about Eternity, I should like to know what the last Mrs Padmore thinks of it - let alone the yellow lady in Upper Burmah. Really, Mr Soulsby might have found out that the bridegroom had been married again and again, and have contented himself with the Prayer Book, which, at any rate, steers clear of these difficulties."

It probably was the recollection of this oratorical miscarriage which governed Bertha's decision. Anyhow, she said that she must and would be married at home, and that the ceremony should be performed by their dear old Vicar, Mr Borum, who had christened her and prepared her for Confirmation.

Few would guess that the last word of the wedding service is "amazement", should the reading take the place of a sermon:

"even as Sarah obeyed Abraham, calling him Lord; whose daughters ye are as long as ye do well, and are not afraid with any amazement."

Allan Quartermain discovered this as he performed the wedding service over Sir Henry Curtis and Nyleptha, Queen of Zu-Vendis during his second expedition to East Africa with Curtis and Commander Good.

16. So it chanced that presently, attended only by two of her favourite maidens, came the Queen Nyleptha, with happy blushing face and downcast eyes, dressed in pure white, without embroidery of any sort, as seems to be the fashion on these occasions in most countries of the world. She did not wear a single ornament, even her gold circlets were removed, and I thought that if possible she looked more lovely than ever without them, as really superbly beautiful women do.

She came, curtseyed low to Sir Henry; then took his hand and led him up before the altar, and after a little pause, in a slow, clear voice uttered the following words which are customary in Zu-Vendis if the bride desires and the man consents:-

"Thou dost swear by the Sun that thou wilt take no other woman to wife unless I lay my hand upon her and bid her come!"

"I swear it," answered Sir Henry; adding in English, "One is quite enough for me."

Then Agon, who had been sulking in a corner near the altar, came forward and gabbled off something into his beard at such a rate that I could not follow it, but it appeared to be an invocation to the Sun to bless the union and make it fruitful. I observed that Nyleptha listened very closely to every word, and afterwards discovered that she was afraid lest Agon should play her a trick, and by going through the invocations backwards divorce instead of marry them. At the end of the invocations, they were asked, as in our service, if they took each other for husband and wife, and on their assenting they kissed each other before the altar, and the service was over, so far as their rites were concerned. But it seemed to me that there was yet something wanting, and so I produced a Prayer-Book, which, together with the "Ingoldsby Legends," that I often read when I lie awake at nights, has accompanied me in all my later wanderings. I gave it to my poor boy Harry years ago, and after his death I found it among his things and took it back again.

"Curtis," I said, "I am not a clergyman, and I do not know if what I am going to propose is allowable - I know it is not legal - but if you and the Queen have no objection I should like to read the English marriage service over you. It is a solemn step which you are taking, and I think that you ought, so far as circumstances will allow, to give it the sanction of your own religion."

"I have thought of that," he said, "and I wish you would. I do not feel half married yet."

Nyleptha raised no objection, fully understanding that her husband wished to celebrate the marriage according to the rites prevailing in his own country, and so I set to work and read the service, from "Dearly beloved" to "amazement" as well as I could; and when I came to "I, Henry, take thee, Nyleptha," I translated, and also "I, Nyleptha, take thee, Henry," which she repeated after me very well. Then Sir Henry took a plain gold ring from his little finger and placed it on hers, and so on to the end. The ring had been Curtis's mother's wedding-ring, and I could not help thinking how astonished the dear old Yorkshire lady would have been if she could have foreseen that her wedding-ring was to serve a similar purpose for Nyleptha, a Queen of the Zu-Vendi.

That chapter in Quartermain's story is called 'A strange wedding'. An even stranger one is described, tongue in cheek, in a review of Cecil B. de Mille's film 'The Crusades' in the 30th August 1935 edition of The Spectator.

17. Richard Coeur-de-Lion, in Mr de Mille's pious and Protestant eyes, closely resembled those honest simple young rowing-men who feel there's something wrong about sex. Richard took the cross rather than marry Alice of France, and when the King of Navarre forced him at Marseilles to marry his daughter (the alternative was to let his army starve) he merely sent his sword to the wedding ceremony, which was oddly enough carried out in English by an Anglican - or possibly American Episcopalian - clergyman in the words of the Book of Common Prayer. There is, indeed, in spite of the subject, nothing Romish about this film.

REFERENCES

1. *The Diary of the Revd Francis Kilvert*, ed. W. Plomer, op. cit., 23rd May 1871.
2. Thomas Hardy, *The Return of the Native*, Macmillan 1878, Ch. The Three Women.
3. R.D. Blackmore, *The Maid of Sker*, op. cit., Ch. 49.
4. Laurence Sterne, *Tristram Shandy*, op. cit., Book 9 Ch. 18.
5. E.F. Benson, *Lucia's Progress*, op. cit., Ch. 1.

6. Dorothy L. Sayers, *Busman's Honeymoon*, Victor Gollancz 1937, Ch. 1.
7. Ibid.
8. Charlotte Bronte, *Jane Eyre*, Smith Elder & Cy 1847, p. 279.
9. George Eliot, *Silas Marner*, op. cit., Ch. 6.
10. Thomas Hardy, *Jude the Obscure*, Macmillan 1896, Ch. 11.
11. Alan Paton, *Cry the Beloved Country*, op. cit., Ch. 12.
12. Agnes Turnbull, *The Bishop's Mantle*, Macmillan N.Y., 1948.
13. Robert Southey, *The Doctor,* op. cit.
14. G.B. Shaw, *Getting Married*, op. cit.
15. The Rt. Hon. G.W.E. Russell, *A Londoner's Log Book*, Elder & Cy 1902.
16. H. Rider Haggard, *Allan Quartermain*, Hodder & Stoughton 1919, Ch. 19 A strange wedding.
17. Graham Greene, reprinted in *The Pleasure Dome*, Secker & Warburg 1972, p. 18.

CHAPTER 15
The Order for the Visitation of the Sick

Sunday May 18th 1828

1. I called after Church on old Harris, who I think is not yet in a dying state, but he thinks he is, and is as much frightened as he was in the winter; but when the fear of death was passed he devoted himself to the world with the same anxiety as he was accustomed to do. I read the prayers for the Visitation of the Sick to him. The world has been this man's idol, and it now vanishes like an evil genius, leaving the wretch desolate and almost despairing. He now says he has given up all thoughts of this world - according to the old rhyme - "when the devil was sick" etc. etc.

2. Within a weeks' time Jeffrey suffered less: he did not know whether it was a result of having taken a variation of the original St Christopher's medication. When he thanked a nurse for her care (her caring mattered to him, he said,) she laughed and replied that she was in the habit of praying with her fingertips. You mustn't fear the pain, she said, I pray that you will cease to fear the pain. At least she hadn't addressed him on the meaning and use of the time of sickness, and the opportunity it afforded him for spiritual profit, as the good sisters at the hospital had. He needed no prodding; he read his Bible and Prayer Book, especially the service for the Visitation of the Sick, as he had been reading and rereading since the beginning of Mary's illness. In his mind he saw before him his fellow parishioners, kneeling together, repeating the litany for the dying: "to deliver the soul of thy servant Jeffrey from the power of the evil one, and from eternal death."

On Thursday of that week, in the dusk of the evening, Father Mabry brought communion and a bit of the service for the Visitation of the Sick from the old Church-of-England Book of Common Prayer: "Sanctify, we beseech thee, this thy fatherly correction to Jeffrey"; "Wherefore, whatsoever your sickness is, Jeffrey, know you certainly, that it is God's visitation. And for what cause so ever this sickness is sent unto you; whether it be to try your patience, for the example of others, . . or else it be sent unto you to correct and amend in you whatsoever doth offend the eyes of your heavenly Father. . ; take therefore in good part the chastisement of the Lord: For (as Saint Paul saith in the twelfth chapter to the Hebrews) whom the Lord loveth he chasteneth, and scourgeth every son whom he receiveth,"

. . . "Now therefore, taking your sickness, which is thus profitable for you, patiently, I exhort you, in the name of God, to remember the profession which you made unto God in your Baptism." Then he examined Jeffrey in the articles of faith;

and without questioning him about his needs and without being exposed to Jeffrey's questions, the good Father Mabry departed.

Then shall the Minister examine whether he repent him truly of his sins, and be in charity with all the world; exhorting him to forgive from the bottom of his heart, all persons that have offended him; and if he hath offended any other, to ask them forgiveness; and where he hath done injury or wrong to any man, that he make amends to the uttermost of his power. And if he hath not before disposed of his goods, let him then be admonished to make his Will, and to declare his debts, what he oweth and what is owing to him; for the better discharging of his conscience, and the quietness of his Executors. But men should often be put in remembrance to take order for the settling of their temporal estates, whilst they are in health.

The Minister should not omit earnestly to move such sick persons as are of ability to be liberal to the poor.

Here shall the sick person be moved to make a special confession of his sins, if he feel his conscience troubled with any weighty matter. After which confession, the Priest shall absolve him (if he humbly and heartily desire it) after this sort. . . .

3. *Visitation of the Sick*

> The Sabbath bells renew the inviting peal;
> Glad music! yet there be that, worn with pain
> And sickness, listen where they long have lain,
> In sadness listen. With maternal zeal
> Inspired, the Church sends ministers to kneel
> Beside the afflicted; to sustain with prayer,
> And soothe the heart confession hath laid bare -
> That pardon, from God's throne, may set its seal
> On a true Penitent. When breath departs
> From one disburthened so, so comforted,
> His Spirit Angels greet; and ours be hope
> That, if the Sufferer rise from his sick-bed,
> Hence he will gain a firmer mind, to cope
> With a bad world, and foil the Tempter's arts.

The Rector of Trowbridge writes to Sarah Hoare from Beccles about Lady Visitors to the sick - 3rd December 1825.

4. Their great doctrine is the universal depravity of the whole human race in consequence of Adam's Transgression. They dwell upon this long and earnestly and they find a ready acquiescence, for who much minds his portion and part of a general debt; yet I believe, the endeavour and the difficulty is in bringing on conviction, and a lively sense of this depravity, and when this feeling is brought on, the rest is easy and at hand. 'As in Adam all die, so in Christ etc.' The great points to be gained are the terrors of conviction and the joys that result from a full sense of justification, and without these I doubt whether these converters of their brethren reckon them safe, at least so I have found in some cases, and one not long since when a zealot of this class told me, I might go to so and so and do what I could,

but he was as dead as a stone and had no feeling of religion more than the bed he groaned upon and she thought so. The poor man's convictions were not lively, and his hopes were humble and his expressions cold and timid - the conversions which they try for and pray for are conversions of the heart, that is of the feelings and they succeed because it is not difficult to excite first the Terrors and then the Exaltations of spirits so agitated and by such people.

Our ministers do not succeed in this manner nor can it be: they are on duty and not as the ladies on a voluntary 'mission'. This is no small matter. In general we think it our business to enquire into and dwell upon the actual sins of the visited and to excite his horrors of them and their consequences, rather than the general depravity of which we can speak so very little and of which our Lord and Redeemer spoke nothing: this is not agreeable to the self love of man and is not the popular way of dealing with him and his offences. Then we ask no questions respecting the feelings, but as well as we can speak to the understanding. We read the service in the Prayer Book and we judge it right to speak of conditions of acceptance which a Calvinist will not admit: we tell men that repentance is necessary and a virtuous and religious life for the future and for this we inform them that grace will be given if faithfully asked and the life regulated by the rules and precepts of ye Gospel.

The philosopher Square and Parson Thwackum discuss the disposition of Squire Allworthy's will, which in his sickness he has revealed to them.

5. About an hour after they had left the sick-room, Square met Thwackum in the hall and accosted him thus: "Well, sir, have you heard any news of your friend since we parted from him?" - "If you mean Mr Allworthy," answered Thwackum, "I think you might rather give him the appellation of your friend; for he seems to me to have deserved that title," - "The title is as good on your side," replied Square, "for his bounty, such as it is, hath been equal to both." - "I should not have mentioned it first," cries Thwackum, "but since you begin, I must inform you I am of a different opinion. There is a wide distinction between voluntary favours and rewards. The duty I have done in his family, and the care I have taken in the education of his two boys, are services for which some men might have expected a greater return. I would not have you imagine I am therefore dissatisfied; for St Paul hath taught me to be content with the little I have. Had the modicum been less, I should have known my duty. But though the Scriptures obliges me to remain contented, it doth not enjoin me to shut my eyes to my own merit, nor restrain me from seeing when I am injured by an unjust comparison." - "Since you provoke me," returned Square, "that injury is done to me; nor did I ever imagine Mr Allworthy had held my friendship so light, as to put me in balance with one who received his wages. I know to what it is owing; it proceeds from those narrow principles which you have been so long endeavouring to infuse into him, in contempt of everything which is great and noble. The beauty and loveliness of friendship is too strong for dim eyes, nor can it be perceived by any other medium than that unerring rule of right, which you have so often endeavoured to ridicule, that you have perverted your friend's understanding." - "I wish," cries Thwackum, in a rage, "I wish, for the sake of his soul, your damnable doctrines have not perverted his faith. It is to this I impute his present behaviour, so unbecoming a Christian. Who but an atheist could think of leaving the world without having first made up his account? without confessing his sins, and receiving that absolution

which he knew he had one in the house duly authorized to give him? He will feel the want of these necessaries when it is too late, when he is arrived at that place where there is wailing and gnashing of teeth. It is then he will find in what mighty stead that heathen goddess, that virtue, which you and all other deists of the age adore, will stand him. He will then summon his priest, when there is none to be found, and will lament the want of that absolution, without which no sinner can be safe." - "If it be so material," says Square, "why don't you present it him of your own accord?" "It hath no virtue," cries Thwackum, "but to those who have sufficient grace to require it. But why do I talk thus to a heathen and an unbeliever? It is you that taught him this lesson, for which you have been well rewarded in this world, as I doubt not your disciple will soon be in the other." - "I know not what you mean by reward," said Square; "but if you hint at that pitiful memorial of our friendship, which he hath thought fit to bequeath me, I despise it; and nothing but the unfortunate situation of my circumstances should prevail on me to accept it."

REFERENCES

1. John Skinner, *Journal of a Somerset Rector*, op. cit.
2. Louise Horton, *Houston*, The White Cross Press 1982.
3. William Wordsworth, *Ecclesiastical Sonnets*, op. cit.
4. *Selected Letters & Journals of George Crabbe,* ed. Thomas C. Faulkner, O.U.P. 1985.
5. Henry Fielding, *The History of Tom Jones*, op. cit., Book V Ch. 8.

CHAPTER 16
The Order for the Burial of the Dead

1. Upon his return to the inn, he found a card inviting him to the funeral of Miss Margaret Bertram, late of Singleside, which was to proceed from her own house to the place of interment in the Greyfriars churchyard, at one o'clock afternoon.

At the appointed hour, Mannering went to a small house in the suburbs to the southward of the city, where he found the place of mourning, indicated, as usual in Scotland, by two rueful figures with long black cloaks, white crapes and hatbands, holding in their hands poles adorned with melancholy streamers of the same description. By two other mutes, who, from their visages, seemed suffering under the pressure of some strange calamity, he was ushered into the diningparlour of the defunct, where the company were assembled for the funeral.

In Scotland, the custom, now disused in England, of inviting the relations of the deceased to the interment, is universally retained. On many occasions this has a singular and striking effect, but it degenerates into mere empty form and grimace, in cases where the defunct has had the misfortune to live unbeloved and die unlamented. - The English service for the dead, one of the most beautiful and impressive parts of the ritual of the Church, would have, in such cases, the effect of fixing the attention, and uniting the thoughts and feelings of the audience present, in an exercise of devotion so peculiarly adapted to such an occasion. But, according to the Scottish custom, if there be not real feeling among the assistants, there is nothing to supply the deficiency, and exalt or rouse the attention; so that a sense of tedious form, and almost hypocritical restraint, is too apt to pervade the company assembled for the mournful solemnity. Mrs Margaret Bertram was unluckily one of those whose good qualities had attached no general friendship. She had no near relations who might have mourned from natural affection, and therefore her funeral exhibited merely the exterior trappings of sorrow.

The priest and clerks meeting the corpse at the entrance of the churchyard and going before it, shall say....

2. It soon came - the blessed day of deliverance, the sad day of bereavement; and in the second week of March they carried him to the grave. He was buried as he had desired: there was no hearse, no mourning-coach; his coffin was borne by twelve of his humbler hearers, who relieved each other by turns. But he was followed by a long procession of mourning friends, women as well as men.

Slowly, amid deep silence, the dark stream passed along Orchard Street, where eighteen months before the Evangelical curate had been saluted with hooting and hisses. Mr Jerome and Mr Landor were the eldest pall-bearers; and behind the coffin, led by Mr Tryan's cousin, walked Janet, in quiet submissive sorrow. She could not feel that he was quite gone from her; the unseen world lay so very near her - it held all that had ever stirred the depths of anguish and joy within her.

It was a cloudy morning, and had been raining when they left Holly Mount; but as they walked, the sun broke out, and the clouds were rolling off in large masses when they entered the churchyard, and Mr Walsh's voice was heard saying, "I am the Resurrection and the Life." The faces were not hard at this funeral; the burial-service was not a hollow form. Every heart there was filled with the memory of a man, who through a self sacrificing life and in painful death, had been sustained by the faith which fills that form with breath and substance.

After Paddy Dignam's funeral.
3. Corney Kelleher stepped aside from his rank and allowed the mourners to plod by.

- Sad occasions, Mr. Kernan began politely.

Mr Bloom closed his eyes and sadly twice bowed his head.

- The others are putting on their hats, Mr Kernan said. I suppose we can do so too. We are the last. This cemetery is a treacherous place.

They covered their heads.

- The reverend gentleman read the service too quickly, don't you think? Mr Kernan said with reproof.

Mr Bloom nodded bravely, looking in the quick bloodshot eyes. Secret eyes, secret searching eyes. Mason, I think: not sure. Beside him again. We are the last. In the same boat. Hope he'll say something else.

Mr Kernan added:

- The service of the Irish church, used in Mount Jerome, is simpler, more impressive, I must say.

Mr Bloom gave prudent assent. The language of course was another thing.

Mr Kernan said with solemnity:

-'I am the resurrection and the life.' That touches a man's inmost heart.

- It does, Mr Bloom said.

He continues with his own private irreligious reflections, but the point has been made.

After they are come into the church, shall be read one or both of these Psalms following: 39 and 90.

4. Lord Peter watched the coffin borne up the road.

"Here comes my problem," said he to himself, "going to earth on the shoulders of six stout fellows. Finally, this time, I suppose, and I don't seem to have got very much out of it. What a gathering of the local worthies - and how we are all enjoying it! Except dear old Venables - he's honestly distressed . . . This everlasting tolling makes your bones move in your body . . . Tailor Paul . . . Tailor Paul . . . two mortal tons of bawling bronze . . . 'I am the Resurrection and the Life . . .' that's all rather sobering. This chap's first resurrection was ghastly enough - let's hope there won't be another this side of Doomsday . . . Silence that dreadful bell! . . . Tailor Paul . . . though even that might happen, if Lubbock finds anything funny . . . 'Though after my skin worms destroy this body . . .' How queer that fellow Thoday looks . . . something wrong there, I shouldn't wonder . . . Tailor Paul . . . 'We brought nothing into this world and it is certain we can carry nothing out . . .' except our secrets, old Patriarch; we take those with us all right." The deep shadows of the porch swallowed up priest, corpse and bearers, and Wimsey, following with Mrs Venables, felt how strange it was that he and she should follow that strange corpse as sole and unexpected mourners.

"And people may say what they like," thought Wimsey again, "about the services of the Church of England, but there was genius in the choosing of these psalms. 'That I may be certified how long I have to live' - what a terrifying prayer! Lord, let me never be certified of anything of the kind. 'A stranger with Thee and a sojourner' - that's a fact, God knows . . . 'Thou hast set our misdeeds before Thee' . . . very likely, and why should I, Peter Wimsey, busy myself with digging them up? I haven't got so very much to boast about myself, if it comes to that . . . Oh well! . . . 'world without end, Amen.'"

5. Fanny Peronett was dead. That much her husband Hugh Peronett was certain of as he stood in the rain beside the grave which was shortly to receive his wife's mortal remains. Further than that, Hugh's certainty did not reach. . . .

We brought nothing into this world and it is certain we can carry nothing out.

It was true that Fanny had brought nothing into this world. On the other hand she had had plenty of things waiting for her when she arrived. It was many years now since Hugh had stopped wondering to what extent he had married for money. . . .

For man walketh in a vain shadow, and disquieteth himself in vain: he heapeth up riches and cannot tell who shall gather them.

Hugh hoped that the children were not too disappointed about Fanny's will. She had left everything to him and nothing to them, which was characteristic of her and perfectly right. . . .

When thou with rebukes dost chasten man for sin, thou makest his beauty to consume away, like as it were a moth fretting a garment.

His own beauty, such as it was, had certainly consumed away some time ago. Others of his contemporaries had done better, he reflected, . . .

The days of our age are three score years and ten.

Fanny had not lived out her appointed span. The cancer came sooner. And he himself had yet another three years to go. Well, Fanny had lived, she had married a distinguished man, she had borne children, she had loved her husband and her children and her grandchildren and her cats and dogs. She had been, he supposed, happy. . . .

Thou hast set our misdeeds before thee: and our secret sins in the light of thy countenance.

It was just as well he reflected that most of her own *were*, fortunately, secret. Yes, he had passed as a good husband. . . .

He passed slowly along the line of cars. He passed Randall's Vauxhall and Felix Meecham's very dark blue Mercedes. Here at last was his own clumsy capacious Standard Vanguard. *O spare me a little, that I may recover my strength: before I go hence and be no more seen.*

Then shall follow the lesson taken out of the fifteenth chapter of the former Epistle of St. Paul to the Corinthians.

6. Margaret Anstruther was buried on the next day but one, to the sound of that apostolic trumpet which calls on all its hearers to rise from the dead, and proclaims the creation on earth of celestial bodies, "sown in corruption, raised in incorruption; sown in dishonour, raised in glory; sown in weakness, raised in power". "Be steadfast, unmovable . . . your labour is not in vain in the Lord." Pauline heard with a new attention; these were no longer promises, but facts. She dared not use the awful phrases for herself; only, shyly, she hoped that perhaps, used by some other heavenly knowledge, they might not be altogether inapplicable to herself. The epigram of experience which is in all dogma hinted itself within her. But more than these passages another stranger imagination struck her heart: "Why are they then baptized for the dead?" There, rooted in the heart of the Church at its freshest, was the same strong thrust of interchange. Bear for others; be baptized for others; and, rising as her new vision of the world had done once and again, an even more fiery mystery of exchange rolled through her horizons, turning and glancing on her like the eyed and winged wheels of the prophet.

The central mystery of Christendom, the terrible fundamental substitution on which so much learning had been spent and about which so much blood had been shed, showed not as a miraculous exception, but as the root of a universal rule . . . "behold, I shew you a mystery", as supernatural as that Sacrifice, as natural as carrying a bag. She flexed her fingers by her side as if she thought of picking one up.

7. The ashes of Rudyard Kipling were buried in Westminster Abbey on 23rd January 1936.

He was interred in Poets' Corner. The service was moving and impressive: "I am the Resurrection," "I know that my Redeemer liveth," and "We brought nothing into this world."

The bier was brought from St Faith's Chapel. It was covered with the Union Jack, on which rested 4 wreathes. Beneath the flag was the marble casket containing the dead poet's ashes. The Prime Minister was among the pall-bearers, and the bier rested between lighted candles at the altar steps. Psalm 121, "I will lift up mine eyes," was sung. The Lesson from 1 Corinthians 15, was in perfect sympathy with Kipling's character, and St Paul's robust pleas for immortality rang through the transept. It was followed by 'Abide with me' and the lovely hymn was rendered with haunting beauty.

The Dean spoke the words of committal, and the white marble urn was removed from the bier and lowered into the grave.

Nearly mid-day 11-12 miles south of One Ton
8. We have found them - to say it has been a ghastly day cannot express it - it is too bad for words. The tent was there, about half a mile to the west of our course, and close to a drifted up cairn of last year. It was covered with snow and looked just like a cairn, only an extra gathering of snow showing where the ventilator was, and so we found the door. . . .

Scott lay in the centre, Bill on his left, with his head towards the door, and Birdie on his right, lying with his feet towards the door.

Bill especially had died very quietly with his hands folded over his chest. Birdie also quietly.

We have everything - records, diaries etc. They have among other things several roles of photographs, a meteorological log kept up to March 13, and considering all things, a great many geological specimens. *And they have stuck to everything.* It is magnificent that men in such case should go on putting everything that they have died to gain. I think they realized their coming end a long time before. By Scott's head was tobacco: there is also a bag of tea.

Atkinson gathered everyone together and read to them the account of Oates' death given in Scott's Diary: Scott expressly states that he wished it known. Scott's last words are:

'For God's sake, take care of our people.'

Then Atkinson read the lesson from the Burial Service from Corinthians. Perhaps it has never been read in a more magnificent cathedral and under more impressive circumstances - for it is a grave which kings must envy. Then some prayers from the Burial Service: and there with the floor-cloth under them and the tent above we buried them in their sleeping bags, - and surely their work has not been in vain.

When they come to the grave, the Priest shall say . . .

9. And now the range of marshes lay clear before us, with the sails of the ships on the river growing out of it; and we went into the churchyard, close to the graves of my unknown parents, Philip Pirrip, late of this parish, and Also Georgiana, Wife of the Above. And there, my sister was laid quietly in the earth while the larks sang high above it, and the light wind strewed it with beautiful shadows of clouds and trees.

Of the conduct of the worldly-minded Pumblechook while this was doing, I desire to say no more than it was all addressed to me; and that even when those noble passages were read which reminded humanity how it brought nothing into the world and can take nothing out, and how it fleeth like a shadow and never continueth long in one stay, I heard him cough a reservation of the case of a young gentleman who came unexpectedly into a large property. When we got back, he had the hardihood to tell me that he wished my sister could have known I had done her so much honour, and to hint that she would have considered it reasonably purchased at the price of her death.

10. The funeral of Stanley Spencer took place today at Cookham. His body was cremated yesterday and the little box containing his ashes was brought to Cookham. . . .

The service in the church concluding, we went out to the churchyard for the burial of the ashes. A little hole in the grass, a foot deep or so, was ready to receive the box. Mr Westropp then read the final passages of the service and, after the words 'earth to earth', and slightly stressing the words 'ashes to ashes', he placed the box in the hole. This part was much less heartrending than the usual lowering of the coffin into a dug grave. . . . Nevertheless the occasion had its poignancy. There was too the beauty of the language. When I heard the sentence: 'I heard a voice from heaven, saying unto me write' (From henceforth blessed are the dead which die in the Lord: even so saith the Spirit; for they rest from their labours), I was much affected.

THE PRAYERS

11. *Boswell*: "When a man is the aggressor, and by ill usage forces on a duel in which he is killed, have we not little ground to hope that he is gone to a state of happiness?"

Johnson: "Sir, we are not to judge determinately of the state in which a man leaves this life. He may in a moment have repented effectively, and it is possible may have been accepted of God. There is in 'Camden's Remains', an epitaph upon a very wicked man who was killed by a fall from his horse, in which he is supposed to say:-

'Between the stirrup and the ground
I mercy ask'd, I mercy found'"

Boswell: "Is not the expression in the Burial Service, -

'in *sure* and *certain* hope of a blessed resurrection,' - too strong to be used indiscriminately, and, indeed, sometimes when those over whose bodies it is said have been notoriously profane?"

Johnson: "It is sure and certain *hope*, Sir, not *belief*."

I did not insist further; but cannot help thinking that less positive words would be more proper.

12. Feet were stilled, hats were removed, hands folded and skirts rustled into quietness as Ashley stepped forward with Carreen's worn Book of Devotions in his hand. He stood for a moment looking down, the sun glittering on his golden head. A deep silence fell on the crowd, so deep that the harsh whisper of the wind in the magnolia leaves came clear to their ears and the far-off repetitious note of a mockingbird sounded unendurably loud and sad. Ashley began to read the prayers and all heads bowed as his resonant, beautifully modulated voice rolled out the brief and dignified words.

"Oh!" thought Scarlett, her throat constricting, "How beautiful his voice is! If anyone has to do this for Pa, I'm glad its Ashley. I'd rather have him than a priest. I'd rather have Pa buried by one of his own folks than a stranger."

When Ashley came to the part of the prayers concerning the souls in Purgatory, which Carreen had marked for him to read, he abruptly closed the book. Only Carreen noticed the omission and looked up puzzled, as he began the Lord's Prayer. Ashley knew that half the people present had never heard of Purgatory and those who had would take it as a personal affront, if he insinuated, even in prayer, that so fine a man as Mr O'Hara had not gone straight to Heaven. So, in deference to public opinion, he skipped all mention of Purgatory. The gathering joined heartily in the Lord's Prayer but their voices trailed off into embarrassed silence when he began the Hail Mary. They had never heard that prayer and they looked furtively at each other as the O'Hara girls, Melanie and the Tara servants gave the response: "Pray for us, now and at the hour of our death. Amen."

Then Ashley raised his head and stood for a moment, uncertain. The eyes of the neighbors were expectantly upon him as they settled themselves in easier positions for a long harangue. They were waiting for him to go on with the service, for it did not occur to any of them that he was at the end of the Catholic prayers. County funerals were always long. The Baptist and Methodist ministers who performed them had no set prayers but extemporized as the circumstances demanded and seldom stopped before all mourners were in tears and the bereaved feminine relatives screaming with grief. The neighbors would have been shocked, aggrieved and indignant, had these brief prayers been all the service over the body of their loved friend, and no one knew this better than Ashley. The matter would be discussed at dinner tables for weeks and the opinion of the County would be that the O'Hara girls had not shown proper respect for their father.

So he threw a quick apologetic glance at Carreen and, bowing his head again, began reciting from memory the Episcopal burial service which he had often read over slaves buried at Twelve Oaks.

"I am the Resurrection and Life . . . and whosoever . . . believeth in Me shall never die."

It did not come back to him readily and he spoke slowly, occasionally falling silent for a space as he waited for phrases to rise from his memory. But this measured delivery made his words more impressive, and mourners who had been dry-eyed before began now to reach for handkerchiefs. Sturdy Baptists and Methodists all, they thought it the Catholic ceremony and immediately rearranged their first opinion that the Catholic services were cold and Popish. Scarlett and Suellen were equally ignorant and thought the words comforting and beautiful. Only Melanie and Carreen realized that a devoutly Catholic Irishman was being laid to rest by the Church of England's service. And Carreen was too stunned by grief and her hurt at Ashley's treachery to interfere.

REFERENCES

1. Walter Scott, *Guy Mannering*, T.C. and E.C. Jack 1815, Ch. 37.
2. George Eliot, *Scenes of Clerical Life*, Wm Blackwood & Sons 1858, Janet's Repentance.
3. James Joyce, *Ulysses*, The Bodley Head 1936, p. 133.
4. Dorothy L. Sayers, *The Nine Tailors*, op. cit., The Third Part.
5. Iris Murdoch, *An Unofficial Rose*, Chatto & Windus 1962, Ch. 1.
6. Charles Williams, *Descent into Hell*, Faber & Faber Ltd. 1937, Ch. 11.
7. Lord Birkenhead, *Rudyard Kipling*, Weidenfeld & Nicholson 1978.
8. Apsley Cherry-Garrard, *The Worst Journey in the World*, Constable 1922, Vol. 2 Ch. XVI.
9. Charles Dickens, *Great Expectations*, Chapman & Hall 1861, Ch. 35.
10. *Diaries of Maurice Collis*, op. cit., 18 December 1959.
11. James Boswell, *The Life of Samuel Johnson*, op. cit., 2nd Vol. April 1783.
12. Margaret Mitchell, *Gone with the Wind*, Tho MacMillan Cy. 1936.

CHAPTER 17
The Thanksgiving of Women
After Child-Birth

Commonly called The Churching of Women.

1. Well Mrs Crump's little grandchild was born, entirely to the dissatisfaction, I must say, of his father; who, when the infant was brought to him in the Fleet, had him abruptly covered up in his cloak again, from which he had been removed by the jealous prison door-keeper; why, do you think? Walker had a quarrel with one of them, and the wretch persisted in believing that the bundle Mrs Crump was bringing to her son-in-law was a bundle of disguised brandy.

"The brutes!" said the lady; "and the father's a brute too," said she. "He takes no more notice of me than if I was a kitchen-maid, and of Woolsey than if he was a leg of mutton - the dear, blessed little cherub!"

Mrs Crump was a mother-in-law; let us pardon her hatred of her daughter's husband.

The Woolsey compared in the above sentence both to a leg of mutton and a cherub, was not the eminent member of the firm of Linsey, Woolsey & Co., but the little baby, who was christened Howard Woolsey Walker, with the full consent of the father, who said the tailor was a deuced good fellow, and felt really obliged to him for the sherry, for a frock-coat which he let him have in prison, and for his kindness to Georgiana. The tailor loved the little boy with all his soul; he attended his mother to her churching, and the child to the font; and, as a present to his little godson on his christening, he sent two yards of the finest white kerseymere in his shop to make him a cloak. The duke had had a pair of inexpressibles off that very piece.

Lord's Day
2. Up, and I to church, where I have not been these many weeks before; and there did first find a strange Reader, who could not find in the service-book the place for the churching of women, but was fair to change books with the Clerke.

Elizabeth Mapp-Flint seeks to give the impression that she is pregnant.
3. Already she had enjoyed precedence as a bride, but this new precedence quite outshone so conventional a piece of etiquette. Benjy partook of it to a minor degree, for fatherhood was just as rare in the Tilling circle as motherhood. He could not look down on Georgie's head, for Georgie was the taller, but he

145

straddled before the fire with legs wide apart and looked down on the rest of him and on the entire persons of Mr Wyse and the Padre. The former must have told his sister, the Contessa Faraglione, of the happy event impending, for she sent a message to Elizabeth of so delicate a nature, about her own first confinement, that Mr Wyse had been totally unable to deliver it himself and entrusted it to his wife. The Contessa also sent Elizabeth a large jar of Italian honey, notable for its nutritious qualities. As for the Padre, he remembered with shame he had suggested that a certain sentence should be omitted from Elizabeth's marriage service, which she had insisted should be read, and he made himself familiar with the form for the Churching of Women.

Dorothy Wordsworth wrote to Mrs Clarkson on July 15th 1803, "Today we have all been at church. Mary was churched and the babe christened."
4. *Thanksgiving after Childbirth*

    Woman! the Power who left His throne on high,
    And deigned to wear the robe of flesh we wear,
    The Power that through the straits of Infancy
    Did pass dependent on maternal care,
    His own humanity with Thee will share,
    Pleased with the thanks that in His People's eye
    Thou offerest up for safe Delivery
    From Childbirth's perilous throes. And should the Heir
    Of thy fond hopes hereafter walk inclined
    To courses fit to make a mother rue
    That ever he was born, a glance of mind
    Cast upon this observance may renew
    A better will; and, in the imagined view
    Of thee thus kneeling, safety he may find.

REFERENCES

1. W.M. Thackeray, *Ravenswing*, O.U.P. 1908, Ch. 6.
2. *The Diaries of Samuel Pepys*, Everyman Library, J.M. Dent 1906, March 29 1668.
3. E.F. Benson, *Lucia's Progress*, op. cit.
4. William Wordsworth, *Ecclesiastical Sonnets*, op. cit.

CHAPTER 18
A Commination

or Denouncing of God's Anger and Judgement against Sinners to be used on the first day of Lent.

The narrator, staying with his friend at Betton Court and perusing volumes of tracts in the Library on a rainy afternoon, comes across a letter from an unnamed clergyman that quotes "That which walks in Betton Wood knows why it walks and why it cries." He persuades his friend to institute enquiries, and he finds a paper his father wrote on the subject from interviewing local people.

1. One, Mrs Emma Frost, was prevailed upon to repeat what her mother had told her. "They say it was a lady of title that married twice over, and her first husband went by the name of Brown, or it might have been Bryan ("Yes, there were Bryans at the Court before it came into our family," Philipson put in), and she removed her neighbour's landmark: leastways she took in a fair piece of the best pasture in Betton parish what belonged by rights to two children as hadn't no one to speak for them, and they say years after she went from bad to worse, and made out false papers to gain thousands of pounds up in London, and at last they were proved in law to be false, and she would have been tried and put to death very like, only she escaped away for the time. But no one can't avoid the curse that's laid on them that removes the landmark, and so we take it she can't leave Betton before someone take and put it right again."

At the end of the paper there was a note to this effect. "I regret that I cannot find any clue to previous owners of the fields adjoining the Wood. I do not hesitate to say that if I could discover their representatives, I should do my best to indemnify them for the wrong done to them in years now long past: for it is undeniable that the Wood is very curiously disturbed in the manner described by the people of the place. In my present ignorance alike of the extent of the land wrongly appropriated, and of the rightful owners, I am reduced to keeping a separate note of the profits derived from this part of the estate, and my custom has been to apply the sum that would represent the annual yield of about five acres to the common benefit of the parish and to charitable uses: and I hope that those who succeed me may see fit to continue this practice."

2. Lady Constantine, if narrowly observed at this time, would have seemed to be deeply troubled in conscience, and particularly after the interview above described. Ash Wednesday occurred in the calendar a few days later, and she went

to morning service with a look of genuine contrition on her emotional and yearning countenance.

Besides herself the congregation consisted only of the parson, clerk, school children, and three old people living on alms, who sat under the reading desk; and thus, when Mr Torkingham blazed forth the denunciatory sentences of the Commination, nearly the whole force of this seemed to descend upon her own shrinking shoulders. Looking across the empty pews she saw thro' the one or two clear panes of the window opposite a youthful figure in the churchyard, and the very feeling against which she had tried to pray returned again irresistibly.

Coleridge wrote a lengthy preface to the excursion into ballad, of which the following is a part, explaining that his interest in the story lay in "finding there a striking proof of the possible effect on the imagination from an Idea violently and suddenly impressed on it."

The mother hates her own daughter, Mary, because she has married Edward, with whom she herself has fallen in love; and now she cannot bear to find that Ellen, Mary's friend, supports and cheers the young couple after their wedding, which she has already cursed. The Commination Curses seem to her a proper occasion to add her own.

3. *The Three Graves: A Fragment of a Sexton's Tale*

    And now Ash Wednesday came - that day
    But few to church repair:
    For on that day you know we read
    The Commination prayer.

    Our late old Vicar, a kind man,
    Once, Sir, he said to me,
    He wished that service was clean out
    Of our good Liturgy.

    The mother walked into the church -
    To Ellen's seat she went:
    Though Ellen always kept her church
    All church days during Lent.

    And gentle Ellen welcomed her
    With courteous looks and mild:
    Thought she, 'What if her heart should melt,
    And all be reconciled!'

    The day was scarcely like a day -
    The clouds were black outright:
    And many a night, with half a moon,
    I've seen the church more light.

    The wind was wild, against the glass
    The rain did beat and bicker;

The church-tower swinging over head,
You scarce could hear the Vicar!

And then and there the mother knelt,
And audibly she cried -
'Oh! may a clinging curse consume
This woman by my side!

Coleridge's friend, Wordsworth, wrote the following sonnet on the service.
4. Shun not this rite, neglected, yea abhorred,
   By some of unreflecting mind, as calling
   Man to curse man, (thought monstrous and appalling).
   Go thou and hear the threatenings of the *Lord*;
   Listening within his Temple see his sword
   Unsheathed in wrath to strike the offender's head,
   Thy own, if sorrow for thy sin be dead,
   Guilt unrepented, parson unimplored.
   Two aspects bears Truth needful for salvation;
   Who knows not *that?* - yet would this delicate age
   Look only on the Gospel's brighter page:
   Let light and dark duly our thoughts employ:
   So shall the fearful words of Commination
   Yield timely fruit of peace and love and joy.

5. Just as he arrived by the garden gate, he saw a cat inside, going into various arched shapes and fiendish convulsions at the sight of his dog George. The dog took no notice, for he had arrived at an age at which all superfluous barking was cynically avoided as a waste of breath - in fact, he never barked even at the sheep except to order, when it was done with an absolutely neutral countenance, as a sort of Commination-service, which, though offensive, had to be gone through once now and then to frighten the flock for their own good.

REFERENCES

1. M.R. James, *The Collected Ghost Stories*, Edward Arnold Ltd. 1931, A Neighbour's Landmark.
2. Thomas Hardy, *Two on a Tower*, op. cit., Ch. 9.
3. S.T. Coleridge, *Poems,* op. cit.
4. William Wordsworth, *Ecclesiastical Sonnets*, op. cit.
5. Thomas Hardy, *Far from the Madding Crowd*, op. cit., Ch. 4.

CHAPTER 19
The Psalms of David

From the Order how the Psalter is appointed to be read:
"Note that the Psalter followeth the division of the Hebrews, and the translation of the great English Bible, set forth and used in the time of King Henry the Eighth and Edward the Sixth."

In 1662 that translation was abandoned in favour of the Authorised Version in the Epistles and Gospels, but not in the Psalms which were at last bound up with the Prayer Book. The Great Bible was chiefly the work of Miles Coverdale and was first published in 1539, ten years before the first Book of Common Prayer. The title-page, said to have been designed by Hans Holbein, shows Thomas Cranmer, below right of the King, placing the Bible into the hands of one of his clergy and saying "Feed the flock of God" (1 Peter 5 v 2). During the next century Coverdale's translation gained a firm hold on the affection of the English people.

1. It was found, it is said, smoother to sing; but this is not a full account of the matter, and it cannot be mere familiarity which gives to the Prayer Book Psalter, with all its errors and imperfections, an incomparable tenderness and sweetness. Rather we may believe that in it we can yet find the spirit of him whose work it mainly is, full of humility and love, not heroic or creative, but patient to accomplish by God's help the task which had been set him to do, and therefore best in harmony with the tenor of our daily lives.

2. No translator had a better ear for the well-turned phrase and for the ring of a sentence. His independent talent appears to best advantage in that occasionally inaccurate yet lovely version of the Psalms which can still be read in the Anglican Prayer Book. The Church of England, fortunate at least in its literary instincts, continued to prefer Coverdale's Psalms even after the appearance of the Authorised Version of the Bible; they are accordingly still sung at matins and evensong, and for this particular purpose could not be bettered. Even in their obscure moments they have the mellow beauty of some ancient, familiar window with slightly jumbled glass; one would scarcely have the imperfections set right.

3. The greater freedom of translation, the introduction of words which may make the sense clearer, the tender rhythm, for the sake of which expansion and paraphrase are not infrequently adopted, are characteristics which with many go far to atone for the inferiority of the version in point of exactness.

[Some examples of expansion:
him that rideth upon the heavens *as it were upon an horse*
like as it were a moth *fretting a garment*
God is a righteous judge, *strong and patient*
day *long, right* early, *round* world
tush, look, fie on thee]

4. Naturally, after all those years singing them, it is the Prayer Book version of the Psalms that still rings in my ears and comes back to me in scraps:

Like as the hart desireth the water-brooks: so longeth my soul after thee, O God.

My soul is athirst for God, yea, even for the living God: when shall I come to appear before the presence of God?

Have mercy upon me, O God, after thy great goodness: according to the multitude of thy mercies do away mine offences.

Wash me throughly from my wickedness: and cleanse me from my sin.

By the waters of Babylon we sat down and wept: when we remembered thee, O Sion.

As for our harps, we hanged them up: upon the trees that are therein.

For they that led us away captive required of us then a song, and melody, in our heaviness: Sing us one of the songs of Sion.

5. But it is when one looks at some of the most famous and best loved of the Psalms that one realizes how working with poetry is, for these translators, a work against the grain. *[The reference is to the new Episcopalian Prayer Book in the U.S.A.].*

In Coverdale's version of Psalm 137, verse 4 is a poignant question: "How shall we sing the Lord's song in a strange land?". This is now "upon an alien soil". In the old version, the alliteration of 'song' and 'strange' points the unendurable contrast; in the new one, the alliterative, syntactical and rhythmic emphasis all falls upon the word 'soil', giving it far more than its due. It is not the fact that they are on 'soil' that bothers the questioners. The meaning seems contorted, for does one think of oneself as singing "upon a soil"? What is the connection? What is "an alien soil"? - something with an inhospitable pH? or moonrock? The old version gives us a simple, emotive and central meaning - "in a strange land" - words that are by no means archaic or hard to understand. A well known utterance is lost, for no reason at all.

And if we look at the new rendition of Psalm 126 we find that some of the best loved and most resonant phrases in the literature of our language have disappeared.

5 Turn our captivity, O Lord: as the rivers in the south.

6 They that sow in tears: shall reap in joy.

7 He that now goeth on his way weeping, and beareth forth good seed: shall doubtless come again with joy, and bring his sheaves with him.

We now have

5 Restore our fortunes, O Lord, like the watercourses of the Negev.

6 Those who sowed with tears will reap with songs of joy.

7 Those who go out weeping, carrying seed, will come again with joy, shouldering their sheaves.

One can accept that the south really refers to the Negev - though the appeal of the south is lost, and the uninstructed may have to hunt through atlases. But "Turn our captivity" is a much deeper utterance than "Restore our fortunes" - which irresistibly smacks of the desires of industrialists whose shares have collapsed. Any connection between the restoration of fortunes and watercourses is to seek - the language gives no clue, whereas in the old version the dramatic "turn" functions as a kind of zeugma. The change of tense from present to past in verse 6 makes the pain less pressing - though the tense shifts again arbitrarily to present tense in the next verse.

It is in verse 7 that one feels the greatest damage has been done. Coverdale's version moves from general to particular, from "they that sow" to the view of an individual sower; presumably to avoid the fashionably dislikeable masculine pronoun, the modern translation makes everything plural, and less intensely focused. The phrase "go out" is simple, but puzzling, as it usually means, colloquially, to go out of doors; "goeth on his way" is clearer. But we have lost the emphasis on the individual who suffers and rejoices; in the older version "bring his sheaves with him" is a beautiful phrase, coming after the affirmation in "doubtless" - an affirmation in the face of bitter sorrow - and the last phrase gives rhythmic emphasis to "bring . . . sheaves . . . him." The climax comes with "sheaves," but the ending "with him" gives point and poignancy; it is the weeping sower who - against reason in one sense, yet in the course of nature, in another - shall ultimately bring the sheaves. The new version gives instead of this poignant simplicity the fussy participle "shouldering" in heavy alliteration with "sheaves"; the attention is not on the fact of the sower's bringing the sheaves with him, but on a group of people's shoulders. The phase makes reader or hearer endeavour suddenly to picture something very literally, and in doing so the triumphant emotional sense is lost. The word *shouldering* shoulders out the sheaves. Could Thackeray have adapted this verse in its new form as he did the old one in that memorable speech in *Henry Esmond*?

"Do you know what day it is?" she continued. "It is the 29th of December - it is your birthday! But last year we did not drink it - no, no. My lord was cold, and my Harry was likely to die: and my brain was in a fever, and we had no wine. But now - now you are come again, bringing your sheaves with you, my dear." She burst into a wild flood of weeping as she spoke: she laughed and sobbed on the young man's heart, crying out wildly, "bringing your sheaves with you - your sheaves with you!"

Could Thackeray have had Lady Castlemaine say "now you are come again, shouldering your sheaves"? Maybe - but he could not have used it thrice - the "shouldering" is too full of comical possibilities. The new translators dislike metaphor, and are much happier with the literalisms which release us from too much bondage to the metaphor. That is probably why so many of their translations veer towards the potentially comic, or to understatement and prosy-ness, as in the new "a day in thy courts is better than a thousand in my own room" - where the addition of the last phrase is irresistibly comic, reminiscent of bed-sitter-land - and who wouldn't rather be anywhere else than shut up in one room for a thousand days?

"The Psalter shall be read through once every month, as it is there appointed, both for Morning and Evening Prayer." Because they were used regularly in

153

worship and were written in memorable verse, the Psalms entered into the hearts and minds of English folk, and became part of their private prayer and everyday speech.

Shakespeare was an early beneficiary.

6. Above all, it was the *Psalms* Sunday by Sunday at Morning and Evening Prayer that made a lifelong impression on him. Psalm xc in the Prayer Book version has it: 'we bring our years to an end, as it were a tale that is told'. It is another of those phrases one does not forget - certainly not Shakespeare, with whom it becomes in years to come,

Life is as tedious as a twice-told tale;

or further on still, in *Macbeth*, that life

is a tale

Told by an idiot.

But the effects are sometimes, intentionally, comic. Psalm xcii has, 'They shall also bring forth more fruit in their age: and shall be fat and well-liking.' In *Love's Labour's Lost*, which has a wider range of Scriptural allusions than any other of the early plays, Rosalind describes the young men of the Court of Navarre, 'Well-liking wits they have: gross, gross: fat, fat'. It is the collocation of the words that clangs. Or when Dromio of Syracuse is all mixed-up, in *The Comedy of Errors*, and says, 'Nay, 'tis for me to be patient: I am in adversity', this would raise a laugh from an audience that regularly heard in church, 'that thou mayest give him patience in time of adversity'.

And there are more examples:

"Death, as the Psalmist saith, is certain to all: all shall die", says Justice Shallow to Silence in King Henry IV Part 2, alluding to Psalm 89 v. 47.

In Part 2 of King Henry VI, the King says to the Duke of Gloster,

"God shall be my hope,

My stay, my guide, and lantern to my feet"

reflecting verses from Psalms 39, 18, 68 and 119.

In King Henry V the King gives thanks for the victory of Agincourt

"O God, thy arm was here;

And not to us but to thy arm alone

Ascribe we all"

paraphrasing the first verse of Psalm 115, and one could go on.

Centuries later a writer still felt it appropriate to incorporate phrases from the Psalms in the conversation of Dorset rustics. Joseph Poorgrass is urged to show himself a man of spirit.

7. "Show myself a man of spirit? . . . Ah well! let me take the name of drunkard humbly - let me be a man of contrite knees - let it be! I know that I always do say, "Please God" afore I do anything, from my getting up to my going down of the same, and I be willing to take as much disgrace as there is in that holy act. Hah, yes! - but not a man of spirit? Have I ever allowed the toe of pride to be lifted against my hinder parts without groaning manfully that I question the right to do so? I enquire that query boldly."

8. "What a pucker everything is in!" said Bathsheba discontentedly, when the child had gone. "Get away, Mary Ann, or go on with your scrubbing, or do something. You ought to be married by this time, and not here troubling me!"

"Ay, mistress - so I did. But what between poor men I won't have, and the rich men who won't have me, I stand as a pelican in the wilderness."

Rowland Prothero's book "The Psalms in human life", published in 1903, gives a comprehensive picture of the way in which the Psalms (not only in Coverdale's version) have provided men and women with thoughts and words by which to express the whole gamut of their relationship with God. Of course, some psalms express feelings which are better overcome, and not all psalms can be used in Christian prayer without ingenious allegorising. But even these can be used to good effect by literary men.

9. "Make them like unto a wheel" is a bitter sarcasm, as all the learned know, against the grand tour, and that restless spirit would haunt the children of men in the latter days; and therefore, as thinketh the great Bishop Hall, 'tis one of the severest imprecations which David ever uttered against the enemies of the Lord - and, as if he had said, "I wish them no worse luck than always to be rolling about" - so much motion, continues he (for he was very corpulent) - is so much unquietness; and so much rest, by the same analogy, is so much of heaven.

10. Dr Haynes, the Archdeacon, records in his diary:

"*Oct. 22* - At evening prayers, during the Psalms, I had that same experience which I recollect from last year. I was resting my hand on one of the carved figures, as before (I usually avoid that of the cat now), and - I was going to have said - a change came over it, but that seems attributing too much importance to what must, after all, be due to some physical affection in myself: at any rate, the wood seemed to become chilly and soft as if made of wet linen. I can assign the moment at which I became sensible of this. The choir were singing the words (*Set thou an ungodly man to be ruler over him and) let Satan stand at his right hand.*

"The whispering in my house was more persistent to-night. I seemed not to be rid of it in my room. I have not noticed this before. A nervous man, which I am not, and hope I am not becoming, would have been much annoyed, if not alarmed, by it. The cat was on the stairs to-night. I think it sits there always. There *is* no kitchen cat."

While on holiday, Mr Davidson, through a chance meeting, decides to visit the chapel at Brockstone Court.

11. Even if Brockstone Court has not been illustrated in *Rural Life* (and I think it has not), I do not propose to point out its excellences here; but of the Chapel a word must be said. It stands about a hundred yards from the house, and has its own little graveyard and trees about it. It is a stone building about seventy feet long, and in the Gothic style, as that style was understood in the middle of the seventeenth century. On the whole it resembles some of the Oxford college chapels as much as anything, save that it has a distinct chancel, like a parish church, and a fanciful domed bell-turret at the south-west angle.

When the west door was thrown open, Mr Davidson could not repress an exclamation of pleased surprise at the completeness and richness of the interior.

Screen-work, pulpit, seating, and glass - all were of the same period; and as he advanced into the nave and sighted the organ-case with its gold embossed pipes in the western gallery, his cup of satisfaction was filled. The glass in the nave windows was chiefly armorial; and in the chancel were figure-subjects, of the kind that may be seen at Abbey Dore, of Lord Scudamore's work.

But this is not an archaeological review.

While Mr Davidson was still busy examining the remains of the organ (attributed to one of the Dallams, I believe), old Mr Avery had stumped up into the chancel and was lifting the dust-cloths from the blue-velvet cushions of the stall-desks. Evidently it was here that the family sat.

Mr Davidson heard him say in a rather hushed tone of surprise, "Why, Mary, here's all the books open agin!"

The reply was in a voice that sounded peevish rather than surprised. "Tt-tt-tt, well, there, I never!"

Mrs Potter went over to where her father was standing, and they continued talking in a lower key. Mr Davidson saw plainly that something not quite in the common run was under discussion; so he came down the gallery stairs and joined them. There was no sign of disorder in the chancel any more than in the rest of the Chapel, which was beautifully clean; but the eight folio Prayer-Books on the cushions of the stall-desks were indubitably open.

Mrs Porter was inclined to be fretful over it. "Whoever can it be as does it?" she said: "for there's no key but mine, nor yet door but the one we come in by, and the winders is barred, every one of 'em; I don't like it, father, that I don't."

"What is it, Mrs Porter? Anything wrong?" said Mr Davidson.

"No sir, nothing reely wrong, only these books. Every time, pretty near, that I come in to do up the place, I shuts 'em and spreads the cloths over 'em to keep off the dust, ever since Mr Clark spoke about it, when I first come; and yet there they are again, and always the same page - and as I says, whoever it can be as does it with the door and winders shut; and as I says, it makes anyone feel queer comin' in here alone, as I 'ave to do, not as I'm given that way myself, not to be frightened easy, I mean to say; and there's not a rat in the place - not as no rat wouldn't trouble to do a thing like that, do you think, sir?"

"Hardly, I should say; but its sounds very queer. Are they always open at the same place, did you say?"

"Always the same place, sir, one of the psalms it is, and I didn't particular notice it the first time or two, till I see a little red line of printing, and it's always caught my eye since."

Mr Davidson walked along the stalls and looked at the open books. Sure enough, they all stood at the same page: Psalm cix., and at the head of it, just between the number and the *Deus laudum*, was a rubric, "For the 25th day of April." Without pretending to minute knowledge of the history of the Book of Common Prayer, he knew enough to be sure that this was a very odd and wholly unauthorized addition to its text; and though he remembered that April 25 is St Mark's Day, he could not imagine what appropriateness this very savage psalm could have to that festival. With slight misgivings he ventured to turn over the leaves to examine the title-page, and knowing the need for particular accuracy in these matters, he devoted some ten minutes to making a line-for-line transcript of it. The date was 1653; the printer called himself Anthony Cadman. He turned to the list of proper psalms for certain days; yes, added to it was that same inexplicable entry: *For the 25th day of April: the 109th Psalm.* An expert would no doubt have thought of many other points to inquire into, but this antiquary, as I have said, was no expert. He took stock, however, of the binding - a handsome one of tooled blue leather, bearing the arms that figured in several of the nave windows in various combinations.

"How often," he said at last to Mrs Porter, "have you found these books lying open like this?"

"Reely I couldn't say, sir, but it's a great many times now."

REFERENCES

1. Unattributed quotation in W.F. Moulton, *The History of the English Bible,* Epworth Press 1937.
2. A.G. Dickens, *The English Reformation,* B.T. Batsford Ltd. 1964.
3. W.F. Moulton, *The History of the English Bible,* op. cit.
4. A.L. Rowse, *A Cornish Childhood,* op. cit., Ch. Church.
5. Margaret Moody, 'How shall we sing the Lord's song', in *The State of the Language,* eds C. Ricks & L. Michaels, University of California Press 1980.
6. A.L. Rowse, *William Shakespeare,* op. cit.
7. Thomas Hardy, *Far from the Madding Crowd,* op. cit. Ch. 42 (Ps. 113 & 36).
8. Ibid, op. cit., Ch. 9 (Ps. 102).
9. Laurence Sterne, *Tristram Shandy,* op. cit., Book 7 Ch. 13 (Ps. 83).
10. M.R. James, *The Collected Ghost Stories,* op. cit., The Stalls of Barchester Cathedral (Ps. 109).
11. Ibid, The Uncommon Prayer Book.

The Village Choir
Thomas Webster 1847

CHAPTER 20
Interlude: 'Psalms and Hymns and Spiritual Songs'

During the first three centuries that followed the publication of the first Book of Common Prayer the only additions made to its use for Sunday worship were the metrical psalms. In King Henry VIII's reign Thomas Sternhold began to put the psalms into simple verse, and in 1562 a collection known as the 'Old Version' by Sternhold and Hopkins appeared. It received official sanction by being bound up with the Prayer Book: "set forth and allowed to be sung in all churches, of all the people together, before and after Morning and Evening Prayer and also before and after sermons, and moreover in private houses for their godly solace and comfort, laying apart all ungodly songs and ballads, which tend only to the nourishing of vice and corrupting of youth," said Convocation on December 20th 1661.

Psalm 67 is rendered thus:

Have mercy on us, Lord
and grant to us thy grace
To show to us do thou accord
the brightness of thy face,
That all the earth may know
the way to godly wealth
And all the nations on a row
May see thy saving health. . . .

Tunes were given, and the metrical psalms became popular because of the ease with which they could be sung; but to the fastidious ear the translation, and perhaps the singing, was appalling:

Sternhold and Hopkins had great qualms,
When they translated David's psalms,
To make the heart right glad:
But had it been King David's fate
To hear thee sing and then translate,
By God! 'twould set him mad!

wrote the Earl of Rochester.

In 1696 a version by Tate and Brady was published also.

John Merbecke had published his "Book of Common Prayer noted" in 1550. "In this book is contained so much of the order of Common Prayer as is to be sung in churches, wherein are used only these 4 sorts of notes. . . .", but after the fifteen years under the Commonwealth, when the Prayer Book was banned, this greater skill of singing the canticles and Coverdale's Psalms seems only to have survived in cathedrals and chapels royal where anthems were also sung, a specific place being allotted to the latter in the 1662 Book. Only the versicles and responses at Morning and Evening Prayer continued to be sung in humbler churches, (the responses being led, not always successfully, by the Parish Clerk) along with the metrical psalms.

As time went by choirs were formed in churches throughout the country. They were accompanied by a variety of instrumentalists, depending on local talent, and, where possible, used the gallery at the west end of the nave.

In the eighteenth century Isaac Watts, the Wesleys, William Cowper and others published hymns they had written, and these quickly became popular. They received official approval for use at church services through a judgement by the Archbishop of York in 1820, when Thomas Cotterill, a Sheffield incumbent, was accused of introducing his own hymn book. He had to withdraw the book, but the Archbishop paid for a new edition out of his own pocket on condition that he supervised the publication. By 1800 organs were starting to replace the violin, cello and bassoon.

As a result of the Oxford Movement, the second half of the nineteenth century saw great changes in the style of Sunday services with surpliced choirs filling the chancel and an organ close by. Coverdale's psalms and the canticles were sung to "Anglican Chant", and from 1861 Hymns Ancient and Modern was available to augment the church's worship. As the English Hymnal expressed it in its first edition in 1906, "Here is a collection of the best hymns in the English language, which is offered as a humble companion to the Book of Common Prayer for use in church." In Anglo-Catholic churches a sung eucharist replaced mattins and choirs sang elaborate settings of the liturgy. However, with the growth of the Parish Communion movement in this century the wheel came full circle as congregations joined enthusiastically in the original settings of John Merbecke.

1. "There was one other feature of that service not to be forgotten. When the sermon was ended, and I had lost sight of the last grass-hopper in my hasty rising, we found that there was to be a hymn. It was the old custom of this church so to conclude Evening Prayer. No one seemed to use a book - it was Bishop Ken's evening hymn, (Glory to Thee, my God this night) which every one knew, and, I think, every one sang. But the feature of it to us was when the Irishman began to sing. From her startled glance, I think not even the red-haired young lady had known that he possessed so beautiful a voice. It had a clearness without effort, a tone, a truth, a pathos, such as I have not often heard. It sounded strangely above the nasal tones of the schoolchildren, and the scraping of a solitary fiddle. Even our neighbour, who had lustily followed the rhythm of the tune, though without much varying from the note on which he responded, softened his own sounds and turned to look at the Irishman, who sang on without noticing it, till, in the last verse, he seemed disturbed to discover how many eyes were on him. Happily, self-consciousness had come too late. The hymn was ended.

We knelt again for the Benediction, and then went back through the summer fields."

2. *A Church Romance*
   (*Mellstock: circa 1835*)
   She turned in the high pew, until her sight

Swept the west gallery, and caught its row
Of music-men with viol, book, and bow
Against the sinking sad tower-window light.

She turned again; and in her pride's despite
One strenuous viol's inspirer seemed to throw
A message from his string to her below,
Which said: "I claim thee as my own forthright!"

Thus their hearts' bond began, in due time signed.
And long years thence, when Age had scared Romance,
At some old attitude of his or glance
That gallery-scene would break upon her mind,
With him as minstrel, ardent, young, and trim,
Bowing "New Sabbath" or "Mount Ephraim."

*Mellstock is the name also used in Hardy's novel, 'Under the Greenwood Tree',
its subtitle being 'The Mellstock Quire'. In his preface to the novel, written in 1896,
he says that the story of the choir and musicians gives a "fairly true picture of what
was common fifty or sixty years ago", and expresses his regrets at the changes
which the novel describes.*

3. One is inclined to regret the displacement of these ecclesiastical bandsmen by
an isolated organist (often at first a barrel-organist) or harmonium player; and
despite certain advantages in point of control and accomplishment which were, no
doubt, secured by installing the single artist, the change has tended to stultify the
professed aims of the clergy, its direct result being to curtail and extinguish the
interest of parishioners in church doings. Under the old plan, from half a dozen to
ten full-grown players, in addition to the numerous more or less grown-up singers,
were officially occupied with the Sunday routine, and concerned in trying their
best to make it an artistic outcome of the combined musical taste of the congregation. With a musical executive limited, as it mostly is limited now, to the parson's
wife or daughter and the school-children, or to the school-teacher and the children,
an important union of interests has disappeared.

The choir assemble.

4. Old William sat in the centre of the front row, his violoncello between his knees
and two singers on each hand. Behind him, on the left, came the treble singers and
Dick; and on the right the tranter and the tenors. Further back was old Mail with the
altos and supernumeraries.
*[Dick was the treble violin, Reuben, his father, the tranter, the tenor violin, and
Michael Mail, the second violin.]*

The Vicar has plans to replace them with his own organ.

5. The tranter cleared his throat after this accidental parenthesis about Leaf, rectified
his bodily position, and began his speech.

'Mr Mayble,' he said, 'I hope you'll excuse my common way but I always like
to look things in the face.'

Reuben made a point of fixing this sentence in the vicar's mind by gazing hard at him at the conclusion of it, and then out of the wndow.

Mr Maybold and old William looked in the same direction, apparently under the impression that the things' faces alluded to were there visible.

'What I have been thinking' - the tranter implied by this use of the past tense that he was hardly so discourteous as to be positively thinking it then - 'is that the quire ought to be gie'd a little time, and not done away wi' till Christmas, as a fair thing between man and man. And, Mr. Mayble, I hope you'll excuse my common way?'

'I will, I will. Till Christmas,' the vicar murmured, stretching the two words to a great length, as if the distance to Christmas might be measured in that way. 'Well, I want you all to understand that I have no personal fault to find, and that I don't wish to change the church music by forcible means, or in a way which should hurt the feelings of any parishioners. Why I have at last spoken definitely on the subject is that a player has been brought under - I may say pressed upon - my notice several times by one of the churchwardens. And as the organ I brought with me is here waiting' (pointing to a cabinet-organ standing in the study), 'there is no reason for longer delay.'

'We made a mistake I suppose then, sir? But we understood the young woman didn't want to play particularly?' The tranter arranged his countenance to signify that he did not want to be inquisitive in the least.

'No, nor did she. Nor did I definitely wish her to just yet; for your playing is very good. But, as I said, one of the churchwardens has been so anxious for a change that, as matters stand, I couldn't consistently refuse my consent.'

Now for some reason or other the vicar at this point seemed to have an idea that he had prevaricated; and as an honest vicar it was a thing he determined not to do. He corrected himself, blushing as he did so, though why he should blush was not known to Reuben.

'Understand me rightly,' he said: 'the churchwarden proposed it to me, but I had thought myself of getting - Miss Daisy to play.'

'Which churchwarden might be that who proposed her, sir? - excusing my common way.' the tranter intimated by his tone that so far from being inquisitive he did not even wish to ask a single question.

'Mr. Shiner, I believe.'

'Clk, my sonny! - beg your pardon, sir, that's only a form of words of mine, and slipped out accidental - he nourishes enmity against us for some reason or another; perhaps because we played rather hard upon en Christmas night. Anyhow 'tis certain sure that Mr. Shiner's real love for music of a partiuclar kind isn't his reason. He've no more ear than that chair. But let that be.'

'I don't think you should conclude that, because Mr. Shiner wants a different music, he has any ill-feeling for you. I myself, I must own, prefer organ-music to any other. I consider it most proper, and feel justified in endeavouring to introduce it; but then, although other music is better, I don't say yours is not good.'

'Well then, Mr. Mayble, since death's to be, we'll die like men any day you name (excusing my common way).'

Mr. Maybold bowed his head.

'All we thought was, that for us old ancient singers to be choked off quiet at no time in particular, as now, in the Sundays after Easter, would seem rather mean in the eyes of other parishes, sir. But if we fell glorious with a bit of a flourish at Christmas, we should have a respectable end, and not dwindle away at some nameless paltry second-Sunday-after or Sunday-next-before something, that's got no name of his own.'

The first time that the organ is used.
6. Thus they parted, and Fanny proceeded to the church. The organ stood on one side of the chancel, close to and under the immediate eye of the vicar when he was in the pulpit and also in full view of the congregation. Here she sat down, for the first time in such a conspicuous position, her seat having previously been in a remote spot in the aisle.

The old choir, with humbled hearts, no longer took their seats in the gallery as heretofore (which was now given up to the school-children who were not singers, and a pupil-teacher), but were scattered about with their wives in different parts of the church. Having nothing to do with conducting the service for almost the first time in their lives they all felt awkward, out of place, abashed, and inconvenienced by their hands. The tranter had proposed that they should stay away to-day and go nutting, but grandfather William would not hear of such a thing for the moment. 'No,' he replied reproachfully, and quoted a verse: '"Though this has come upon us let not our hearts be turned back, or our steps go out of the way."'

So they stood and watched the curls of hair trailing down the back of the successful rival, and the waving of her feather as she swayed her head. After a few timid notes and uncertain touches her playing became markedly correct, and towards the end full and free. But, whether from prejudice or unbiased judgement, the venerable body of musicians could not help thinking that the simpler notes they had been wont to bring forth were more in keeping with the simplicity of their old church than the crowded chords and interludes it was her pleasure to produce.

Sydney Smith writing in the year 1800 in the preface to a collection of his sermons commends the beneficial effect of organs.
7. I am very glad to find that we are calling in more and more the aid of music to our service. In London, where it can be commanded, good music has a prodigious effect in filling a church; organs have been put up in various places in the country, and, as I have been informed, with the best possible effect. Of what value, it may be asked, are auditors who come there from such motives? But our first business seems to be, to bring them there from any motive which is not undignified or ridiculous, and then keep them there from a good one: those who come for pleasure may remain for prayer. . . .

That many greater causes are at work to undermine religion I seriously believe; but I shall probably be laughed at when I say that warm churches, solemn music, animated preaching upon practical matters, and a service some little abridged *[in his day mattins, litany, ante-communion and sermon]* would be no contemptible seconds to the just, necessary and innumerable invectives which have been levelled against Rousseau, Voltaire, D'Alembert and the whole pantheon of those martyrs to atheism who toiled with such laborious malice, and suffered odium with such inflexible profligacy, for the wretchedness and despair of their fellow creatures.

Contemporary with Sydney Smith, Mary, who has been brought up in the Scottish church, experiences worship in the English.

8. They had now reached the church - a grave antique-looking building, whose grey ivy-mantled tower proclaimed, not worldly pomp, but heavenly hope, while its meek low-browed porch seemed to echo the hallowed invitation of Him, whose temple is all space, "Come unto me, all ye that are weary and heavy laden, and I will give you rest."

Mary loved the simple ritual of her native land, but she felt and acknowledged the excellence and impressive solemnity of England's church service. Perhaps in every form of Christian worship, the devout heart will find something suited to its wants; in none will it find all things in perfect accordance with its feelings.

The service was performed in a simple and reverent manner. The prayers were not, perhaps, what is called "beautifully *read*!" but they were felt as the breathings of a lowly, penitent, and devout spirit, in deep prostration in the awful presence of its God. But how discordant - how *unholy* sounded to Mary's unaccustomed ear, the irreverent responses of the clerk, as he gabbled over those sacred echoes which, if heard at all, ought to come from the hearts and lips of a praying people.

The sermon was delivered with the same scriptural simplicity and fervent unction, as coming from the heart of one deeply impressed with the importance of the divine truths he proclaimed, and earnest in enforcing their moral influence in the personal holiness of all who profess to believe them. The organ was good, and Mary felt how well its sublime melody was adapted to solemnize the mind in its approach to God. But the singing was (as is commonly the case) meagre and defective; and surely all must admit that no *merely* instrumental music, however fine that may be, can be so acceptable to the Hearer of prayer and of praise as the voices of his intelligent creatures, combining symphony of voice with sympathy of heart, such as *ought* to be in every Christian congregation. The one, however exquisite, is but the mere vibration of matter on the outward senses, but to render

"The deep worship of the living soul,"

"in the noble psalms of David, as sung by the mingled voices of a large congregation, swelling often to a sublime volume of sound, elevating the mind and quickening the feelings beyond all studied excitements of art," is as the melody of heaven begun upon earth.

Ernest sees the changes taking place as a result of the Oxford Movement.

9. On Sunday Ernest went to church as a matter of course, and noted that the ever-receding tide of Evangelicalism had ebbed many a stage lower, even during the few years of his absence. His father used to walk to the church through the Rectory garden, and across a small intervening field. He had been used to walk in a tall hat, his Master's gown, and wearing a pair of Geneva bands. Ernest noticed that the bands were worn no longer, and lo! greater marvel still, Theobald did not preach in his Master's gown, but in a surplice. The whole character of the service was changed; you could not say it was high even now, for high-church Theobald could never under any circumstances become, but the old easy-going slovenliness, if I may say so, was gone for ever. The orchestral accompaniments to the hymns had disappeared while my hero was yet a boy, but there had been no chanting for some years after the harmonium had been introduced. While Ernest was at Cambridge, Charlotte and Christina had prevailed on Theobald to allow the canticles to be sung;

and sung they were to old-fashioned double chants by Lord Mornington and Dr Dupuis and others. Theobald did not like it, but he did it, or allowed it to be done.

Then Christina said: 'My dear, do you know, I really think' (Christina always 'really' thought) 'that the people like the chanting very much, and that it will be a means of bringing many to church who have stayed away hitherto. I was talking about it to Mrs Goodhew and to old Miss Wright only yesterday, and they *quite* agreed with me, but they all said that we ought to chant the "Glory be to the Father" at the end of each of the psalms instead of saying it.'

Theobald looked black - he felt the waters of chanting rising higher and higher upon him inch by inch; but he felt also, he knew not why, that he had better yield than fight. So he ordered the 'Glory be to the Father' to be chanted in future, but he did not like it.

'Really, mamma dear,' said Charlotte, when the battle was won, 'you should not call it the "Glory be to the Father" you should say "Gloria".'

'Of course, my dear,' said Christina, and she said 'Gloria' for ever after. Then she thought what a wonderfully clever girl Charlotte was, and how she ought to marry no one lower than a bishop. By and by when Theobald went away for an unusually long holiday one summer, he could find no one but a rather high-church clergyman to take his duty. This gentleman was a man of weight in the neighbourhood, having considerable private means, but without preferment. In the summer he would often help his brother clergymen, and it was through his being willing to take the duty at Battersby for a few Sundays that Theobald had been able to get away for so long. On his return, however, he found that the whole psalms were being chanted as well as the Glorias. The influential clergyman, Christina, and Charlotte took the bull by the horns as soon as Theobald returned, and laughed it all off; and the clergyman laughed and bounced, and Christina laughed and coaxed, and Charlotte uttered unexceptionable sentiments, and the thing was done now, and could not be undone, and it was no use grieving over spilt milk; so henceforth the psalms were to be chanted, but Theobald grisled over it in his heart, and he did not like it.

During this same absence what had Mrs Goodhew and old Miss Wright taken to doing but turning towards the east while repeating the Belief? Theobald disliked this even worse than chanting. When he said something about it in a timid way at dinner after service, Charlotte said, 'Really, papa dear, you *must* take to calling it the "Creed" and not the "Belief"'; and Theobald winced impatiently and snorted meek defiance, but the spirit of her aunts Jane and Eliza was strong in Charlotte, and the thing was too small to fight about, and he turned it off with a laugh. 'As for Charlotte,' thought Christina, 'I believe she knows *everything*.' So Mrs Goodhew and old Miss Wright continued to turn to the east during the time the Creed was said, and by and by others followed their example, and ere long the few who had stood out yielded and turned eastward too; and then Theobald made as though he had thought it all very right and proper from the first, but like it he did not. By and by Charlotte tried to make him say 'Alleluia' instead of 'Hallelujah,' but this was going too far, and Theobald turned, and she got frightened and ran away.

And they changed the double chants for single ones, and altered them psalm by psalm, and in the middle of psalms, just where a cursory reader would see no reason why they should do so, they changed from major to minor and from minor back to major; and then they got 'Hymns Ancient and Modern,' and, as I have said, they robbed him of his beloved bands, and they made him preach in a surplice, and he must have celebration of Holy Communion once a month instead of only five times in the year as heretofore.

REFERENCES

1. J.H. Ewing, *Mrs Overtheway's Remembrances*, op. cit.
2. Thomas Hardy, *Collected Poems*, op. cit.
3. Thomas Hardy, *Under the Greenwood Tree*, Macmillan & Co. Ltd.1903.
4. Ibid.
5. Ibid.
6. Ibid.
7. Sydney Smith, *Collected Sermons*, Edinburgh 1800.
8. Susan Ferrier, *Marriage*, Wm Blackwood 1818.
9. Samuel Butler, *The Way of All Flesh*, Grant Richards 1903.

CHAPTER 21
Forms of Prayer to be Used at Sea

These forms are in addition to the ordinary services of Morning and Evening Prayer. The first two, to be used daily, are for the protection of "the Fleet in which we serve" and the post Communion collect, "Prevent us, O Lord, in all our doings with thy most gracious favour. . . ." Then follow prayers and psalms to be used in storms and tempests and after victory.

The retired sea-captain, Edward Cuttle, is anxious about a young friend who has gone to sea, and about whom he has had no news for many months.

1. The captain did not go to bed for a long time. He walked to and fro in the shop and in the little parlour, for a full hour, and appearing to have composed himself by that exercise, sat down with a grave and thoughtful face, and read out of a Prayer Book the Forms of Prayer appointed to be used at sea. These were not easily disposed of; the good Captain being a mighty slow gruff reader, and frequently stopping at a hard word to give himself such encouragement as "Now, my lad! With a will!" or, "Steady, Edward Cuttle, Steady" which had a great effect in helping him out of any difficulty. Moreover, his spectacles greatly interfered with his power of vision. But not withstanding these drawbacks, the Captain, being heartily in earnest, read the service to the last line, and with genuine feeling too; and approving of it very much when he had done, turned in under the counter with a serene breast and most benevolent visage.

2. "A good inspection, Mr Bush," said Hornblower, returning to the quarterdeck. "The ship is in better order than I hoped for. I shall expect the improvement to continue. You may rig the church now."

It was a God-fearing Admiralty who ordered church service every Sunday morning, otherwise Hornblower would have dispensed with it, as befitted a profound student of Gibbon. As it was, he had managed to evade having a chaplain on board - Hornblower hated parsons. He watched the men dragging up mess stools for themselves, and chairs for the officers. They were working diligently and cheerfully, although not with quite that disciplined purposefulness which characterised a fully trained crew. His coxswain Brown covered the compass box on the quarterdeck with a cloth, and laid on it, with due solemnity, Hornblower's Bible and prayer book. Hornblower disliked these services; there was always the chance that some devout member of his compulsory congregation might raise objections to having to attend - Catholic or Nonconformist. Religion was the only power which could ever pit itself against the bonds of discipline; Hornblower remembered a theologically minded master's mate who had once protested against his reading the benediction, as though he, the King's representative at sea - God's representative, when all was said and done - could not read a benediction if he chose!

He glowered at the men as they settled down, and began to read. As the thing had to be done, it might as well be done well, and, as ever, while he read he was struck once more by the beauty of Cranmer's prose and the deftness of his adaptation. Cranmer had been burned alive two hundred and fifty years before - did it benefit him at all to have his Prayer Book read now?

Bush read the lesson in a tuneless bellow as if he were hailing the foretop. Then Hornblower read the opening lines of the hymn, and Sullivan the fiddler played the first bars of the tune. Bush gave the signal for the singing to start - Hornblower could never bring himself to do that; he told himself he was neither a mountebank nor an Italian opera conductor - and the crew opened their throats and roared it out.

Frank, Emmeline and Kate, with small brother Edwin, caught by the tide, have climbed on to a ledge, where they hope to be able to wait until the tide recedes or someone hears their cries for help.
3. Not a word had passed between them as to the danger, yet they felt what was in each other's mind, and no one broke the silence till little Edwin spoke: "Miss Townsend and Jane don't think where I am."

Kate bent down and kissed the little fellow's forehead, and wondered how far he understood his situation; then a thought like his came across her, and she murmured, "O mamma! O, poor Constance."

Frank had all this time been looking out intently on the sea; but on hearing this exclamation, he turned and looked on his sisters, and marking their trembling lips and frightened eyes, he said, "Shall I read something?" He took his little Prayer Book from his waistcoat pocket, and uncovering his head, read, in a low solemn tone, strangely accompanied by the surging rush of the waves, the prayers to be used at sea, beginning with, 'O most glorious and gracious God' -

The girls clasped their hands more tightly together. In their lives never had they so followed any prayer.

4. *Forms of Prayer at Sea*
To kneeling Worshippers no earthly floor
Gives holier invitation than the deck
Of a storm-shattered Vessel saved from Wreck
(When all that Man could do availed no more)
By Him who raised the Tempest and restrains:
Happy the crew who this have felt, and pour
Forth for His mercy, as the Church ordains,
Solemn thanksgiving. Nor will *they* implore
In vain who, for a rightful cause, give breath
To words the Church prescribes aiding the lip
For the heart's sake, ere ship with hostile ship
Encounters, armed for work of pain and death.
Suppliants! the God to whom your cause ye trust
Will listen, and ye know that He is just.

REFERENCES

1. Charles Dickens, *Dombey & Son*, Chapman & Hall 1848, Ch. 49.
2. C.S. Forester, *A Ship of the Line*, Michael Joseph 1938, Ch. 7.
3. C.M. Yonge, *The Castlebuilders*, op. cit., Ch. 12.
4. William Wordsworth, *Ecclesiastical Sonnets*, op. cit.

CHAPTER 22
Finale: Excellent References

The tributes paid to the Book of Common Prayer throughout its history are manifold, and not least in our own day, when its supplanting in a multitude of churches by the Alternative Services Book has given it the status of an endangered species, and what has been taken for granted is being taken away.

Hilaire Belloc, (not the most obvious choice for Cranmer's laudator) writes of the prime author of the Prayer Book.

1. For Cranmer in those years was - unknown to himself - growing to be that artist whose pen touched with magic, years after, the prayers of the new establishment: of an English liturgy which no man in those earlier years could have dreamt of. There was never a writing man yet in prose or verse whose talent did not come to him before his twentieth year, and though Cranmer knew it not, though no man praised him for it throughout all his life, such talent was given him in the writing of English that he made permanent what, but for his prose, could not have lived: the Anglican Liturgy.

See him, then, a youth bent over the desk with peering, short-sighted eyes close to his paper and with slow pen forming himself to that which, after thirty years, was to reach so great a height. See him carefully chiselling the phrase.

For the genius of Cranmer in this supreme art of his - the fashioning of rhythmic English prose - was not of that spontaneous kind which produces great sentences or pages in flashes, as it were, unplanned, surging up of themselves in the midst of lesser matter; he was not among prose writers what such men as Shakespeare or Ronsard are among the poets - voluminous, uneven, and without conscious effort compelled to produce splendours in a process of which they are themselves not aware. He was, on the contrary, a jeweller in prose, a man who sat down deliberately to write in a particular way when there was need or opportunity for it, but who, on general occasions, would write as might any other man. We have a great mass of what he did, in long letters to Boleyn, to the King and to Cromwell, careful arguments transcribed at length in his disputations, as in the famous one with Gardiner on the Real Presence; it is always scholar's work, careful and lucid. But when he sits down to produce a special effect all changes. He begins to carve with skill and in the hardest material. He is absorbed in a particular task, creative, highly conscious, and to his sense of beauty vastly satisfactory.

Cranmer being of such a kind in his work, that work reached heights which none other reached - not even Tyndale, whose great sweeps of rhythm underlie what was, a century after his death, to become the standard English Bible. But, unlike Tyndale

- the other and older great master of prose in that generation which fixed the English tongue - Cranmer's work was deliberately limited, as its very nature demanded. It was set in small frames, as it were, and put apart from all the rest he did. Left to himself, I think he would have spent all his energies upon that one occupation in which he must have known himself to be a master, although contemporaries but vaguely appreciated his unique powers in that one field. For he was not a man to give an impression of power. Indeed, he did not impress at all. He shrank, withdrew, was suave and unguent - also by nature mild in his external manner. His presence did not suggest genius of any kind. When he was forced into public life there fell upon him that penalty of public life, the fixing on a man of a label which has little to do with his real self. He passed for a courtier or a protestant hero: he was no more than a poet. But the effect of a poet is enduring.

He was not of those to whom a fountain of creation fills and who declaim, as it were, great matter. His art was of the kind which must work very slowly and in secret, isolated; his sentences when he desired to produce his effect must be perfected in detail, polished, lingered over, rearranged, until they had become so that one could feel them with the finger-nail and find no roughness. But when he was composing a letter, a proclamation - anything which had to be done for workaday business and where there was no time or occasion for lengthy toil - you hardly ever find in Cranmer's work even occasional beauty. Once or twice a phrase stands out, but in the great mass of what he has left he is as dull, turgid and confused as all his generation were; repeating himself, writing at vast length, using exaggerated terms, and seeming incapable sometimes of finishing his sentence at all. But when he says to himself: "Now I have something special to do; here I am on my mettle, I must produce some final thing" - *then* he constructs with a success only paralleled by the sonnets of Shakespeare.

I say "constructs". Though we could not do the same ourselves, yet we can see how the hand is at work and how every word is thought out, each rhythm discovered, and the contour of the whole cameo carved. There is not in all that he has thus left of perfect English one lengthy passage; most of the Collects, which, with the isolated phrases of the Litany are his chief triumph, consist in single sentences - but they are sentences which most men who know the trade would give their eyes to have written. And since that endures which is carved in hard material, they have endured, and given endurance to the fabric - novel and revolutionary in his time, the institution at the root of which he stands - The Church of England.

The poet's genius and labours are his own, and yet he himself is a product of his age - a beneficiary if the times are right, - which also helps to explain the magic of the Prayer Book.

2. A liturgy compiled, as the Book of Common Prayer was compiled, during a period prior to the divorce of spoken and written styles benefits enormously from the enrichment of vocabulary, the concern for precise formulation of thought, the regard for shape, which are the attributes of the written style, coupled with the feeling for natural idiom, the sinewy immediacy, the directness, which belong to the spoken style. In twentieth century English the two sets of qualities are not easily married together without incongruity, without an effect of wobble between different kinds and levels of style. In the sixteenth and seventeenth centuries, the marriage could still be true and harmonious.

3. *The Book of Common Prayer 1549*
   This is just what you might expect
   a Prayer Book to be like. This is
   What we always thought about rain;
   about dying, and marriage, and God.
   We needed only the help which
   the right placing of a relative pronoun
   could manage. Words, then, said what they meant;
   they bit. A man was a houseband
   until death departed him.
   And all was for common use:
   printed in Fleet Street,
   at the sign of the sun,
   over against the conduit.

Behind the felicities of Cranmer's prose lay a process, begun with Chaucer, of mingling native English prose rhythms with those of Latin and the Romance languages, possessed of a more polysyllabic vocabulary; and this reached its consummation in the Prayer Book and the Authorised Version. The native elements, trochaic roll (eg. make thy chosen people joyful) and stressed monosyllables (eg. ways, like lost sheep) are combined with the more exotic rhythms of the Latin, but the sublimest effects are produced by the former. More details are given in a lecture by Professor A.C. Clark, "Prose Rhythm in English", published by O.U.P. in 1913.

4. The familiarity of the Bible and the Prayer Book is now declining. So much the worse for us. How much the worse may be clearly seen if we compare the petitions and prayers, written by living hands, which are sometimes used in churches on special occasions, with the words of the Prayer Book itself. Even in our prayers we are timidly hesitant as though we were candidates at an election-meeting anxious to compromise, to conciliate all comers, and, therefore, not to commit ourselves. Who now would have the courage to open with: 'Stir up, we beseech thee, O Lord, the wills of thy faithful people . . . . .'? Or who would dare to write: 'That it may please thee to strengthen such as do stand; and to comfort and help the weak-hearted; and to raise up them that fall; and finally to beat down Satan under our feet'? 'To *beat down Sa*tan . . .' - where, except in Churchill at war, shall we find the passionate energy that can drive a stress on to three consecutive syllables? We are half-afraid of emphasis as we are half-afraid of poetry. 'Lighten our darkness, we beseech thee, O Lord; and by thy great mercy defend us from all perils and dangers of this night . . .' If you or I were given the grace to write that, some astringent compromiser would object to it as rhetorical and sentimental, and say that 'perils and dangers' was repetitive.

If borrowing from another writer's work be a testament to his merits, Cranmer received such not long after his death from the greatest British playwright of all. Phrases from the Church services are constantly echoed in Shakespeare's plays.
5. Prince Henry says to Falstaff, 'I see a good amendment of life in thee'; Falstaff says to Bardolph, 'Do thou amend thy face, and I'll amend my life.' The phrase 'amend our lives' comes from the Litany. At the Holy Communion the priest says

in the Exhortation 'confess yourselves to Almighty God with full purpose of amendment of life.' The point of these phrases would, of course, be redoubled with an audience that knew them and where they came from. And they would derive all the more amusement when Falstaff turns them round to his own lusty purposes. When the Prince sees a good amendment of life in him, the old rascal rejoins with, - 'Why Hal, 'tis my vocation, Hal; 'tis no sin for a man to labour in his vocation.' He has the whole Prayer Book with him: the Catechism enjoins the duty 'to labour truly to get mine own living'; the Epistles tell us to give ourselves to some vocation; the Homily against Idleness bids everyone 'in some kind of labour to exercise himself, according as the vocation whereunto God hath called him shall require'. This is by no means the end of the old reprobate's variations on themes from Prayer Book and Bible. 'Oh, if men were to be saved by merit . . . .', he sighs: this goes back to St Paul's Epistle to the Romans and justification by faith, not works, as the Homily on Fasting - a nice authority for a Falstaff - lays down. Or again we hear him preaching, with all sorts of reverberations from Scripture and the Collects:

Well, God give thee the spirit of persuasion, and him the ears of profiting, that what thou speakest may move, and what he hears may be believed.

The phrase from the Litany, 'O God, we have heard with our ears', must have fastened itself in the mind of many an Anglican besides William Shakespeare. But out it comes with Sir Hugh Evans: 'What phrase is this, "He hears with ear"? Why, it is affectatious' - the joke being that it is a Welsh parson who does not recognise it. Anyone familiar with the Prayer-Book services will recognise in

their best conscience

Is not to leave't undone, but kept unknown,

the echo from the General Confession, 'we have left undone those things which we ought to have done' - a sentence we can never forget. There are similar phrases and echoes from all the services, from Baptism and Holy Matrimony - references to which are numerous - to the Commination Service and the Churching of Women. He had attended them all, many times. We learn that for him there were only two sacraments, Baptism and Holy Communion - not a trace of the Catholic teaching in which his parents had been brought up, nor had he any knowledge of the Vulgate. He was an orthodox, conforming member of the Church into which he had been baptised, was brought up and married, in which his children were reared and in whose arms he at length was buried. . . . . .

The rhythms of the majestic phrases of Bible and Prayer Book, heard all the days of one's youth, enter into the blood-stream: one cannot get them out of one's head, even if one would: they come back into the consciousness again and again unbidden, at every kind of juncture, in accordance with laws of association too subtle for description.

Protagonists of the Prayer Book are accused of being concerned primarily with its aesthetic qualities. But even for the unbeliever there is more to it than that.

6. We live continually in and through words. Memories of words, poetic and sacred, travel with us through life. The loss of lively and natural access to the Authorised Version of the Bible and Cranmer's Book of Common Prayer is a

literary loss comparable to losing touch with Shakespeare. It is also, whether or not one believes in God, a spiritual loss. Good works of art convey wisdom and understanding, and make places and spaces for pure unselfish contemplation and recollection. The great traditional words of the Bible and the Prayer Book are high instances of sacred art, of beauty as sacrament. These words have been treasured and understood for centuries by people whose use made of them timeless language, perfectly comprehensible and illuminating, a part of ordinary life for educated and uneducated alike. Now an ephemeral parochial 'modernism' threatens to cut us off from these sources of spiritual and literary nourishment. Such a loss could be irrevocable. I cannot imagine that believers and unbelievers will be able to 'live by' the new texts as they did by the old. The Bible and the Prayer Book were great pieces of literary good fortune, when language and spirit conjoined to produce a high unique religious eloquence. These books have been *loved* because of their inspired linguistic perfection. Treasured words encourage, console and save.

7. We feel that the Church may not sufficiently appreciate that these two works are part of a literary and imaginative heritage which can only decay if they are not used as they were intended to be used. The Book of Common Prayer cannot, like Shakespeare's plays, become a set text for every school and university; it cannot be performed except as it was meant to be performed - as liturgy. The Authorized Version of the Bible, the idioms of which have passed into common speech, unless it is read as scripture in our churches, will become inaccessible, and those many vital metaphors and figurative expressions with which it has enriched the language must inevitably decay with its disuse.

No one, Christian or non-Christian, who cares for language and its ethical and imaginative function in society, can view this position with equanimity. We are not persuaded by arguments against continuity, for it seems to us that it cannot be good to cut people off from a living consciousness of their past. Such consciousness is most innocently and immediately served by the traditional usage in ceremonies which the whole community requires - baptism, marriage and burial - of a liturgy and scripture with which over four centuries everyone has become familiar.

It is absurd to contend that these liturgies are less meaningful today than when they were linguistically contemporary, if only because, from their inception, subsequent generations have kept them alive and understandable simply by usage. They can be rendered meaningless only by disuse.

Such disuse, then, will inevitably destroy far more than the doctrinal attitude from which the Prayer Book derived. We think that this is not widely enough understood. The Book of Common Prayer was composed at a peculiarly happy moment in the development of the English language. The translators of the Authorized Version of the Bible felt this themselves, and used a conservative and sometimes archaic language in order to demonstrate the importance of continuity.

We are concerned about the effect of recent innovations among all sections of the community, most of whom had their first, and sometimes only, experience of imaginative prose and its wider implication in the context of ordinary life, through their acquaintance, however cursory, with the Prayer Book and the Authorized Version of the Bible. Because we believe in the primary importance of language as a means of communication, we urge the Church to look seriously at its responsibility in this matter.

As for the believer.

8. My own life would have been so much the poorer without the Book of Common Prayer that I feel a kind of horrified pity for an Anglican and Episcopalian posterity which may have to do without it. It is hard to describe my own experience in adolescence, of growing up in cramped and rather poor surroundings, without the plastic and performing arts, without nearly enough access to literature - in an environment where, with the very large exception of natural beauty of landscape, there was little to persuade one that life was not banal, and gritty, and dull. And in the circumstance I was at least once a week compelled to be moved by a public ritual which had the stature of great art (though that was not its purpose), which was not commonplace and not dull and not mean. The Book of Common Prayer gave me insistent constant contact with something much greater than myself - and unlike attendance at an artistic performance, it forced me very literally and publicly to participate in it, whether that were my immediate fancy or not. It really constituted my first and deepest acquaintance with what is classical in spirit as differentiated from Romantic. I was reached through language which shaped my own sense of language, and my own life. It has been essential to my own love of literature, and hence to my career. Much more important, ultimately, it has been essential to my life as a believer, and the development (though that is a poor and misleading word) of my Christian life, as far as I understand and try to practice Christianity. This language was a perpetual instruction about the nature of God - one knew one was speaking to a God who is very great indeed, and that it is perpetually necessary to long for and reach out to something which is greater and better than the surface satisfactions of ordinary life - something beyond content- ment, beyond success, beyond cheerfulness or happiness. I knew inescapably some things which my lighter will might not have chosen to know. I knew what penitence was (even if impenitent); the liturgy told me and made me enact it. I knew what joy was, and a refreshed turning to God (even if not joyful, not returning); the language forced me to know. Although as I have said it provided me with great art, I always knew that that was not its function. It was not there to provide easy channels for adolescent or adult flickering velleities, to be a resort for the feelings. It came to me and changed me, this tough compelling language, which demands that its meanings be practised even in the uttering of the words.

A strong liturgy perpetually communicates the relationship of man to God and God to man, and it needs a language which will include, celebrate and evoke a range of emotions and attitudes which only language can convey - until we arrive at the point of the mystics, loving God without language, a state not to be found by bypassing the use of language at the outset. There is a real danger in devising rituals which are trivial or flabby, which do not press upon the hearer's attention or ring along the nerves. The language of the old BCP is comforting in the older sense - strengthening, offering bark and steel for the mind and soul. The language of the new liturgies is comfortable in the upholsterer's sense: "To rest, the Cushion and soft Dean invite." It will never make one uncomfortable, in itself, for it is not stirring; any sense of discomfort must be brought by the individual, or any terrific sense of joy and wonder. The new liturgy does not make any palpable demands, does not shanghai anyone into drama. Indeed, if the worshipper comes into church really penitent or really joyful, the language of the service will tend rather to defuse the intenser emotions, while the inarticulate and unfocused feelings which may arise in the worshipper on weekdays will not be made articulate and concentrated for him on a Sunday. The old liturgy is being rejected not for archaism or dryness but fundamentally because it exerted too much dramatic force on the emotions. This liturgy will not make anyone feel what he is not feeling already - any emotions must be brought and dealt with by the worshipper himself, for the service withdraws from that task. It is thus ironically, for all its devisers' emphasis on community, a liturgy for a late Romantic age, a liturgy which lets the sincere desires of individual souls pretty well alone, and is not going to be so impertinent as to shape and change them.

9. To know what was generally believed in all ages, the way is to consult the Liturgies, not any private man's writing. If you would know how the Church of England serves God, go to the Common Prayer Book, consult not this or that man.

10. About my own beliefs there is no secret. To quote Uncle Toby: "They are written in the Common Prayer Book."

Praise for the Book of Common Prayer invites comparison, but in the spirit of Mr Pleydell, Guy Mannering's companion at Sunday worship in the Kirk of Scotland.
11. The sermon was not read - a scrap of paper containing the heads of the discourse was occasionally referred to, and the enunciation, which at first seemed imperfect and embarrassed, became, as the preacher warmed in his progress, animated and distinct; and although the discourse could not be quoted as a correct specimen of pulpit eloquence, yet Mannering had seldom heard so much learning, metaphysical acuteness, and energy of argument, brought into the service of Christianity.

"Such," he said, going out of the church, "must have been the preachers to whose unfearing minds, and acute, though sometimes rudely exercised talents, we owe the Reformation."

"And yet that reverend gentleman," said Pleydell, "whom I love for his father's sake and his own, has nothing of the sour or pharisaical pride which has been imputed to some of the early fathers of the Calvinistic Kirk of Scotland. His colleague and he differ, and head different parties in the Kirk, about particular points of church discipline, but without for a moment losing personal regard or respect for each other, or suffering malignity to interfere in an opposition, steady, constant, and apparently conscientious on both sides."

"And you, Mr Pleydell, what do you think of their points of difference?"

"Why, I hope, Colonel, a plain man may go to heaven without thinking about them at all; - besides, *inter nos*, I am a member of the suffering and Episcopal Church of Scotland - the shadow of a shade now, and fortunately so; - but I love to pray where my fathers prayed before me, without thinking worse of the Presbyterian forms because they do not affect me with the same associations." And with this remark they parted until dinner-time.

But it remains a fact that:

12. In England even the least churchly of men look back upon the village church which they attended in youth with affection; they know the words of the Prayer Book and revere them, even when they have given up belief. The Englishman about to be killed by an Afghan tribe recalls

the gray little church across the park,
The mounds that hid the loved and honour'd dead;
The Norman arch, the chancel softly dark,
The brasses black and red.

The literature of England is full of allusions to the village church. I do not recall a single Scottish poem that deals lovingly with the village kirk.

And we can understand Coleridge saying:

13. I never distinctly felt the heavenly superiority of the prayers in the English Liturgy, till I had attended some kirks in the country parts of Scotland.

Already in the reign of King Charles I George Herbert had described 'The British Church' as standing between the two extremes of Calvinism (Presbyterianism) and Roman Catholicism.

14. *The British Church*

I joy, deare Mother, when I view
Thy perfect lineaments, and hue
Both sweet and bright.

Beautie in thee takes up her place,
And dates her letters from thy face,
When she doth write.
A fine aspect in fit aray,
Neither too mean, nor yet too gay,
Show who is best.

Outlandish looks may not compare:
For all they either painted are,
Or else undrest.

She on the hills, which wantonly
Allureth all in hope to be
By her preferr'd,

Hath kiss'd so long her painted shrines,
That ev'n her face by kissing shines,
For her reward.

She in the valley is so shie
Of dressing, that her hair doth lie
About her eares:

While she avoids her neighbours pride,
She wholly goes on th' other side,
And nothing wears.

But dearest Mother, (what those misse)
The mean thy praise and glorie is,
And long may be.

Blessed be God, whose love it was
To double-moat thee with his grace,
And none but thee.

Lady Ponsonby writes to Lady Canning.
15. I must own to you when I last wrote I took it into my head from the little word you said about Miss Stanley that you had an inclination towards the Roman Church and I dreaded to hear it was thus. I am *so* relieved to find that it is not so.

In many ways the direction and the beaten track may be easy to follow and there may be a false charm in the repose of giving up the pain and toil of using one's own poor weak judgment and relying on that of another, but with all the said variances and conflicts in our distracted Church, we need not (it seems to me) feel impelled to think for an instant of leaving it, as long as the Prayer Book is left.

Dame Rose Macaulay writes to Fr Johnson S.S.J.E.
16. I'm glad you think that the line of prayer chosen should be congenial to one's particular capacities and leanings, I do, too. That's why I always shun those rather florid, sentimental prayers and meditations; they might sink one altogether. There is much in Roman Catholic devotions that I can't stand; *nothing* in what a contemptuous convert called "Cranmer's little work".

W.H. Auden in his Commonplace Book.
17. The poor Roman Catholics have had to start from scratch, and, as any of them with a feeling for language will admit, they have made a cacophonous horror of the Mass. We had the extraordinary good fortune in that our Book of Common Prayer was composed at exactly the right historical moment. The English language had already become more or less what it is today, so that the Prayer Book is no more difficult to follow than Shakespeare, but the ecclesiastics of the sixteenth century still possessed a feeling for the ritual and ceremonious which today we have almost entirely lost. Why should we spit on our luck?

Small wonder that the clergy should be exhorted to be loyal to the Prayer Book.
18. Another Thing which I have in special Charge from my Lord to recommend unto you is, that you would daily use the *Liturgy of the Church* with all possible Devotion and Solemnity, in all its Offices, and at all the appointed Times; not presuming to curtail any Part of it in Favour of your own Inventions, or upon any other Occasion whatsoever. There are many Arguments to induce Men to have a special Regard for our Liturgy, and to value it as a principal Part of that Sacrifice, which the church offers in the House of God. I shall forbear to tell you of the

Clergy, how excellent the Composition is, how devout and comprehensive the Prayers and Supplications, how sweet and exalted the Hymns and Thanksgivings, how charitable and compassionate the Intercessions for all Sorts of Men; in a Word, how excellent and divine the Matter, the Method, and the Decorum of the whole Liturgy is. So that neither *Rome* nor *Muscovy, Osburgh* nor *Amsterdam*, have any Thing in their Publick Services, that can enter into comparison with it. And as I do but glance upon the Excellency of it, (which would afford an endless Theam) so I shall speak very little of the Merit and Fate of it, which ought surely in some measure to enhance our Value of it: So true a Friend, (as I may term it) and so constant a Martyr of our Church and Religion. It has undergone the Fate of the great Catholic Verities, it has been crucified between Thieves, upon the Right Hand and upon the Left, as all the Articles of our *Nicene* Creed have been. And we have not yet forgotten, that it had the Honour to fall by the very same Hands as the Church and Monarchy itself.

John Wesley agrees with Sir Leoline Jenkins' comparison in his preface to "The Sunday Service of the Methodists, adapted from the Common Prayer of the Church of England", published in 1792.
   "I believe there is no liturgy in the world, either in ancient or modern language, which breathes more of a solid, scriptural, rational piety, than the Common Prayer of the Church of England."

In the light of these comparisons it is tempting to think that much might have been gained by extending the practice of the "Polestar".
19. . . . Divine service was read as usual by the chief engineer. It is a curious thing that in whaling vessels the Church of England Prayer Book is always employed, although there is never a member of that Church among either officers or crew. Our men are all Roman Catholics or Presbyterians, the former predominating. Since a ritual is used which is foreign to both, neither can complain that the other is preferred to them, and they listen with all attention and devotion, so that the system has something to recommend it.

In time of war the writer Charles Morgan gave a broadcast talk on the subject of the Village Church.
20. One of the symbols of this saving continuity - and no less a symbol because it was sometimes resisted - was the whole ceremony of church-going. It came at the end of that long Sunday afternoon and was undertaken often enough in no very willing or pious spirit. Left to oneself, one might have chosen the garden, not the sermon, and yet, when the decision was made and the little procession had set out, the power of ritual asserted itself - not yet the ritual of the Church, but that of the fields, the bells, the angle of the sun, of other figures approaching down the convergent lanes of the hill opposite. In the churchyard, if the five-minute bell had not yet begun, there was a pause for neighbourly conversation, and it was possible to wander among the graves and read again an inscription which, long ago, had been learned by heart. Inside the church itself was a mingling of daylight and lamplight, a pallor of glass which would presently darken, a low gleam of stone and wood; and all these things bespoke the hour and the month, and were part of the order of the seasons.

When the service began, it borrowed from the approaching night a sweet solemnity, which, for a child at any rate, it had not in the morning in the same degree. It is not possible to say of the two orders of prayer that one is greater than the other, but the order for the evening has appeared to many as the more intimate, the *Nunc dimittis* and the Third Collect having an unequalled power to speak from the suppliant's heart. And to-morrow,* after the reading in the morning of that matchless Epistle which begins: "After this I looked, and behold, a door was opened . . .", the evening will bring, unless another psalm be used for Trinity-Sunday, "The Lord is my shepherd", of which the fourth verse is: "Yea, though I walk through the valley of the shadow of death, I will fear no evil. . . ." The miracle of the Prayer-book, if allowed to speak in its own order plainly, is that it speaks both timelessly and to the occasion; and there can be no Englishman who hears that psalm, the last for the evening, but will cast his mind back to another June four years ago and, seeing now upon what a threshold we stand, wonder. So it was, in the past, when the peril was not of nations - the words of the Prayer-book would often pass us by, almost unheeded, a splendour of accustomed sound, and men would say that the words must be simplified for children or that the petitions must be adapted to modern needs; then, suddenly, because it had not been changed, because every phrase in it was a familiar emblem, the Prayer-book, in our greatest need, would speak, as it were a voice within us, of that darkness in which we were lost and that light which we had forgotten.

* The reference is to Trinity-Sunday, June 4th, 1944. The troops went in to the beaches on Tuesday the 6th.

An eloquent tribute to the Prayer Book comes from a contemporary writer.
21. Within Anglicanism the influence of the Bible was channelled and reinforced by the influence of a second book, scarcely less important in the formulation of Anglican tradition: the Book of Common Prayer. It was the genius of Cranmer to bring together into a single volume many different things: the texts necessary for the Sunday Eucharist, the texts for the daily office, the service for ordination, the occasional offices which accompany the believer from birth to burial. Thus there was in the hands of any churchmen who could read, a book which linked private with public prayer, which showed the Bible as a text to be used in worship and which embraced the whole range of human life, personal as well as social. It represented a balanced and inclusive vision of Christian prayer and worship. . . .

Here in the Book of Common Prayer was a vision of the Church as a corporate reality at once of time and eternity, the context in which the individual finds his way to God, presented in pages of memorable prose, straightforward yet solemn.

It is fitting that our last excellent reference for the Book of Common Prayer should come from the writings of Canon R.C.D. Jasper, for many years the chairman of the Liturgical Commission that brought forth the Alternative Services Book. He concludes his history of the Prayer Book revision in the nineteenth century with these words.
22. By 1900, the 1662 Book had been vindicated. In spite of its imperfections, it had withstood all attacks; and, because it had stood firm, the doctrinal standards of the Church of England remained unimpaired. It had established itself - to quote Alexander Knox once again - as "the decus and tutamen (adornment and protection) of professional and vital Christianity". All parties professed a loyalty to it,

although action sometimes belied the profession. Even those who wished to revise it or supplement it only wished to make it, in their own eyes, a better book and more acceptable to other people. But no-one ever expressed a desire to cast it aside and put something else in its place. It did remain the Book of *Common* Prayer, for priest and people alike. "To the Prayer Book the Anglican Church owes the hold she retains on the English people. They are not attracted merely by the fact that the Church is established by law; it may be doubted whether her catholicity allures the bulk of the laity; and assuredly her standard of preaching is not the force which keeps men from other Communions. But the Book of Common Prayer is unique, a κτημα εισ αει (possession for ever). Amid the fierce contentions of the Churches it gave the Church of England unity, strength, and a way to the hearts of men such as no other Church could boast."[1]

[1] A.F. Pollard, *Thomas Cranmer and the English Reformation, 1489-1556* (London, 1906), pp. 222-3.

REFERENCES

1. Hilaire Belloc, *Cranmer*, Cassell & Cy 1931.
2. Stella Brook, *The Language of the Book of Common Prayer,* André Deutsch 1965.
3. David Scott, *A Quiet Gathering*, Bloodaxe Books 1984.
4. Charles Morgan, *The Writer and his World*, op. cit.
5. A.L. Rowse, *William Shakespeare: A Biography*, MacMillan 1963.
6. Iris Murdoch, 'Essay', in *P N Review* 13, Carcanet Press.
7. Letter from the Principal of St Hugh's College, Oxford and others, *The Times* 14th November 1979.
8. Margaret A. Moody, 'How shall we sing the Lord's song' in *The State of the Language* op. cit.
9. John Selden, *Table Talk*, ed. S.W. Singer, Wm. Pickering 1847.
10. C.S. Lewis, *Mere Christianity*, Geoffrey Bles Ltd. 1952.
11. Sir Walter Scott, *Guy Mannering*, op. cit.
12. Wallace Notestein, *The Scot in History*, Jonathan Cape 1946.
13. S.T. Coleridge, *Table Talk and Omniana,* op. cit.
14. George Herbert, *The Temple*, Cambridge 1633.
15. Lady Ponsonby, *A Lady in Waiting to Queen Victoria*, J.H. Sears & Cy 1927.
16. Rose Macaulay, *Letters to a Friend*, op. cit., 16th November 1951.
17. W.H. Auden, *A Certain World*, Faber & Faber 1971, Liturgy, Reform of.
18. William Wynne, *The Life of Sir Leoline Jenkins,* op. cit.
19. Sir Arthur Conan Doyle, *Tales of Pirates and Blue Water*, John Murray 1922, The Captain of the Polestar.
20. Charles Morgan, *Reflections in a Mirror,* (2nd Series) op. cit., The Village Church.
21. A.M. Allchin, *Anglican Spirituality.*
22. R.C.D. Jasper, *Prayer Book Revision in England 1800-1900*, S.P.C.K. 1954.

EPILOGUE

Our business has been with words, words to be used in common. The rubrics (i.e. directions) in the Prayer Book therefore order the minister to "read with a loud voice", "with an audible voice", to "rehearse distinctly", to "pronounce with a loud voice", words that can be shared through being heard. But, as Charles Simeon advised young clergymen, "Pray the prayers, and don't read them only", if the congregation are to find in their corporate worship all that Thomas Cranmer hoped they would.

Richard Steele writes in The Spectator of 18th August 1711 about worshipping at St James Garlick Hill (by happy chance the present headquarters of the Prayer Book Society) when the Reverend Philip Stubbs was Rector:
1. "Mr Spectator,

The well Reading of the Common Prayer is of so great Importance, and so much neglected, that I take the Liberty to offer to your Consideration some Particulars on that Subject; And what more worthy your Observation than this? A thing so Publick, and of so high Consequence. . . .

You must know, Sir, I've been a constant Frequenter of the Service of the Church of *England* for above these four Years last past, and 'till *Sunday* was sevennight never discover'd, to so great a Degree, the Excellency of the Common Prayer. When being at St *James's Garlick-hill* Church, I heard the Service read so distinctly, so emphatically, and so fervently, that it was next to an Impossibility to be unattentive. My Eyes and my Thoughts could not wander as usual, but were confin'd to my Prayers. I then consider'd I address'd myself to the Almighty, and not to a beautiful Face. And when I reflected on my former Performances of that Duty, I found I had run it over as a matter of Form, in comparison to the Manner in which I then discharged it. My Mind was really affected, and fervent Wishes accompanied my Words. The Confession was read with such a resign'd Humility, the Absolution with such a comfortable Authority, the Thanksgivings with a Religious Joy, as made me feel those Affections of the Mind in a manner I never did before. To remedy therefore the Grievance above complain'd of, I humbly propose, that this excellent Reader, upon the next and every Annual Assembly of the Clergy of *Sion College*, and all other Conventions, should read Prayers before them. For then those, that are afraid of stretching their Mouths, and spoiling their soft Voice will learn to Read with Clearness, Loudness, and Strength. Others that affect a rakish negligent Air by folding their Arms, and lolling on their Book, will be taught a decent Behaviour, and comely Erection of Body. Those that Read so fast as if impatient of their Work, may learn to speak Deliberately. . . ."

Of course, the congregation not only listen, but join in the common prayer, and so need to be instructed in what they are about. Soon after his accession, King Charles II issued a 'Gracious letter touching Catechising' which stressed the importance of this. In all places where there was an afternoon service either the Church Catechism should be explained to the people, or a text preached in such a way "as may conduce to the exposition of the liturgy and the prayers of the Church (as occasion shall be offered), the only cause that they grew in contempt among the people being this, that they were not understood." Perhaps the congregation has shown as many imperfections as the clergy, especially in previous ages when church attendance was obligatory or considered proper. As Edward wrote of the Olympians (those Uncles and Aunts who, sharing the same house, yet lived in a different world),

2. "No irresistible Energy haled them to Church o' Sundays; yet they went there regularly of their own accord, though they betrayed no greater delight in the experience than ourselves."

However, when priest and people go willingly to church, there is Charles Simeon's "finest sight short of heaven": "a whole congregation using the prayers of the Liturgy in the true spirit of them."

Today many members of the Church of England are deprived of this experience. Where Prayer Book services are advertised, we often find surprising omissions and alterations. Louis MacNeice in his poem "Sunday Morning" wrote, "Man's heart expands to tinker with his car", but, the clergyman's, it seems, to tinker with the liturgy. Church notice boards proclaim Family Service, Healing Service, Ecumenical Service, Prayer and Praise, Songs of Praise. Like Cleopatra, the Church of England displays an infinite variety, and anomy reigns - the very opposite of Cranmer's intention. The A.S.B. provides variations enough, but, not content with these, and in spite of solemn promises, today's clergyman often makes up his own special "hymn sandwich", and offers no further sustenance in the village church on the Lord's Day.

3. "It was that verse about becoming again as a little child," wrote Philip Larkin, "that caused the first sharp waning of my Christian sympathies. If the Kingdom of Heaven could be entered only by those fulfilling such a condition, I knew I should be unhappy there . . . . having to put up indefinitely with the company of other children, their noise, their nastiness, their boasting, their back answers, their cruelty, their silliness." Fortunately for the Christian, scholars would criticise Larkin's interpretation of Jesus' words, but we can sympathise with his sentiments, especially when the main Sunday service focuses its attention on the children; and we can wonder whether Sunday School and catechising and parental training of children to behave at adult services were not better ways.

It is not my purpose to provide a detailed criticism of those services that are now legitimate alternatives to the Book of Common Prayer, yet the lover of the Prayer Book is bound to regard the present situation of the Church of England as tragic, because so many of its clergy have defected from the Prayer Book and have established worship according to the A.S.B. at all, or at all the main, Sunday services of the church. *La Trahison des Clercs*, the title of Julien Benda's reflections in 1927 on the thinkers and writers of the previous fifty years who had betrayed

Europe's traditional values describes what the majority of the laity see in the behaviour of the clerks in Holy Orders in our own country in the last two decades. However, they have found it difficult to protest effectively, not knowing their rights for the most part, and not knowing the answers to their parson's little learning of liturgiology (Mix one large volume of Dix with leaflets of Buchanan). Meanwhile a new generation of clergy is coming on the scene, which has not used the Prayer Book in church or at school nor has been instructed in it at theological college. As time passes, churchfolk will grow accustomed to their loss and to the new services, for our minds do acquiesce in deprivation and do adjust, if we allow them. But those made of sterner stuff will continue to use the Common Prayer privately at home and go many miles to find a church which uses it for Sunday worship, reluctantly forsaking their own parish church. They will do battle within the scope provided by the church representation rules, and especially on the Parochial Church Council, and will find "mutual society, help and comfort" as members of the Prayer Book Society.

During the Commonwealth, Anthony Sparrow, a former Fellow of Queen's College, Cambridge, was appointed to the living of Hawkedon in Suffolk, and was ejected after holding it for no more than five weeks because of his loyalty to the Prayer Book. In 1655, while the Prayer Book was still proscribed, he published "A Rationale upon the Book of Common Prayer of the Church of England," a book to help the laity understand and use the Prayer Book in their private devotions. "As for those that love it, and suffer for the love of it," he wrote in the Preface, "this will show them reasons why they should suffer on, and love it still more and more."

Still during the Commonwealth, in July 1659, Sir Leoline Jenkins wrote to Mr Athanasius Davies, who had bravely continued to use the Prayer Book:
4. "Sir,

Upon information from divers friends of your extraordinary care and conscience in the work of your ministry, I think myself bound to congratulate you. I joy to hear, that your holy exercises are according to the Order, and in the form of the Church of England; which form (I mean the Liturgy) as it is of most advantage and comfort to practical and sober Christians, so it is most scorned and persecuted by ignorant and newfangled men. Wherefore we should be more in love with it now, and set our hearts at rest in this resolution, that we desert not a truth because it is persecuted, nor entertain an error because it seems prosperous, or embraced and countenanced by men in power; for there hath never been any truth of consequence, but hath met with adversaries, and scarce any error or absurdity that hath not found abetters."

He might have been writing to lovers of the Prayer Book today.

REFERENCES

1. *The Spectator,* Everyman Edition op. cit.
2. Kenneth Grahame, *The Golden Age,* op. cit., Young Adam Cupid.
3. Philip Larkin, *Required Writing,* Faber & Faber 1983, The Savage Seventh p. 111.
4. William Wynne, *The Life of Sir Leoline Jenkins,* op. cit.

AUTHOR AND BOOK INDEX

COPYRIGHT PERMISSIONS

The publishing world has undergone many changes in recent years, and, as a result, finding the owners of copyright has often proved difficult. I apologise in advance for any omissions or wrong assignations. These will certainly be corrected in future editions, should they be brought to my attention. In the meantime, I wish to thank the following for permission to produce extracts from material under copyright:

A.M. Allchin, for *Anglican Spirituality*.

Allen Lane for Richard Adams, *The Girl in the Swing*.

Andre Deutsch Ltd. for Stella Brook, *The Language of the Book of Common Prayer* (1965).

A.P. Watt Ltd. on behalf of the Executors of Ernest Raymond for Ernest Raymond, *The Witness of Canon Welcome*, and *The Story of My Days*.

Barrie & Jenkins for Anthony Quayle, *A Time to Speak*;
P.G. Wodehouse, *Young Men in Spats, Eggs, Beans and Crumpets*, and *Jeeves and the Feudal Spirit*.

Bloodaxe Books Ltd. for David Scott, 'The Book of Common Prayer' from *A Quiet Gathering*.

Bodley Head for Geoffrey Lowis, *Fabulous Admirals*.

B.T. Batsford Ltd. for A.G. Dickens, *The English Reformation*.

Chatto & Windus for Iris Murdoch, *An Unofficial Rose*;
J.L. Carr, *A Day in Summer*.

Louise Collis for *The Diaries of Maurice Collis* edited by her and published by Wm. Heinemann Ltd.

Curtis Brown Ltd. London and the author for Priscilla Napier, *A Late Beginner*, published by Michael Joseph.

Eric Glass Ltd for Beverley Nichols, *A Village in a Valley*.

Evergreen Books for Susan Goodyear, *Cathedral Close*.

Faber & Faber Ltd. for W.H. Auden, *A Certain World*;
P.D. James, *Devices and Desires*, *An Unsuitable Job for a Woman*, and *A Taste for Death*;
Charles Williams, *The Greater Trumps*, *War in Heaven*, and *Descent into Hell*.

The Gomer Press for A.H. Jones, *His Lordship's Obedient Servant*.

Hamish Hamilton Ltd. for Isabel Colegate, *The Shooting Party*;
James Lee-Milne, *Another Self*.

The Hamlyn Publishing Group Ltd. for Winston Churchill, *My Early Life*, published by Collins.

Harrap Publishing Group Ltd. for Margaret Craven, *I Heard the Owl call my Name*.

Rupert Hart-Davis for Arthur Calder-Marshall, *No Earthly Command*.

Hodder & Stoughton for W.R. Matthews, *Memories and Meanings*;
  Elizabeth Goudge, *The Joy of Snow*.

Hogarth Press for Laurie Lee, *Cider with Rosie*.

Louise Horton for *Houston*, published by the White Cross Press.

Jonathan Cape Ltd. for Barabara Pym, *Some Tame Gazelle*;
  Alan Paton, *Cry the Beloved Country*;
  Wallace Notestein, *The Scot in History*.

MacDonald for Edward Short, *I Knew My Place*.

James McGibbon for 'Why are the clergy...' from Stevie Smith, *Collected Poems*,
  Penguin 20th Century Classics.

Macmillan Ltd. for Margaret Mitchell, *Gone With the Wind*;
  David Williams, *Murder in Advent*;
  Charles Morgan, *Reflections in a Mirror*;
  Pamela Hansford Johnson, *The Humbler Creation*;
  A.L. Rowse, *William Shakespeare*.

The Macmillan Publishing Group N.Y. for Agnes S. Turnbull, *The Bishop's Mantle*
  (1948).

Martin Secker & Warburg Ltd. for Eric Bligh, *Tooting Corner*;
  Graham Greene, *The Pleasure Dome*.

Michael Joseph Ltd. for C.S. Forester, *A Ship of the Line*.

Dame Iris Murdoch and the Carcanet Press for an excerpt from *PN13*.

Mr John Osborne and *The Spectator* for 'Great Sighs of Today', *The Spectator*,
  22 December 1984.

Oxford University Press for M.V. Hughes, *A London Girl in the 1880's*;
  M. Millgate, *Thomas Hardy: A Biography*;
  Charles Williams, *Thomas Cranmer of Canterbury*.

Peters, Fraser & Dunlop Group Ltd. for Rose Macaulay, 'Churchgoing: Anglican'
  from *Personal Pleasures*, published by Gollancz;
  Hilaire Belloc, *Cranmer*, published by Cassells;
  D.M. Greenwood, *Clerical Errors,* published by Headline Publishers.

The Principal of St Hugh's College, Oxford, for a letter to *The Times*, November 1979.

Random House for Eileen Baillie, *The Shabby Paradise*, published by Hutchinson.

The Regents of the University of California and Professor Margaret Anne Moody
  for 'How shall we sing the Lord's Song?' from *The State of the Language*,
  eds C. Ricks & L. Michaels, 1980 edition;
  The Rt. Hon. Enoch Powell, 'Further Thoughts: Grammar and Syntax', 1990
  edition.

Sheed & Ward for G.K. Chesterton, *Autobiography*.

S.P.C.K. for R.C.D. Jasper, *Prayer Book Revision in England*;
  C.H. Smyth, *The Genius of the Church of England*.

Victor Gollancz/New English Library for Dorothy L. Sayers, *The Nine Tailors*, and
  Busman's Holiday;
  Edmund Crispin, *The Moving Toyshop*.

Weidenfeld & Nicholson for J.G. Farrell, *The Hill Station*;
  Lord Birkenhead, *Rudyard Kipling*.

Wm Heinemann Ltd. for Paul Scott, *Staying On*.